WINN LIBRARY
Gordon College
Wenham, Mass. 01984

W9-BXB-720

Religion and Schooling

DISCARDED
JENKS LRC
GORDON COLLEGE

377.1
C 579

A Blaisdell Book in Education

CONSULTING EDITOR

John I. Goodlad
*University of California
Los Angeles*

Religion and Schooling

A Comparative Study

A. STAFFORD CLAYTON
INDIANA UNIVERSITY

Blaisdell Publishing Company

A DIVISION OF GINN AND COMPANY

WALTHAM, MASSACHUSETTS · TORONTO · LONDON

377.1
C 5 79

ACKNOWLEDGMENT

The inquiry reported in this book was supported by a grant
from the United States Office of Education, under its
Cooperative Research Program, and the book is based in part
on the report of Cooperative Research Project No. F-017
entitled *Historical and Social Determinants of Public
Education Policy in the United States and Europe.*

Copyright © 1969 by Blaisdell Publishing Company,
A Division of Ginn and Company.
All rights reserved. No part of the material
covered by this copyright may be produced
in any form or by any means of reproduction.
Library of Congress Catalog Card Number: 68–24612
Printed in the United States of America.

Foreword

The decade of the 1950's was a period of intense soul-searching in American education. Early in the decade, books such as those by Albert Lynd, Arthur Bestor, Robert Hutchins, and Paul Woodring (all in 1953) were sharply critical of progressive education. By the end of the decade, the schools had been poked at and probed from every angle, and constructive reform was underway. James B. Conant had come out in support of the comprehensive high school; millions of dollars were going into updating and restructuring the curriculum of elementary and secondary education. An educational reform movement had begun.

A significant part of this movement remained obscure and is only now coming into focus. Education as a field of solid inquiry is coming of age. Education is being seen as central to the welfare of mankind, the nation, and the individual. The study of education increasingly is being recognized as requiring the attention of our very best minds. To be a philosopher, psychologist, economist, or sociologist *of education* is now, as never before, to be respectable in the academic world. The demand for good educationists far exceeds the supply.

The Blaisdell series in education was initiated at about the time that the present period of constructive reform in education was beginning to replace the critical soul-searching of the 1950's. Those of us who planned the series anticipated rapid advance in educational studies and resulting benefits for educational practice. We wished to accelerate these developments through commissioning and publishing fine manuscripts. The same care that characterizes the well-known Blaisdell books in mathematics and the sciences goes into editing, designing, and binding the handsome new volumes in education. The several books so far published are unsurpassed in format and attractiveness.

But, of course, the proof of a book is in its content. The intent, from the beginning, has been to define the scope of education as a field of study and practice. Volumes published to date fall into two general classifications. One group focuses rather directly on content and processes of teaching. Published examples are *Readings in Art Education* (1966) by Elliott W. Eisner and David W. Ecker, *History and the Social Sciences* (1967) by Mark M. Krug, and *The Study of Literature in High School* (1968) by Geraldine Murphy. The second group seeks to advance insight into broader educational phenomena: the school as a social institution, the making of educational policy, the organization of schools, and so on. Examples in this classification include the first book in the series, *The Secondary Phase of Education* (1965) by Lawrence W. Downey, *The Middle School* (1967) by Samuel Popper, and the present volume, *Religion and Schooling.*

A. Stafford Clayton holds a doctorate from Columbia Teachers College. He taught at Talladega College, Alabama, and at Western Illinois State College, and for the past twenty years has been a professor in the Department of History and Philosophy of Education at Indiana University.

I came to the reading of Professor Clayton's manuscript with some reluctance. The controversial issues pertaining to religion and the schools are far from new; there is a substantial body of writings dealing with them; and these writings almost always include the same pivotal court cases. In spite of the controversial nature of the field and the rich source materials available, the content of books on this subject rarely is brought alive. But I became absorbed in Professor Clayton's manuscript at the outset, despite my misgivings. I found myself lingering over historical passages which presented material that was fresh for me; I believe it will be fresh for most readers.

This volume illuminates problems which have both deep historical roots and profound contemporary significance. These problems are as fascinating for scholars as they are challenging for today's educational administrators. Professor Clayton provides substance for both in this addition to the list of Blaisdell Books in Education.

JOHN I. GOODLAD

Contents

Religion and Schooling

CHAPTER 1

An Approach to the Problem

More and more the American people are being called upon to consider the relationships between organized religion and the public schools. Court decisions in recent years have interpreted the First Amendment as it bears upon programs of released time, bus transportation, the offering of prayers, Bible reading, and the use of public funds for textbooks for parochial school students. A variety of responses has been made in various communities. Recently, new relations between the public and the private sectors of American education have been called for by federal legislation of 1963 and 1964 and especially by the Elementary and Secondary Education Act of 1965. How we shall use public funds for the improvement of education and yet maintain a separation of state and church is unclear. In a number of instances at different levels of decision, various operative policies are being worked out.

How the public school should bring its practices under the direction of some common public policy is becoming a vital concern to many individuals and groups throughout our society.

This book is an effort to contribute to the discussion and forming of American policy by looking at the conditions and consequences of policies in three European countries. Each of these — England, the Netherlands, and Sweden — has clearly introduced its culture and its people into the American scene. Moreover, these countries have not only had a long history of struggle between church and state, but in more recent years have come to grips with the demand for clearly defined national policy. On the one hand they have responded to the demand that the schools promote religious belief, and on the other hand they have sought to provide a maximum suitable education for all of their people. If the meaning of European patterns of relating religion and schooling was clearly revealed, Americans would have a broader background for approaching their own problems.

Nevertheless, an argument frequently runs beyond this appeal to broader experience. There are those who think that the United States should in some sense follow the policies of a European nation.

On the most divisive issue among us — that of public aid to independent education — a calm study of the procedures in other democratic countries should calm fears and renew intelligent discussion. Whenever everyone is out of step but Johnny, it behooves Johnny to look at his own feet. In nearly every other nation with principles like our own, government has entered into partnership with religious groups in the matter of primary interest to all — the education of youth. While we will find our own solution, the experience of our peers should help.[1]

Should we then select from European patterns of policy those judged by some interest to be most appropriate to the American situation? Should we manage the conflict of interests in our society after the fashion of some European country? Are we to think that the United States is going through, or should be going through, the various stages which European nations may have lived through in developing their present policies? Does the argument mean that the American people have not, or should not have, departed so far from their European ancestors that they should endeavor to synthesize a unique pattern of response to ancient and recurrent problems? Do policies and their attendant consequences in selected European countries suggest what we might well avoid in the design of American policy? This book assembles evidence enabling us to judge in what ways we may learn from European experiences.

Since the main problems in America come to a focus in policies about elementary and secondary schools, our attention centers on schools at a corresponding level abroad. However, in Europe there is typically a wide variety of schools intermediate between elementary schools and the university. While the high school and junior college of the United States resemble in some ways the gymnasium, lyceum, and preparatory schools of European countries, American schools also serve other purposes than preparing for the university. Although movements toward a comprehensive school are found in England, the Netherlands, and Sweden, they are based in each country on the educational traditions and needs of that society. The variety of schools and the changing designs of education in these countries should warn against oversimplified attempts at comparisons.

Although many aspects of educational policy are relevant to and help to clarify the handling of religious questions, the focus of this inquiry is found in two areas. We are concerned with policies about (1) the support of religious schools from public funds and (2) the teaching of religion in schools under the control of public educational authorities. The difficulty here is that in many European countries the line between private and public schools is far from definite and clear. A dual system, involving the mixture of public and private schools, exists, and various measures of state support and state control of private and religious schools are common. To the degree that public support and control are involved in private religious schools, those schools and the policies regarding them fall within the scope of this inquiry.

It should also be noted that national policy in each of the countries studied is conditioned by the organization of education in each country. In England, for example, one can identify a national policy, but its meaning is to a major extent dependent upon local conditions and interpretations provided by local education authorities, leadership in the schools, and the particular characteristics of a region. In contrast, although the Netherlands has regional differences, the country is more compact, and the pattern of educational control much more centralized. This does not mean that there are no opportunities for local initiative in school affairs. It does mean that in the Netherlands one looks much more to the details of legislative enactment to provide the direction of education. The States-General performs what in many other countries would be done by regional or local educational authorities or school boards. Sweden endeavors to apply to questions of national policy in an increasingly unified school system the fullest use of the products of investigation and research covering the whole nation. The country is in the process of far-reaching school reform guided by the recommendations of various commissions, chief among them the 1957 School Commission, but also including a commission studying the relations between church and state. Additionally, in Sweden 99 percent of the people belong at least nominally to the Church of Sweden, and one is by right of birth a member of the Church of Sweden. Differences in social context and educational organization demand that we look in depth into the conditions of policies in each country.

Inquiry into national policy in each country is guided by certain tasks indicating what is looked for, the kind of sources consulted, and the nature of the interpretations and appraisals made by the investigator. The tasks are stated here in an order moving from those which are primarily descriptive to those in which a set of criteria is at work enabling one to reveal more fully the meaning and consequences of the policies in the life of the people.

TASK 1. In each country we examine the nation's laws and the directives of the ministry or department of education and other policy-making bodies or offices in order to state the framework of national policy.

TASK 2. For each country we seek to identify broadly the main historical and social conditions to which present policies are responsive.

TASK 3. We aim to discover the pressures that have been brought to bear upon the development of present policy. Ideally we seek to know who has influenced some aspect of policy, from what position of power in the society, toward what outcome, and with what effectiveness. The study selects from the quantity of materials dealing with religion and education those expressions of individual, or more typically, group interest which reveal the articulate voices in the settlement of current or recent policy. It accepts the view that if we are to reveal the way policy is produced, we should see it in the concrete exercise of power in certain directions in selected instances.

TASK 4. The study seeks to identify efforts to modify current policy — to find out who is seeking to change present policy in what direction and for what purpose. These changes may range from refinements within the general norms of present practice to more fundamental changes urging the redirection of national policy.

TASK 5. The study searches out those investigations and reports of research which bring to the assessment of policy some measure of educational expertness. These studies may be made by individuals or by groups — by committees, commissions and the like — and are frequently sponsored by educational, religious, or governmental agencies.

TASK 6. The inspection of written materials is supplemented by observation of the meaning of policy in the concrete life of the school. The question is: When one looks at practices in schools as distinct from enactments and arguments about policy, what does one learn about the meaning of policy in the day-to-day life of the schools? This involves, of course, the selection of schools which represent the range of practice. It also involves the observation of the total atmosphere of the school and a considerable range of its activities as well as the particulars of religious education at various class levels.

TASK 7. Central to the interpretation of policies in regard to religion and schooling are various aspects of the meaning of freedom. It is necessary to speak of this task at greater length.

In the United States we have affirmed two interrelated principles: the separation of church and state and the principle of religious freedom. The European countries with which we are concerned have not founded their policies on the principle of separation although they have long-standing traditions of religious freedom. Each of these countries has a history of an established church. The Church of England and the Church of Sweden are still established churches, although the character of their establishment differs in many respects from its character in the past. In the Netherlands the presence of confessional political parties is very different from the American conception of the separation of religion and politics. Our questions concern what is meant by religious freedom in these countries and how its meaning relates to other civic and intellectual freedoms that are of central importance to democratic education.

One aspect of the meaning of freedom relates to freedom from ignorance. One is not free to make enlightened choices about matters in which he is inadequately informed. The learner must know that to which he is committed else his belief is blind and slavish. Many would say that we in the United States have not paid adequate attention in the public schools to the problems of developing religious literacy. Religion is taught, if at all, as a corollary of other subjects. In European countries religion is a subject of study in its own right. In this inquiry we are interested in how it is managed so that it meets educational values and standards. We are concerned with policies concerning the understanding of different forms of Christian religion, of non-Christian religions, of the varieties of dissent. We seek to understand how the teaching of religion in these countries comes to grips with the demand for religious commitment and for objectivity in teaching. We are interested in how religious freedom is related to the development of critical belief and conviction.

Another aspect of educational policy concerns the place and character of forms of worship in school in relation to the demand for religious literacy and conviction while maintaining the freedom of the individual to think for himself, to exercise intellectual and moral integrity. In regard to religious worship, as well as the teaching of classes in religion, we are interested in how respect for differing views is handled.

Since religious freedom has generally been conceived to include the freedom of parents to send their children to schools of their choice, we are interested in how policies cognizant of this right are related to other policies concerning freedom. Policies recognizing the right of the parent in this regard may conflict with those supporting other fundamental values. The freedom of the learner to extend the range of his choice, to learn in school to respect in full measure the views of others, to cultivate habits of free inquiry and of deliberation in the presence of conflicting ideas may be submerged in the pursuit of a policy emphasizing only part of the fuller meaning of freedom. We are interested in determining how various European policies may extend or limit the school's role in providing a full and free interplay between diverse religious interests.

We are also concerned with how the freedom of one church or religious group is related to the freedom of another. In this regard we are interested in policies dealing with equality of opportunity for religious groups. We seek to discover how the opportunity of one church, or religious group, or combination of both, to extend its message through educational activity relates to the educational opportunities of other groups. Since the freedom of one group may support or deny the freedom of another, we look for evidence of whether freedom and equality of opportunity are directly or inversely related. The critical tests seem to appear in the ways educational policies provide for religious minorities and for diversity in religious experience.

TASK 8. Apart from the content of policies, we shall examine the ways European countries have gone about the business of policy building.

The extent and quality of attention given to educational problems and policies in many countries of Europe are impressive to an American observer. Education is a common topic in the news, on radio and television broadcasts, in the platforms of political parties, in the study of national affairs, in legislative debates, and in everyday conversation. The discussion of educational policy is relatively well informed and frequently reflects the interests of the component elements of the nation's power structure.

We would do well to try to specify some of the influences contributing to this enlightened discussion of educational policy. For example, in England a series of commissions has been appointed by the government to study educational problems. Some of the most valuable materials on English educational policy are found in the reports of the various advisory councils of the Ministry of Education. These reports have been helpful in focusing the attention of the country on key considerations. Similarly, in Sweden commissions have been appointed to look into the adequacy of educational policy, to collect data, and to interpret the educational needs of a particular period of national life. These advisory groups in both countries have had considerable influence on legislative action. They have molded and refined the discussion of crucial issues both in the legislature and throughout the country. Much of this discussion has focused upon how religion shall be managed in the schools.

Another example may be helpful. English policy requires that each local education authority appoint a committee to develop an agreed syllabus for religious instruction. These committees are made up of laymen, educators, and clergymen of the various faiths, and thus different points of view are brought to the conference table. The consequences of this process of developing an educational program through the give and take of traditionally conflicting interests are of considerable importance. Societies in which religious interests are segregated, in which basic educational problems may not be commonly confronted, are deprived of the essential condition for the cooperative development of policy.

In the conduct of the study, statements elaborating these eight tasks were used to explain the project to others, particularly to those who helped to assemble the evidence. Clearly my associates and consultants are not to be held responsible for the particular structure of the study, the formulation of the tasks, or the interpretations of evidence. However, without the help of colleagues who could select and penetrate into the areas where evidence was to be sought, the tasks would have been formidable.

The reader should be forewarned that the selections and interpretations involved in this study are conditioned by the author's judgments. Inquiry into educational policy is never free from the selection and interpretation of the inquirer as he defines the problem and accumulates data and evidences. This does not mean that such inquiry rests only on subjective and arbitrary grounds. It does suggest that the basis for these appraisals should be recognizable, that they should in some measure be available for public inspection, and that as far as possible the influence of the values at stake in these judgments be indicated. These are major demands, and undoubtedly all value-involved inquiry falls short of their fulfillment. Yet they need to be posted as a directive framework for the understanding of the problem and the interpretation of its findings.

In this study the general perspective of the author may be suggested by a few statements offered here in highly abbreviated form. Although they merit much fuller discussion, they provide some clues as to the framework brought to the inquiry.

The values of a free people represented by thoughtful use of such terms as freedom, equality, open-mindedness, integrity, and respect for the views of others may be fruitfully used to interpret a nation's policy about religion and schooling. Granted that we are not in complete agreement in our interpretations of these values, nevertheless free peoples have had enough experience with their meanings in concrete situations to suggest their use as criteria in weighing and assessing issues in public policy. These values, enlisting the loyalty and support of a free people, provide an operative framework for the study of problems that have long been approached by more narrowly defined interests.

The use of the educational values of a free people to transcend the limitations of partisan strife is not to be understood as hostility to religious interests. It is to be distinguished from a narrow and militant secularism which seeks to be promulgated as another kind of religion through the public schools. Here there is no effort to reduce the religious impulse to the status of superstition or to cancel out of a culture its roots in religious experience and institutions. However, the role of the church in the determination of public educational policy should be brought within the range of scrutiny provided by the educational values of a free people.

With these considerations in mind, the author has undertaken the study of public policy concerning religion and schooling from a point of view which is independent of particular church affiliation. The study represents an effort to provide an alternative to the view that one must bring an active and committed participation in a specific church to the forefront of the discussion of policy in this area. It is the educational interest and the educational values which remain in the fore and which seek to provide for the maximum growth of religious experience for all.

NOTES

1. Joseph N. Moody, "A Catholic View of Contemporary Conflict," in *The Outbursts That Await Us* by Arthur Hertzberg, Martin E. Marty, and Joseph N. Moody (New York: The Macmillan Co., 1963), p. 120.

CHAPTER 2

Religion and the Schools in England

When an American educator visits an English school at the opening of the school day, he is confronted with a situation that is radically different from anything he has been accustomed to in the United States. He arrives at the time of the daily act of worship.

The visitor may join some of the masters as they sit at the sides of the assembly hall, or he may stand in the yard while the worship service is conducted outdoors, or he may be asked to join the processional as a simple wooden cross made by the students in the school's shop is carried by one of the students to the platform. He may participate in the singing of a hymn, the reading of a collective response, the offering of a prayer. He will typically find the ceremony brief, dignified, and worshipful. If the headmaster has announcements or other academic concerns to take up with the entire school, he will separate these matters from the period of worship.

The students will probably be brought actively into the act of worship, perhaps by one of them reading from the Bible or from some other appropriate expression of Christian belief. If the headmaster does not conduct the assemblage, the master who instructs in religious education will probably do so.

The visitor may join a group of students and a master who go to another room provided for Roman Catholics. He will probably not encounter any instance of a student's withdrawing from this religious activity, or any instance of a master's withdrawal from it, although either might occur and would be accepted as a matter of course.

The visitor may come to a school in which the act of religious worship is performed in a rather perfunctory manner. He may visit a school in which worship occurs in homerooms since the school has no place in which the entire school body can assemble. In some of these rooms it may be difficult to identify an act of worship. The visitor will sense that the quality of the school's religious attitude, as well as its academic atmosphere, is a function of the headmaster's convictions and sense of values. Most heads and teachers support the daily act of worship since it sets the tone of the school and unites its efforts with those of the historic English Christian tradition. Yet, evidence points also to considerable opposition to worship in school and suggests that its acceptance as a national policy would be difficult to achieve today.

The Statutory Provisions of 1944

In England and Wales an act of Parliament states the conditions under which public funds are provided for the support of church schools.[1] The act also requires religious worship and religious instruction in all schools within the national system. This is the only subject of the curriculum prescribed by an act of Parliament. In schools provided wholly by public authorities the instruction is to follow an agreed syllabus drawn up by conferences of representatives of the churches, the teachers, and the local educational authorities. In schools established by churches and continued under church control, though supported in part by public funds, religious instruction is in accordance with the teaching of the church which founded the school.

This general framework of policy concerning religion and schooling was established by the Education Act of 1944, frequently referred to as the Butler Act. R. A. Butler, who later held the office of Foreign Secretary, was then president of the Board of Education and was largely responsible for the content of the bill as well as for the processes which secured its enactment. When in 1944 the Board of Education became the Ministry of Education, Butler became the first Minister of Education.

The Education Act of 1944 has been amended by the education acts of 1946, 1948, and 1953; the Education Act of 1959 extended provisions laid down in the earlier enactment. However, these acts have not altered the basic policies instituted by the Butler Act.

Provisions for the support of church-established schools from state funds and for the teaching of religion in the public schools are not isolated phenomena. They are parts of a government's efforts to achieve a comprehensive program of school reform. The Education Act of 1944 established a basic pattern for a national system of education and drew into this national system in one degree or another a variety of schools of different backgrounds which were already in existence. This act established basic policies for achieving certain goals in primary, secondary, and further education and laid out schedules for achieving the changes that were called for. It developed in considerable detail and with much care for avoidance of misunderstanding the rules by which these policies and goals were to be achieved. The act established administrative machinery for extending the range of educational opportunity from infancy to adulthood, for providing special educational treatment for those needing it, and for maintaining a high quality of schooling.

An integral part that in a sense provided the conditions by which a national program of educational reform could be advanced was a settlement of the religious question. English policies about religion and schooling are not discrete and self-contained. These statements about the place of religion in public education are part and parcel of a larger effort to extend educational opportunity of an appropriate quality to a larger number of the people.

The act includes various strands from previous education acts; for example, it continued the existence of "local education authorities" (L.E.A.'s) which provide much of the structural unity of English education and are brought in many respects under the direction and continued influence of the Ministry. These L.E.A.'s refer to the county and county borough councils which were earlier empowered to deal with local educational support and control in place of various boards of education. The Butler Act provides that the L.E.A.'s should establish and control "county schools," those which Americans would call "public schools." Since the act also provides that schools established by the churches would be brought within the national system, it contains a dual system of schools: county schools directly under the control of public authorities and voluntarily aided schools under the management of church-appointed bodies.

In both county and voluntary schools Section 25 of the act mandates that the school day shall begin with an act of collective worship to be attended by all students. Only if the L.E.A.'s for the county schools or the managers or governors of voluntary schools think it impractical because of the nature of the school premises may there be any exception. In addition, religious instruction must be given in each school of either type. Only if a parent requests withdrawal from worship or religious instruction or both may any student be excused.

The act goes on to describe the way in which a student who is withdrawn shall be provided with opportunity to receive religious instruction elsewhere during school hours. It informs L.E.A.'s that their responsibilities in regard to secular instruction in voluntary schools should not interfere with provisions for religious instruction. In county or voluntary schools an effort should be made to provide for religious observances by the religious body chosen by the parent, but this should not entail expenditure by the L.E.A.

The act of collective worship "shall not, in any county school, be distinctive of any particular religious denomination, and the religious instruction . . . at a county school . . . shall be given in accordance with an agreed syllabus adopted for the school or for those pupils and shall not include any catechism or formulary which is distinctive of any particular religious denomination." (Section 26)

The fifth schedule to the act provides for the way in which the L.E.A. shall receive help in developing the agreed syllabus and the teaching materials and methods appropriate to it. The L.E.A. shall appoint the members of an advisory council to produce a syllabus and if such a council produces unanimous recommendations, the L.E.A. is bound to "have regard" for them.

The fifth schedule provides more detailed directions for the preparing and use of the agreed syllabus. The L.E.A. shall appoint to advisory councils or committees members of religious denominations that represent the circumstances of the area. The Church of England, the teachers, and the L.E.A. itself should be represented. It is "the duty of the conference to seek unanimous agreement upon a syllabus of religious instruction." They may adopt more than one syllabus and designate for whom it should be used. Further provisions allow for subcommittees and for the adoption of the resulting syllabuses by the L.E.A.'s. If unanimous agreement is not reached or the Minister is not satisfied, he shall appoint a committee of experienced persons to prepare the syllabus. Thus the L.E.A. is the arm of the Ministry, and the Ministry will see to it that a syllabus is produced.

A further provision is made for the review of any agreed syllabus and for the further use of the Ministry's authority to see to it that an agreed syllabus is achieved and adopted. L.E.A.'s should also reconsider any temporary syllabus, convene a conference which is to seek unanimous agreement, and if this fails, the Minister shall appoint a committee to prepare the syllabus. In short, the act mandates the L.E.A.'s to see to it that a syllabus to which all agree is provided.

Section 30 of the act provides that "no person shall be disqualified by reason of his religious opinions, nor of his attending or omitting to attend religious worship, from being a teacher in a county school or in any voluntary school." Nor shall he be required to give religious instruction or be discriminated against in salary or promotion or any other way for not giving this instruction or for refraining from attending religious worship. This provision is qualified in regard to teachers in two types of voluntary schools, and to these distinctions we now turn.

A voluntary school is one maintained wholly or partly by the local authority, but not established by it; its voluntary foundation is recognized by certain clauses concerning its management and by provisions for certain privileges concerning the appointment of staff, the conduct of religious observances and teaching, rights of property, and the like. Many schools which were initially established by a particular church or church society have been supported by public funds since the establishing society or denomination found itself unable under modern conditions to provide adequate support for these schools. Various arrangements have been tried over the years to relieve this situation. The problem faced by Butler and Chuter Ede, who was Parliamentary Secretary to the Ministry of Education, and their associates was to find some practical policy for bringing church schools into a confederation of national schools.

Voluntary schools are divided into three categories: controlled schools, aided schools, and special arrangement schools; it is provided that the Minister will decide to which category a school belongs after an application by the school is made to him.

A controlled school is one in which the L.E.A. takes over the responsibility for all the expenses of maintaining the school, including alterations and additions to bring it up to certain standards. In exchange for this support, the control of the school is to be vested in the L.E.A. through its appointment of two thirds of the members of the managing or governing body while one third is appointed by the body which founded the school.

Religious instruction is to be given in accordance with an agreed syllabus, unless at the request of the parents it may be given in accordance with the trust deed, that is, the charter of the school.[2] In this case, for not more than two periods a week such instruction is given by "reserved teachers." These are teachers who have prepared to give denominational instruction. A formula determines how many of these teachers should be appointed for schools of differing sizes; not more than one fifth of the teaching staff may be reserved teachers. The foundation managers or governors have the power of concurring or of vetoing the L.E.A.'s selection of reserved teachers, who shall also be dismissed as reserved teachers if the foundation governors or managers find the teaching ineffective or unsuitable to the contract founding the school. The appointment and dismissal of other teachers — teachers of the secular subjects — is under the control of the L.E.A., but a section of a 1945 act "make[s] it appear that teachers are in the service of the managers or governors and not of the local education authority." [3]

In aided schools and in special agreement schools, in contrast to controlled schools, religious instruction is under the control of the managers or governors of the school and must accord with the terms of the trust deed of the school or with the practice observed in the school before it became a part of the national system as a voluntary school. This means in effect that it is a denominational or church-directed school. In an aided school two thirds of the managing or governing body are to be appointed by the foundation establishing the school and one third by the L.E.A. The employment of teachers is to be regulated by the rules of management or articles of government for the school — that is, teachers are in the employment of the managers or governors. In aided schools if teachers of denominational religious instruction fail to give instruction efficiently and suitably, they may be dismissed by the managers or governors without the consent of the L.E.A.[4] If parents desire it, religious instruction according to an agreed syllabus must be provided.

Various provisions for determining the financial support of these schools are given in the Butler Act and modified in subsequent acts. In general, under the 1944 act the church or denomination was to undertake to meet half the costs of structural improvements and external repairs while the L.E.A. paid the salaries and the costs of running the school. The act of 1959 cuts the contribution of the church from one half to one fourth; subject to certain limitations,[5] the act provides 75 percent of the cost of a new secondary aided school if the need for it can be shown to result from the enrollments in primary aided schools.

Special agreement schools include those in which adjustments were needed in order to provide funds for the fulfillment of an agreement made in the Education Act of 1936. In this act subsidies were available for denominational efforts to build reorganized schools. L.E.A.'s could for a limited period pay from 50 to 75 percent of the cost of building secondary schools. The outbreak of war in September 1939, had interrupted the fulfillment of these agreements, and in the 1944 act these agreements initiated as an emergency measure were revived.[6] Since special agreement schools are denominational schools, their policies in regard to religious instruction are those of the aided schools.

A number of other schools, some established by church interests and others by nonsectarian trust foundations, are brought less directly into relationship with the national system. Direct grant grammar schools, independent schools of the British "public school" tradition, and schools preparatory for these public schools are essentially what Americans call private schools. Although they may be in part aided and controlled by the government in the sense of being recognized as efficient, they are independent of policies concerning religion and schooling laid down for county and voluntary schools.

In short, British policy continues a dual system of private and state-controlled schools in a highly elaborated and detailed way. It has been characterized as a masterpiece of synthesis, the balanced putting together of opposed tendencies. "The Act itself was at once a synthesis and an instrument for forging various syntheses necessary to the growth of a social democracy; it seeks to create, Mr. Butler observed, a synthesis between order and liberty, local initiative and national direction, voluntary agencies and the State, and the private life of the school and the public life of the neighbourhood." [7]

From Enactment to Practice

English policy thus recognizes different types of schools which have developed within the English tradition, and provides for different kinds of relationships of these schools to the Ministry and to the sources of public funds. It allows privately established schools as well as those established by public authorities to find a place in the national system. Thus the various churches — Roman Catholic, Anglican, and Dissenting or Free Churches — choose the kind of relationship their schools are to have within the national system.

This has worked out so that in 1960 about 77 percent of a total school population of almost seven million were enrolled in county schools; slightly more than 12 percent were enrolled in Church of England schools; slightly less than 8 percent were enrolled in Roman Catholic schools; about 2 percent were enrolled in schools of other denominations (Table 1). The Roman Catholic Church chose to retain control over the schools which it founded. Of almost 8,000 Church of England schools, about 42 percent were aided; about 57 percent were controlled, that is, came under the control of the L.E.A.'s. Of the schools of the Free Churches, about 300 became controlled and 150 became aided.

These figures should be interpreted in the light of a number of conditions. About one of every ten of the population of Britain is Catholic. Anglican schools are essentially rural; 90 percent of Roman Catholic schools are urban. As Table 1 shows, the Roman Catholic schools enroll more than 100,000 more pupils in their aided schools than do the Anglicans. The average size of an Anglican school numbers 111; that of a Roman Catholic school, 261; and that of a county school, 283.[8]

In addition to the Anglican, Roman Catholic, and Free Church schools there is a small but increasing number of students in separate Jewish schools. Before World War I over 9,000 children attended Jewish schools.[9] This figure declined after the first war but has increased again since the 1940's. According to a series of

TABLE 1   The Status and Denomination of Schools in England and Wales, January, 1960*

	JUNIOR AND INFANT		ALL-AGE		SECONDARY		TOTAL	
	Schools	Pupils	Schools	Pupils	Schools	Pupils	Schools	Pupils
CHURCH OF ENGLAND								
Aided	2,999	326,651	175	24,642	139	43,642	3,313	394,935
Controlled	4,212	401,540	181	22,839	83	26,329	4,476	450,708
Special agreement	2	285	1	165	25	9,667	28	10,117
Not determined	15	2,372			2	690	17	3,062
Total	7,228	730,848	357	47,646	249	80,328	7,834	858,822
ROMAN CATHOLIC								
Aided	1,246	290,765	479	126,606	254	90,713	1,979	508,084
Controlled	1	39			1	138	2	177
Special agreement			1	435	90	38,392	91	38,827
Total	1,247	290,804	480	127,041	345	129,243	2,072	547,088
OTHER VOLUNTARY								
Aided	52	6,416	5	949	93	46,538	150	53,903
Controlled	125	14,706	14	1,622	165	76,311	304	92,639
Special agreement					1	255	1	255
Total	177	21,122	19	2,571	259	123,104	455	146,797
COUNTY	13,555	2,890,999	425	90,092	4,948	2,390,483	18,928	5,371,574
ALL SCHOOLS	22,207	3,933,773	1,281	267,350	5,801	2,723,158	29,289	6,924,281

* From Tudor David, Church and School (London: Councils and Education Press, 1961), p. 20.

articles published in 1961, more than 6,000 students were in attendance at Jewish aided schools; 4,000 of them in London, the rest mostly in Manchester, Birmingham, and Liverpool. These are largely Orthodox Jewish children. There are an estimated 32,000 Jewish children aged five to fifteen in London, and 16,000 in the other large cities.[10]

The Status of Religious Education in the Curriculum

One of the effects of the Education Act of 1944 is to give the study of religion in the school's schedule of studies a place on a par with — or, some think, above — other studies. The study of religion does not have to be confined to hours at either the beginning or the end of the school day. These unfavorable times for religious instruction had been the rule in earlier legislation. Furthermore, in the Butler Act the study of religion in county schools is subject to inspection by the Ministry as is any other subject. Section 77 (5) provides for the inspection by Her Majesty's inspectors of religious instruction in schools maintained by L.E.A.'s. In voluntary schools, where denominational religion is taught, inspection is arranged by the governors.

Of more importance in bringing the study of religion to a level comparable with other subjects is the providing for examinations in religion within the British pattern of examinations. Much of education in England, as in other European countries, is characterized and ruled by examinations which select and channel the careers of boys and girls. A subject which does not have examination status is typically considered inferior in academic importance. The upgrading of religious education by enabling students to elect it within the pattern of subjects in which they will be examined for entrance to higher or continued education is most significant in elevating the status of the study of religion. Closely related to this is the elevation of religion as a field of study for those preparing to teach.

Furthermore, English policy affords religion a privileged place among the subject matters of instruction. It is the only subject prescribed by Parliament. The mandated act of worship provides for an experience in religion as well as for knowledge of the scriptures and of Christian doctrine. The government does not specify other subjects to be taught, or how the syllabus in them is to be developed, nor does it make necessary an opportunity to practice them. However, religion is the only subject for which statutory right of withdrawal exists.

Interdenominational Christianity

As we have seen, English policy governing religious instruction in county schools involves the building of an agreed syllabus by an educational committee in the county, and care must be taken to see that the content of this syllabus shall not favor any particular denomination. The instruction is to be interdenominational Christianity. Although the term "Christian" is not used in the statutes, it is clear from the context of the entire matter that both the act of collective worship and religious instruction were to strengthen the Christian framework of English tradition and experience. During the debate in Parliament, Chuter Ede pointed out the "general recognition that even if parents themselves have in the course of life encountered difficulties that have led them into doubts and hesitations, they do desire that their children shall have a grounding in the principles of the Christian faith as it ought to be practised in this country." [11] The main emphasis in religious instruction falls upon an understanding of the Bible as a whole, a more detailed knowledge of the Gospels and the life and teaching of Jesus, and a knowledge of the common creeds and sacraments of the Christian churches.

This means that the school should teach the common essentials of Christian doctrine. "The purpose of an agreed syllabus is that the religion taught in the unsectarian schools maintained or aided by the state should be Christianity which all the Churches profess." [12] The instruction is to encompass the doctrines upon which the Protestant churches can agree. Thus the emphasis is not to teach about religion in the sense of an objective presentation of factual material, avoiding partiality to any particular view. Rather, the teaching is based on the importance of Christian interdenominational faith and doctrine. While this instruction may not exclude knowledge of other religious traditions, the main justification of religious instruction is not that a citizen of the modern world should understand the cultures of the world, including their religions, and hence should be objectively informed about them. Of course, the teaching of Christian doctrine and belief does not formally exclude knowledge of other religions, but the rationale of English policy clearly centers on Christian conviction rather than intercultural understanding.

The central responsibility of interdenominational Christian religious instruction consists in teaching the English Bible. When those working in religious instruction are questioned about the basis of selection of material, the usual response refers to that which is relevant to the Bible.

> Is it to be assumed that the syllabus should be mainly or wholly Biblical? Such a question must not be taken to imply the exclusion of other material relevant to the origin and dissemination of the Christian faith — church history, for example, to which agreed syllabuses have very properly given a considerable place, or the Apostles' Creed, which patently is not the distinctive tenet of any Church or Churches. But unquestionably the Churches regard the teaching in the Bible as the primary source of Christian doctrine, and Christianity takes its rise from the historical facts recorded in the New Testament.[13]

The policy affirms the centrality of knowledge of the Bible to Christian faith, and religious instruction in England refers primarily to teaching the Protestant Bible.

When one asks further about what is included within an interdenominational interpretation of the Protestant Bible, one is typically referred to the Apostles' Creed. As expressed by an experienced and highly qualified inspector of religious education in an interview, "We have found no real difficulty in determining the common basis for religious education. Denominational doctrinal differences may be distinguished from what all adhere to within the framework of the Apostles' Creed. We need to work at making common Christianity meaningful, and we no longer get excited about differences in the interpretation of the essential truth." The point is that immersion as held by the Baptists is representative of a particular denominational doctrine which is not to be included in religious instruction, while the assertions of belief of the Apostles' Creed are taken to be undenominational (that is, interdenominational) .

The problem here concerns which interpretation of the meaning of the Creed is to be used to determine when instruction is denominational and when it is interdenominational. Typically the response indicates that a wide range of interpretations may be used. For instance, the section, "He descended into Hell," may be interpreted "more literally" or "more figuratively." However, the impression is given that more "fundamentalistic" interpretations are not as desirably Christian as others. There appear to be some limits to the range of desirable interpretations of the meaning of the Creed. It also suggests that those who prefer to be known as Christians on the basis of the quality of life that is lived rather than on the basis of belief in creeds may also be excluded from the main current of English Christianity. The point is that interpretations of interdenominational Christianity seem to refer to those forms of Christian belief which are recognized to fall within the mainstream of English denominational effort.[14] We shall return to this point in ensuing discussions.

It is clear that the meaning of "religious instruction" takes for granted that it will be Christian and Protestant, and the meaning of "Christian" is given in doctrinal terms. This may be seen clearly in a statement concerning religious beliefs given in a pamphlet of the Ministry of Education in 1949, reprinted in 1961.

The Christian religion, perhaps more than some others, has concerned itself with social duties on earth. It has exalted the dignity of human personality. It has stressed the brotherhood of man and emphasized the need of good works, as a necessary part of men's duty to God. For Christians, men are brothers because God is their Father and good works are justified not only by their fruits but because they fulfill God's will and contribute to the Kingdom of Heaven.

This raises for the good citizen the problem of theological belief. To hold a spiritual faith does not bind a man to every article of a particular creed, but there are some essentials on which no religion can compromise. It must, for instance, accept a code of right and wrong, based on absolute values. Christians, and some others, would add that it must acknowledge a personal God who, having created the world, retains a just and merciful interest in every one of His creatures.[15]

Statements of this kind make it clear that the role of religious education is not merely to inform children and youth about the Bible and the essentials of undenominational Christian tradition. It aims to secure belief in doctrines taken to be held in common by the main churches in the culture. English policy seeks believers, membership in a "worshipful community," and in this sense religion is given a special place in the curriculum, and a position which is not given to other academic studies. In subsequent pages we shall be concerned with the extent to which this policy is endorsed today.

Withdrawal from Religion

The conception of freedom involved in this policy of undenominational religion is contained in the provision for parents to withdraw their children from religious instruction or worship or both and in the provision that teachers shall not be discriminated against because of refraining from the religious worship or instruction in schools. It is exemplified in county schools by the withdrawal of Roman Catholic students from the program of worship and religious instruction under the agreed syllabus. Thus a student is not compelled to participate in worship or religious instruction which is not acceptable to his parents.

Aside from the withdrawal of Roman Catholic and Jewish students attending county schools, apparently very few students are withdrawn. The reasons for this lack of withdrawal are not totally clear. Perhaps parents of secularistic tendencies are not strongly enough convinced of their views to withdraw their children. Perhaps they prefer to have their children experience and understand that from which they themselves differ. Perhaps those most convinced of their point of view send their children to independent schools. Perhaps the voice of dissent in modern England is muted through a complex of cultural factors that have placed dissent on the defensive. At any rate, one hears repeatedly that there are very few instances of withdrawal of children from the agreed syllabus program and that in existing cases one finds no discrimination, academic or social, against those who are withdrawn.

Whether this means that a full sense of freedom is operative in English policy is another question. It is clear that policy in England assumes that one is not free in religious matters simply by being left alone. "Nothing could be more fatal than to use any subject to mould the child to a pattern — except the negligence that leaves him to be moulded accidentally, but no less indelibly, by the base and dangerous chance influences that abound in the modern world of propaganda and cheap and effortless amusements." [16] The conception of freedom involved in English policy does not hold that education should refrain from molding the child in the dominant religious pattern of his culture.

It is also clear that this policy is grounded in the view that if one is to attain religious and intellectual freedom, he must know the traditions in which he is nourished or from which he is departing. Enlightenment, not ignorance, is a condition of freedom, and it is less than a full measure of freedom to be free from that which one does not understand.

A question remains, however, concerning the range of religious belief and experience in which the young are enlightened. A school program cannot include all of the religious interpretations and beliefs which a culture makes available; it must be selective. Nevertheless, the criteria for selection may value maximally the opportunity for the individual to be as fully informed as possible so that he can make up his own mind. Or they may value most centrally the preservation of what has already been established. To put it in terms of educational policy, the school may provide a widest possible range of alternatives for the free choice of the individual; or it may provide a range of interpretations within the limits of a framework about which there is no choice.

English policy, as we have noticed, assumes the production of "believers" or "members in a worshipful community." There may be a range of interpretation of doctrine within the church; there may be a choice between Christian churches; but the weight of English policy favors individual choice only within the framework of the acceptance of traditional and dominant creedal beliefs.

The Act of Worship

It has been pointed out that English policy affords a central place for the teaching of interdenominational Protestant Christianity. In the act of 1944, religious instruction was upgraded and an experience in an act of worship was mandatory. Religion was to be practiced as well as taught in the school. It was not just to be taught about; it was to be taught in the sense of seeking believers. In this sense religion was given a special place in the curriculum. English policy does not merely direct that the young be informed about the religious basis of English culture. It prefers that they be brought into a living worshipful community.

This policy gives religion a distinctive place in the content of schooling in the sense that neither the content of religious education nor the performance of the act of worship is to be left to the vagaries of local educational authorities, teachers, or community interests. Furthermore, it expresses the judgment that worship without study of "divinity" will not do. The young are to be informed, participative members of a worshipful community. Moreover, the act of worship not only provides an opportunity for an orderly beginning of the school day. It "sets the tone," as one is frequently informed, for the entire program of the school. It is intended that a Christian spirit pervade the atmosphere and work of the school.

It is commonly understood in English schools that the act of worship is not to be diluted with the rest of the business of running a school. It is not to serve as an opportunity merely to carry on the secular announcements of the school's activities. On the contrary, the act of devotion is present to counteract the "secular" movements and tendencies in modern English life. This does not mean that the ingredients of the service itself are to be deliberately anti-secularistic in tone. It does mean that English educational policy is not neutral in regard to cultural movements that bear upon traditional religious beliefs and values. It means that the weight of educational policy is to be thrown into an effort to have the Christian spirit, in the sense in which we have identified it, serve as the preferred basis for interpreting value problems in the school.

The 1957 revision of the report of the research committee of the Institute of Christian Education says that the Parliamentary requirement of daily worship has not done more harm than good, as some had feared, but has directed attention to form and content as well as to meaning and purpose in worship. They "perceive no tendency to foster a 'school religion,' impoverished in itself and mischievous in so far as it might offer a substitute for worship in the churches." The report finds that the hymns and prayers of all churches are drawn upon, and although there is some indifference, presumably on the part of some headmasters, most desire to have their schools "worship God in spirit and in truth." [17]

In a sense English educational policy responds to the general character of religion in Britain as described by some students of the English scene. Michael Argyle, for instance, has observed what he finds to be the differences between religion in the United States and in England.

. . . in America religion is more liberal and more secularized, and it is attuned to the values of the prosperous middle class. In Britain religion has maintained its traditional character, and changes in society and personality have resulted in a decline of interest. [18]

In general, churches in England have far fewer secular activities associated with them; they have, rather, maintained their "traditional character." Educational policy is to support this traditional character. It is to bring the young, through knowledge of Christian tradition and forms, as well as through participation in the act of worship, into the fold of Christian worshippers.

The policy is to do more than this, however. Not only is the Protestant Bible to be taught, but Christianity, as defined by those who give a "mainstream," though not necessarily orthodox, interpretation to the Apostles' Creed and the like, should be taught. It also means that the schools should seek to encourage identification with and eventual membership in the church.

While teachers may withdraw from the expression of Christian commitment, the expression of Christian convictions is sanctioned by civic law. It has been observed that although there is no lawful test of religious identification for the selection or promotion of educators (teachers or masters), it is more likely in certain instances that an educator who expressed an active concern with Christian belief and worship would be appointed a headmaster. The effect of British policy is to provide through the L.E.A.'s a considerable preference for Christian leadership if the local community favors it. The National Union of Teachers reports as recently as January and July 1964, cases in which teachers applying for positions felt they were discriminated against by questions concerning willingness to accept classes in religious instruction.[19] As Diana Dewar reports in her recent *Backward Christian Soldiers,* "The head teacher of a large mixed infants school . . . , a committed Christian, told me she would feel most unhappy if any of her staff felt unable conscientiously to teach religion. She said, 'I would ask them to get a transfer.' "[20]

An example may show the thoroughly Christian character of many English schools. In a county junior school, the equivalent of an elementary public school in the States, the teacher pointed with considerable pride to the extensive handwork of the children. The schoolrooms contained an imposing array of products made by the children showing their use of paper, paints, and weaving materials. Many figures of religious significance were displayed: angels, biblical costumes, illustrated copies of Bible verses — many more than would be found in most Sunday School classrooms in America. In response to a comment concerning the extent of religious themes present in the artistic and creative work of these children, the teacher observed that one should visit the school in the Christian season or on other holy days, for then one would see much more fully their use of Christian themes. To an American visitor, it was difficult to visualize a school more full of Christian faith and doctrine.

English policy provides, if the local education authorities and the educators wish it, a school program that encourages at many points and at levels appropriate to the child's development, an identification with a Christian outlook and with a church. Speaking of the agreed syllabuses published since the 1944 act, the Institute of Christian Education says:

> . . . Increasing attention is paid in them to worship and the aim of the teaching is declared to be that children should understand and accept the Christian faith and follow the Christian way of life, while in more recent syllabuses the hope is expressed that school worship and religious instruction will, in the words of the Introduction to the Lindsey syllabus, 'increasingly lead pupils to become and remain full members of a worshipping community outside the school.' [21]

Historical Conditions

The Education Act of 1944 is clearly designed to provide a basis for continuing, with modifications, a historic policy in English education. Although new provisions for the control of schools were set up, the provisions for religious instruction and the subsidy of church schools built upon an enduring tradition that education should be Christian. The church since the days of the cathedral school and the charity school has had a major role in English education. When the state entered the field in the nineteenth century, the church had a record of centuries of effort in behalf of schools. The act of 1944 in appealing to a spirit of tolerance and respect for others offered a concrete basis in policy and practice for an acceptable settlement of what had earlier torn English communities apart. When one looks at the current policy in the light of those of the past, one appreciates both the continuity and the new dimensions of the 1944 settlement.

In English history a number of schools have fulfilled different purposes, and the Statute of Artificers of 1406, taken by some to be the first English education act, says "every man or woman, of what state or condition that he be, shall be free to set their son or daughter to take learning at any school that pleaseth them within the realm." [22] Nevertheless, the main direction of early English policy was that education was the business of the church alone. According to W. O. Lester Smith, in the centuries up to the Renaissance there was no secular control or content of education, and there was no alternative to the policy that education is inseparable from religion.

Asher Tropp in his history of the teaching profession reminds us of the qualifications to be used in the choice of a master for the charity schools.

He was to be:
1. A member of the Church of England, of a sober life and conversation, and not under the age of twenty-five years.
2. One that frequents the Holy Communion.
3. One that hath a good government of himself and passions.
4. One of a meek temper and humble behavior.
5. One of a good genius for teaching.
6. One who understands well the grounds and principles of the Christian religion, and is able to give a good account thereof to the minister of the parish, or ordinary, on examination.
7. One who can write a good hand, and who understands the grounds of arithmetic.
8. One who keeps good order in his family.
9. One who is approved by the minister of the parish (being a subscriber) before he be presented to be licensed by the ordinary.[23]

In establishing these qualifications, the Society for the Promotion of Christian Knowledge, which was formed in 1698, thus sought to ensure that the teachers of the charity schools would be soundly based in Anglican faith.

The place of the established Anglican Church in the founding and control of schools is further exemplified in one of the Canons of 1604 which states: "No man shall teach either in public school or private house, but such as shall be allowed by the Bishop of the diocese or Ordinary of the place . . . being found meet as well for . . . right understanding of God's true religion. . . ." As Smith says, "This division of the nation into Anglicans *versus* the Rest . . . had permanent disruptive consequences in our national life, and was a prime cause of the denominational quarrels which have bedevilled our modern educational system." [24]

Subsequent movements associated with the Puritan revolution did not fundamentally alter the presupposition that ecclesiastical authority was basic to the control of education although they provided some of the seeds which much later developed into movements favorable to toleration. The Puritan regime continued the intolerance of the Anglican.

> The Reformation had destroyed the medieval conception of a world governed by Pope and Emperor; its place had been taken by a nationalism in which Church and State were regarded as equivalent and coterminous . . . Anglicans were merely putting this doctrine into practice when they demanded that all education within the Realm should conform to a particular pattern: so, in their turn, were the Calvinist Puritans of the Long Parliament. Although the two combatants differed in their interpretation of Christianity and in their politics, they were in complete agreement in believing that there should be one Church-State and that parents should be obedient to its decrees concerning the education of their children.[25]

It was only after the famous Clarendon Code of the Restoration Parliament, the consequent rise of the Dissenting academies, and the movements toward toleration (the Toleration Act of 1689) that challenges to the older Anglican and Puritan orthodoxies appeared.

The Clarendon Code with its penal laws keeping Dissenters and Roman Catholics from any lawful part in the government of local and national level and forcing them to have their children educated in the Established Church was "designed to break the political and educational influence of non-Anglicans for all time." [26] In addition, its consequence was to put the religious question squarely into the social structure of English life for the center of dissent was found in middle and lower classes while Anglicanism was representative of the gentry.

The religious settlement of 1944 should beyond doubt be seen against the background of the long and bitter struggle between competing interests, among others, the Anglicans and the Nonconformists. It had its roots in the earlier traditions of ecclesiastic control of education and in the repressive conflicts of the sixteenth and seventeenth centuries. However, it became much more acute in the latter part of the eighteenth century because of the rapidly changing economic and social conditions in English life. Industrialization and the growth of factory towns made the situation more critical. In all of this struggle the fundamental question was not whether religion should be taught or public subsidy given for denominational schools. The question was rather how these arrangements should be managed and which competing interest should be satisfied.

This is shown by what one study calls the "battle royal" between Joseph Priestley and Dr. Brown of Newcastle in 1765. "Brown urged the establishment of a centralised authority in education which should secure national patriotism and religious orthodoxy, while Priestley's plea was for voluntaryism in education holding that the vital thing in education was to ensure a progressive variety of opinion." [27] Yet Priestley held religion to be central in the broader curriculum which he was urging. Those who opposed the establishment most fervently were also deeply committed to Christianity as the core of education, although they meant a purified form of the faith.

The nineteenth century is generally regarded as of crucial importance in the development of English educational policy for it began to see the active participation of the state in connection with the educational activity of the churches. Recognizing that voluntary efforts were insufficient to provide for the needs of the vast numbers of children in industrial areas, Parliament in 1833 granted state subsidies for the first time. The money was provided through the two church school societies: the National Society for Promoting the Education of the Poor in the Principles of the Established Church, founded in 1811, and the British and Foreign School Society, established by Nonconformists in 1814. These societies, representing the deep division in religious life, were the main agencies for common education in the greater part of the nineteenth century. Their conflicting conceptions of religion and of instruction in religion led to prolonged and bitter controversy.

This controversy was a center of concern in Parliament. The Whig government in 1839 initiated a plan for state control including the creation of a committee for distributing Parliamentary grants, the setting up of a system of inspection of schools receiving grants, and the founding of a nonsectarian normal school. Intense opposition by the Church of England led to the dropping of the proposal for the state school for the training of teachers. There was long and bitter struggle over the question of inspection, eventually settled by a compromise affording the Church the right to nominate inspectors. The period was characterized by slow advances by the state as it began to attain a more active partnership with the churches.

One of the interesting episodes in the development of a national system concerns the Liverpool experiment in the years 1836–1842. In Liverpool there were large numbers of Roman Catholic children, for many Irish had moved into the manufacturing districts of England. Since at least one fourth of the population was Roman Catholic, there were far more poor children than could be provided for by voluntary efforts. In these years the Liberals had gained enough political strength in Liverpool that they were able to control the Town Council. As a result of these factors, among others, "Corporation Schools" were established in which children of Roman Catholic, Anglican, and Nonconformist faiths were educated together in publicly owned schools. The Bible was studied in a form appropriate to the church membership of the pupil and religious instruction given under the representatives of the various churches. The management of these municipal elementary schools was entrusted to an education committee appointed by the Town Council.

According to the Proceedings of the committee initiating this policy:

As respects the management of the Schools, there is no doubt some difficulty in arranging plans for their future conduct so as to change them from their former exclusive character, and make them accessible to and desirable for the instruction of all classes of Christians. This change is imperative on a body representing all the different Religious Sects of Christians all of whom contribute to the maintenance of the Schools. The Committee feel no doubt of being able to arrange Plans for the conduct of the Schools which by the exercise of a little mutual concession, and liberal, they may say Christian, feeling will prove generally satisfactory and promote the general object of a useful moral and religious Education of the Poor. The Committee feel they have undertaken a very serious duty, and that they could not therefore without a violation of that trust for which they are responsible delegate the management of the Schools to other hands, however respectable, and especially to the Clergy of one particular persuasion.[28]

This atmosphere of mutual concession and liberal and Christian feeling was not to be dominant in subsequent events.

It is remarkable that more than one hundred years before the Butler Act an effort had been made to educate children of all faiths in public schools, and subsequently this experiment was to be rejected as a pattern of national policy. The full story of this incident provides interesting suggestions about the current opinion that any settlement in 1944 that did not involve the dual system was inconceivable.

In the period of the Liverpool experiment Roman Catholic authorities did not insist that children of their faith should attend only Roman Catholic schools. At that time a cardinal of the Roman church said:

I think that in this country and in Ireland such an arrangement could be made, that both Protestants and Catholics could attend anything in the form of an University or Public School, without any harm ensuing, good might perhaps be done. I think also that in the lower branches of education it might easily be managed to give them a common education, reserving the religious education of their respective classes to their own pastors.[29]

Furthermore, the Holy See, not yet having hardened its position, was able to resolve that:

. . . no judgment should be definitely pronounced in this matter; and that this kind of education should be left to the prudent discretion and religious conscience of each individual bishop. . . .[30]

The clergy should be vigilant and cautious and should try to obtain by degrees a better order of things. They should refrain from such controversy that might interfere with desirable educational policies.

However, in 1842, as the conservative reaction set in and control passed to a conservative council, it was decreed that the children should be instructed in the doctrines of the Church of England and that *all* the children would read the authorized version of the Bible and join in (Anglican) prayer. As a result, the Roman Catholic children, under the leadership of their clergy, withdrew from the schools.

It is also clear from the historical account that the intolerance and intemperance of some parts of the press and of some of the influential Anglican clergy were important contributing reasons for the reversal of policy. The attitude of the Anglicans was consistently opposed to any compromise that would lessen the influence of the establishment on the control of education. An "intelligent, if not altogether unbiased observer" reported in 1841:

Toryism and Churchism are in the ascendant, and reign with undisputed sway. The Liberal party are disheartened, and have virtually (not virtuously) abandoned the contest. Bigotry, encouraged by the want of opposition, speaks out more and more boldly. . . . More complete spiritual subjection I never saw.[31]

The conservative clergy were particularly opposed to the experiment in Liverpool if it was represented as having any directive impact upon national policy.

The development of educational policy in these years was dominated by an unfortunate involvement in the activities of a political election. Much distortion of the basic merits of the educational question developed as exaggerated claims, wild accusations, and bitterness of an electoral campaign dominated the field. So much passion was aroused that the question of providing an education for the increasing numbers of poor children was virtually submerged.

As a result, a proposal made in 1850 that Roman Catholic children might attend common public schools for secular instruction only was rejected from all sides. The atmosphere was the reverse of that which characterized the initiation of the experiment. A commentator observed that " 'from 20,000 to 30,000 of the juvenile population of Liverpool were growing up in a state of comparative barbarism, and worse than barbarism, inasmuch as they inherit vices from which the barbarian savage is free.' " [32] Thus a chapter in English policy which might have forecast an integrated national pattern of common schooling ended with the reinforcement of the pattern of voluntary schools and an increasing inadequacy to provide for the ever larger numbers of children to be educated.

The long story of controversy between the churches and those who sought to achieve a national system of education in which clerical control of the schools would be limited cannot be told here. These were among the profoundly disturbing issues: the increase of lay influence; the right of parents to obtain exemption from religious instruction for their children; efforts to obtain legislation providing government support for the growing need for adequate schools; the question of government subsidy dependent on results of examinations in the three R's; the place of religious instruction in the curriculum, and more specifically in the timetable of the school; the question of inspection of religious instruction; proposals to establish neutral teacher training schools. Apparent throughout are various strands of conditions bearing upon the character of the current national system of education: (1) The state's move to establish schools and to control religious instruction in state subsidized schools was distrusted and resented. Movements to have religious education pass into the hands of teachers rather than clergy were resisted. (2) Denominational efforts were seen as an integral part of any national educational endeavor. The "dual system" was seen as inevitable. (3) An emphatic Nonconformist preference looked to control of schools by elected bodies with provisions for unde-nominational religious instruction. (4) A secularist or neutral school system was such a radical departure from tradition that it failed to receive any substantial measure of public support. (5) The association of church membership and power with various segments of the social structure — Anglicans with the gentry, Nonconformists with the trade and commercial town groups, Roman Catholics with the urban workers — tied the question of religion and schooling to conflicting social class and political interests.

The Elementary Education Act of 1870, establishing the "School Board Era" in English education, was a landmark in the growth of the national system. It set a pattern which has continued ever since, for it established a publicly controlled system of elementary schools side by side with the church schools. It thus enacted the dual system, and at the same time underscored the problem of the place of religion in the state schools. Its solution to this problem included the famous Cowper-Temple clause according to which: "No religious catechism or religious formulary which is distinctive of any particular denomination shall be taught in the school," referring, of course, to the public elementary school.[33] Thus the state was not neutral toward religious education; it provided the basis for undenominational teaching. Those matters upon which the churches could agree would be central in religious teaching. However, the question of the desirability of this clause was in 1944, and is still today, controversial, some holding that it is highly prejudicial to true religion.

The Forster Act of 1870 also contained the important conscience clause, "the guarantee of religious freedom," as it is commonly called. In any schools receiving state subsidy parents have the right to withdraw their children from religious instruction.

Just as the question of religion dominated the settlement of the Forster Act, so the same question was crucial to the Balfour Act of 1902, which enacted a state system of secondary schools.

Its provisions included: the expansion of the tax base so that local taxes ("rates") could be used in support of church schools; increased control by L.E.A.'s over church schools; the reassertion of the Cowper-Temple and conscience clauses; and guarantees that church schools could teach religion in accordance with their trust deeds. It led among other things to the refusal of some to pay their "rates" and "Rome on the rates" became the Nonconformist battle cry. Religious education became a central political question as the Liberal forces were mustered against the Conservative bill. Thus, although the lines of policy eventually assembled in the 1944 bill were being slowly developed, the friction and strife involved in the religious controversies delayed the fundamental extension of educational opportunity until after the experiences of World War II.

Events of the 1930's and early 1940's, including the debates associated with the Government White Paper of 1943 and the passage of the 1944 education bill, reveal a network of interrelated events and beliefs making possible a settlement in 1944 that could not have been achieved in the earlier great education acts of 1870 and 1902. After the highly charged struggle associated with the 1902 act came a period in which many, disillusioned with the fraction and strife, sought to stay clear of the problems associated with religious education. One senses a period of disillusionment especially in regard to the abortive efforts of the Liberals to reverse some of the provisions of 1902.

However, in the 1920's certain events began to pave the way for a new approach to the matter. One of these was the initiative taken by the local authorities working with the churches to develop an agreed syllabus for religious instruction. The Cambridgeshire syllabus, appearing in 1924, offered a way to deal with religion so that instruction might be greatly improved in county schools. Associated with this beginning of the development of agreed syllabuses was the growth in the capacities of the teaching profession to teach religion. Teachers, consolidating their professional standing, as shown in the growth of the National Union of Teachers (N.U.T.),[34] were more and more able to teach

"Scripture" or "divinity" as an educational subject matter. The development of syllabuses in the West Riding of Yorkshire, Cambridgeshire, Leicestershire, Oxfordshire, Hampshire, and Middlesex led to the application of educational principles and controls to the teaching of religion. Teachers rather than clergy came more and more to control the teaching of religion.

The report of the consultative committee on secondary education, 1938, commonly called the Spens Report, gave considerable attention to the matter in its chapter entitled "Scripture." The Institute of Christian Education, founded in 1935, sought, as did the Spens Report, to cultivate an effective and expert teaching of religion in the undenominational sense. The Spens Report indicates the new hope and the new direction for the teaching of Scripture.

It considers the "wide and genuine recognition of the value and importance of religious education" and "that the time is favourable for a fresh consideration" of the matter. It sought "an approach to the subject which can enlist the disinterested enthusiasm and give scope to the professional ability of teachers." Although teachers differed in their personal convictions, they had faith that the approach of the agreed syllabuses (developed by local education authorities) would be a fruitful solution for secondary schools. Religious education would be "justified as a regular part" of the curriculum only if it "included some serious study to which teachers have given not less thought and skill than to their other studies." Moreover, there was no "large body of opinion definitely favorable to an entirely secular secondary education."

The report continued by making clear an educational justification for the teaching of religion by means of the agreed syllabus.

It is often maintained that the study of the Bible should have a place in the curriculum for its literary value alone. We do not wish to underestimate that value. The English Bible is one of the glories of the literary heritage bequeathed to the English-speaking peoples. For that reason there is much to be said in favour of the inclusion of portions of the Bible in the syllabus of English literature. But it is also true that no boy or girl can be counted as properly educated unless he or she has been made aware of the fact of the existence of a religious interpretation of life. The traditional form which that interpretation has taken in this country is Christian, and the principal justification for giving a place in the curriculum to the study of the Scriptures is that the Bible is the classic book of Christianity and forms the basis of the structure of Christian faith and worship. The content of the Bible has, therefore, inevitably its own dignity and associations. It can neither be treated merely as a part of English literature, nor can it be merged in the general study of history, though its meaning is, in the first instance at least, historically conditioned.[35]

Here is a clear statement of the educational, as distinct from the ecclesiastical, policy upon which the agreed syllabus program rests.

The Bible, the report continues, "contains a body of perfectly intelligible ideas, which can be systematically presented and studied" and a teacher can present these ideas so that "the difficulty of appearing to take sides in traditional controversies may be avoided." Its study provides an "intellectual discipline" which is "historical and objective." Teachers should, of course, manifest their religious faith but this will enable them more effectively to reply to students' questions "without incurring the suspicion of either insincerity or prejudice — personal or denominational."

Although in later years some questions were to arise about the adequacy of the new approach, one senses in the Spens Report a fresh breeze blowing through, or perhaps, over, the older controversies.

It seems clear to one following the long story of religious controversy that the experiences of the war years were crucial contributing factors in producing the 1944 settlement. Careful study and preparation for the framing of the bill, prolonged consultation, and skillful search for compromise on the part of Butler and his colleagues were indispensable contributing factors. In addition, the realization of the need for educational reconstruction was brought more fully home to all. Evacuation of children brought to light extremely unfavorable social and educational conditions. Professor Savory pointed out in the House of Commons the lack of knowledge of the elements of Christianity among evacuated children.[36] The unity of effort called for by the war and the common interest in securing a suitable education for all contributed to making the time favorable to reform. The need for rebuilding of schools was evident and called for the cooperation of all segments of life.

Moreover, the climate of opinion called for a truce in the old religious struggle. Converging circumstances suggest that the contending parties were sensing that little further benefit would result from the older intransigencies. They were, in a sense, ready for a settlement. Britain had come through the holocaust and was not willing that older adamant resistance should stand in the way of educational reconstruction. "It has been remarked that in great national crises there is often a new responsiveness to the central realities of religion, with a corresponding decline of interest in matters which, though perhaps less fundamental, have been the subject of divisive controversy." [37] As F. H. Hilliard puts it:

> . . . The opposition between the values inherent in our democratic way of life and those which had manifested themselves on the one hand in Nazism and on the other in Communism, itself made apparent the need for re-affirming and re-stating to the younger generation the nature and the basis of the values which form the foundations of democratic society as we in the West understand it.[38]

In the record of parliamentary debate it was repeatedly stated that these foundations were grounded in Christian principles. "It will be of little use to fight, as we are fighting today, for the preservation of Christian principles if Christianity itself is to have no future." [39] Despite the fact of a considerable amount of religious indifference, the people were said to be "perfectly aware that the totalitarian state . . . leaves something vital out, and there is a dim but almost universal understanding that the world will slither down again unless we all find a light to guide us by, a light that can be trusted. Throughout the whole of our schools a light ought to be made to shine." [40] It was readily assumed that this light was to be provided by the moral and spiritual values based in Christian principles.

Furthermore, it was commonly believed that the dual system, although inadequate in its existing form for what needed to be done, was none the less to be accepted as the basis for the postwar tasks of educational reconstruction. Butler, referring to the analysis of the White Paper of July 1943, argued that the existing "system is incompatible with the effective organization of the schools of the country and with the wise and economical use of teaching power." [41] Butler had taken the position that " the State, concerned though it is to ensure a sound religious basis for all education, cannot take on itself the full responsibility for fostering the teaching formularies distinctive of particular denominations designed to attach children to particular worshipping communities." [42] The government was trying to bring the church schools "into as close a degree of partnership as possible" and to eliminate as much friction as possible.[43] Hence, managers of church established schools were to choose between becoming controlled or aided schools.

In the preparations for the 1944 bill and particularly in the Parliamentary debate, Butler made clear an essential condition, as he saw it, to the new settlement. "Throughout the history of church schools (in general) . . . two interweaving strands are discernible, namely, an ever-changing adjustment of the measure of public assistance to enable them to meet the ever-growing costs of education, accompanied by a steadily increasing measure of public control." [44] Butler was trying to make it clear to all parties that "any further increased public aid must be accompanied by increased public control" and that this was a traditional English policy. Any settlement which did not take adequate account of this policy would "imperil its general acceptance, and might bring about a reaction as detrimental to the churches as to the cause of education itself." [45]

It was clear that the three major church groups for which a compromise had to be reached were the Anglicans, the Free Churchmen, and the Roman Catholics. The secular solution, as we have seen, did not offer a suitable basis for the continuation of traditional English policy, although strong opposition was expressed to church schools by trade unionists and other sections of the community. Of the three church groups, the Free Churches found a large measure of satisfaction in the continuance of the Cowper-Temple clause and the provision for the withdrawal of children at the request of parents. Further, the right of teachers to withdraw from religious education and worship, together with the agreed syllabus approach to religious instruction, enabled them to see a number of their schools accept the status of controlled schools.

As Butler has observed in his foreword to Marjorie Cruickshank's book, when the Anglicans were able to accept the Cowper-Temple principle and the principle of election between controlled and aided schools, an effective compromise within the context of the preservation of traditional Anglican principles was found. Anglicans were more favorably disposed toward an earlier attempted settlement — the Green Book — which provided a firmer recognition of religion in the schools, the abolition of the Cowper-Temple clause in secondary modern schools, and the abolition of the limitation on the number of reserved teachers (specialists in denominational religion). Cruickshank's account indicates extended discussion between Anglicans and between Anglicans and other government and Free Church leaders. William Temple, Archbishop of Canterbury and Primate of the Church of England, seems to have been largely responsible for the acceptance, although unenthusiastic, of the 1944 act. "Our main task," he said, "is surely not to be fighting a rearguard action in perpetual retreat until we are driven off the field by the competition of the resources of the State, but to take care that we are interpenetrating with our influence all that the State itself is doing.[46]

The Roman Catholics were, by and large, even more reluctant to accept the compromises Butler was proposing. They favored the Scottish solution, full government support of religious schools. They were, and continue to be, fundamentally opposed to the Cowper-Temple clause in principle and as an ingredient of the compromise. On the other side, the National Union of Teachers as well as the Free Churches were unalterably opposed to these preferences. However, "the most determined opposition to the proposed settlement came from the Roman Catholics." [47] Finally, very favorable provisions for long-term loans allowed the Roman church to enter the agreement although it felt that it had not obtained full justice.

The 1959 act extended the grants to aided secondary schools to 75 percent where these schools continued the education of children at existing primary schools, and grammar, technical, and modern secondary schools were now qualified for the grant. It was carrying out the fuller support of denominational schools intended by the Butler Act. This was a major assistance to the Catholic schools and enabled the Anglican schools, depending on the character of their dioceses and the vigor of their leaders, to consolidate and improve their quality. Although county schools and the giving of undenominational religious instruction predominate, the church schools have been harmoniously drawn into the national picture.

Cruickshank concludes that although the problem of complete justice in the sense of equal financial support still remains, the problem in the past "was confused by political and sectarian issues, but today public opinion is indifferent to religious feuds, and the political parties are no longer divided on a matter which can now be debated calmly and rationally." [48] We have yet to note whether this meaning of justice and of calm rationality in managing the religious question are as settled as these words indicate.

The Enactments of 1959

In a revealing series of articles published originally in *Education* in 1961 and subsequently as a pamphlet,[49] the 1959 act was seen as bringing the settlement of fifteen years earlier back to the negotiating table. Churches were being forced to re-examine and clarify their policies. Although in educational conferences as well as in political debate the religious question was avoided,[50] the matter was receiving considerable attention by the churches. "A foreign observer would not readily glean that more than one child in five in England and Wales attends a church school and that 12 per cent. of school building today is in the hands of the Churches." [51]

The 1959 act, according to this view, had wider implications for the major church groups. The Roman Catholics, who are generally credited with being the main force behind the more generous provisions of the 1959 act, had applied themselves diligently to achieve more schools at all levels and more support for them. The Free Churches were reappraising the policy whereby three out of every four of their schools had become controlled schools. In the Church of England the more recent view was that "a school which was not aided lost the capacity to impart a truly Christian education." [52] Among Free Churchmen this view was also coming to prevail.

More specifically, the Roman Catholics have given overriding priority to their schools. They have held fast to the policy affirming that every Roman Catholic child should be in a Roman Catholic primary or secondary school. "Their numbers are increasing more than the rest of the population; it has been said, in fact, that the 'Roman Catholic part of the educational system is the only one which is permanently expanding at the base.' " [53] A strong effort was made to secure more financial support, and an action committee worked vigorously to bring Parliamentary support to a fuller measure of what the Roman church wanted. Nonconformist opposition was seen as weakening, and the Anglican view was more receptive to the Roman Catholic position. In the opinion expressed in Tudor David's articles, the Church of Rome will effectively press for support approaching, although short of, 100 percent. The biggest single problem is the need for teachers. [54] To meet this need, the Roman Catholic Church is making a big effort, marked by the suggestion that the "wastage" of Roman Catholic teachers into non-Roman Catholic schools be stopped. All in all, one sees clearly a picture of vigorous and determined action to achieve a much fuller measure of support for Roman Catholic educational aims.

In appraising the present standing of the Free Churches, the articles by David suggest that there is a fundamental shift from the position of the "old guard" to a new educational policy. John Huxtable, a leading Free Churchman, is quoted as having said, "The gulf between what the Free Church experts in education desire, and what the guardians of Free Church tradition declare, is dangerously wide." The new opinion is "that far from there being anything wrong with the denominational school a Christian education cannot properly or adequately take place outside it." [55] This appraisal should be seen in the context of the historic position of Nonconformity which favored relinquishing their own schools to the control of L.E.A.'s and opposed the church schools of the dual system.

Although the main thrust of the Free Churches in recent years has been to improve the agreed syllabus approach as they see it and to relate this to the life of the church, the Free Churches have also developed organizations seeking to present more effectively their point of view about educational policy. To this end they have established an education policy committee composed of nine members, chiefly full-time officials from each of the main denominations. This high echelon committee was created largely in response to the request of the Ministry of Education for a body of Free Churchmen equivalent to the Church of England School Council with which the Minister could negotiate. There is also a central joint education policy committee composed of Anglican and Free Church representatives which seeks to arbitrate differences between these Protestant interests.

Further, since both Anglicans and Roman Catholics have local policy-forming bodies based on their dioceses, the Free Church Federal Council has been forming local educational policy committees (E.P.C.'s) under the supervision of a secretary for education. These E.P.C.'s are to work with their counterparts in the Anglican dioceses. It has been emphasized that they "do not exist and must not be used for opposition to Church Schools of any kind 'on principle.'" They are to realize that for education to become "secular and materialistic is, in our day, a greater danger than that it should become denominational." [56]

Since, according to David, the same directive for the E.P.C.'s also stated, "We are all concerned about the growing influence of Rome and the possibility of a Roman Catholic Education system within our national system has some ugly implications," [57] problems associated with a policy of recommending denominational schools for Anglican and Free Churches but not for Roman Catholics are apparent. However, the 1963 report of the Free Church Federal Council contains this statement:

> The Roman Catholics have made it known that they will shortly press for the extension of the present grants to apply to schools of all kinds. We are watching this matter closely in cooperation with the Anglicans. We feel that a purely negative approach will achieve little and create much bitterness. While we regret that this question has been raised again so soon, we feel that it is a challenge to us to seek a new and creative approach to the whole question of Church schools and religious instruction in County schools, within the context of the ecumenical movement and bearing in mind the common foe of secularism.
>
> Informal conversations are being held at the highest level between the three branches of the church. There is clearly a desire on all sides to avoid controversy and a determination to come to a common mind before any question of new legislation arises in political quarters. [58]

Thus the contention continues but is presently held at a level that avoids the older divisive political struggle.

Of the Jewish population in England, probably most hold that integration is the only suitable answer for their group. However, Jewish groups are also organized to secure their interests in aided schools. An increasing number of Orthodox Jews contend that within the pattern of schools in England they have an even better case than others for educating a Jewish child in a Jewish school under a policy of fuller support for denominational schooling. Most Jewish children receive religious instruction in part-time classes offered by Jewish religious organizations. [59]

The articles by Tudor David provide an interesting picture of the enrollments in the various schools within the national system. As the graphs showing the percentage of changes from 1950 to 1960 in county, Roman Catholic, and Anglican schools make clear, these years have seen a marked proportionate decline in

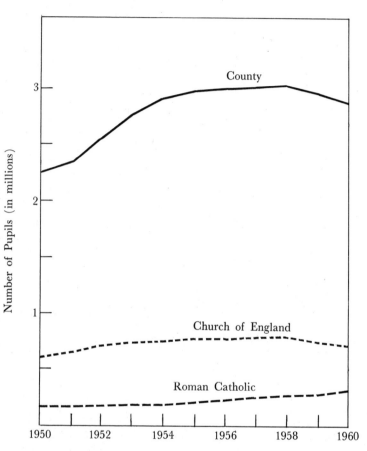

FIGURE 1. The number of primary school pupils attending county, Church of England, and Roman Catholic maintained schools, 1950–1960. (From Tudor David, *Church and School* [London: Councils and Education Press, 1961], p. 5.)

Church of England school enrollments. Furthermore, "The Anglicans had 1,750,000 in their schools in 1911; 50 years later they have only half that number and in their aided schools only 400,000 children. The RCS have 550,000 in their schools (all aided) compared with less than 300,000 fifty years ago." [60]

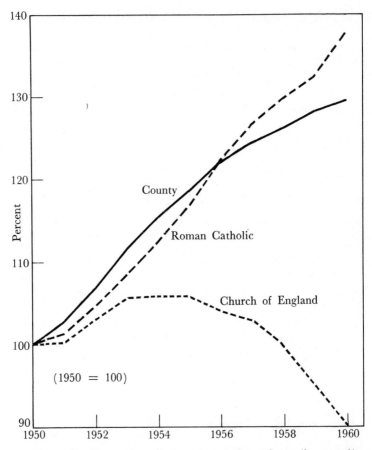

FIGURE 2. Percentage change in number of pupils attending county, Church of England, and Roman Catholic schools, 1950–1960. (From David, *Church and School*, p. 15.)

Anglicans, according to this analysis, are now reappraising their position. Some leading Anglican educators now take the view that they should reverse the tendency toward aided schools and should create modern schools able to impart "a truly Christian education."

The *New York Times* for August 16, 1964, reports that a record total of 777,000 children are now enrolled in Roman Catholic schools in England, an increase of 23,000 in the last year. In the same period the number of teachers rose to 30,500, a gain of 1,000. Furthermore, Diana Dewar in *Backward Christian Soldiers,* drawing upon *Catholic Education — A Handbook, 1962–3* reports that "During the 1960's Catholic children are expected to account for 63 per cent of the total estimated increase in the school population of school age, and by 1974 . . . [they will account] for one sixth of all children of compulsory school age." Archbishop Beck's view is: "If the forecast was reasonably accurate the Government should allocate the bulk of future expenditure in education to providing new schools for Catholics." [61]

The theological view supporting the new Anglican position holds that:

> The Bible asserts that God is the Lord of the world and that man, denying that sovereignty, is in a state of sin. It goes on to proclaim that God has acted for the salvation of man so that he may achieve his true purpose. Much modern thought would deny these truths, asserting that man is only in need of enlightenment and not of redemption. The world belongs to man, it is said, and by a process of emancipation from superstition, he is progressing to lordship over the world. Original sin is denied and a proper environment is held to be all that is necessary for the solution of social problems. Some modern psychological theories are based on these assumptions and to use the Bible selectively to support or illustrate them subjecting it to their demands or to those of a humanistic outlook is unjustifiable.[62]

This position holds that "nothing short of an integrated Church School will do." As a result, "Thirty new aided secondary modern schools are to be built, and the Church's building programme at 80 million pounds is now double that contemplated four years ago." [63] According to a report of a lecture in November 1963 by Kathleen Bliss, General Secretary of the Church of England Board of Education, the Church of England continues to maintain twenty-seven colleges for teachers and since the war has pledged three million pounds to these colleges for capital development.[64]

As Stuart Maclure says in the introduction to Tudor David's

articles, "the motive force behind the Education Act of 1959 came largely from the Roman Catholics"; hence it might be well to look more fully into the processes by which Roman Catholic interests were promoted in the negotiations of the 1959 act. David says that the significance of this act for the Roman Catholics was the dispelling of the view that the subsidy provisions of 1944 were permanent. It also "opened the prospect that in due course further concessions to aided schools were more than likely to be enacted." [65] Such successes were evidence of "a remarkable capacity for painstaking planning and relentless application in order to achieve their purpose." [66]

Without going into the history of the repression and restoration of Catholic schools [67] or the consideration of the place of Catholic schools in English policy of 1944,[68] we note the remarkably complete record compiled by Bishop Beck, presently Archbishop of Liverpool, of his leadership in preparing for the 1959 act.

A series of articles dealing with the costs of schools appeared in *The Clergy Review,* "house magazine" for Roman Catholic clergy, from 1955 to 1960.[69] These articles analyze the difficulties created by Ministry of Education directives setting limits to the building of schools because of financial problems. In the execution of policy the denominations must make their case to the L.E.A., which then submits a program to the Ministry, where it is almost invariably pruned as a whole (not by selecting parts; there is no suggestion of favoritism) in the light of the financial conditions reported from the Chancellor of the Exchequer. Bishop Beck took strong exception to Ministry directives setting new stringencies which would mean that the Catholics would be unable to improve their existing, unfavorable position. Needs in new housing areas were not being met; Catholic claims of conscience were not being sufficiently regarded. Until 1952 only 3 percent of capital for school buildings was allocated to Catholics whereas 7 percent of the school population was Catholic. Later, and perhaps as a result of Bishop Beck's presentations to the Ministry together with representations made at the diocesan level, Catholic proportions in the building programs rose sharply to 7 and then to 10 percent. The articles make the case for diocesan pressure on the L.E.A.'s and, somewhat vaguely, for pressure applied to parliamentary candidates to see where they stand on the aid question.

Other articles appeared in *Catholic Education*,[70] now replaced by the *Catholic Education Handbook*, published by the Catholic Education Council, of which Archbishop Beck is chairman. These articles, of which the one appearing in 1959 is especially important for our purposes, contain detailed accounts of the negotiations in which Bishop Beck engaged. They include the memoranda exchanged with the Ministry and with the Anglican Bishops, the appraisals of Nonconformity opposition, and the meetings with Catholic and other legislators to make clear the case for greater support of Catholic schools. Associated with these efforts was the formation of a Catholic action committee "to provide and distribute information and propaganda in connection with our schools' campaign."[71] The action committee, appointed with the approval of the hierarchy to support its cause in press and Parliament, is credited by Bishop Beck with being "the most important co-ordinating influence in the campaign."[72]

Bishop Beck makes it clear that Catholic policy aspires to full support of their schools by the state by quoting a statement of the Cardinal: "We would be happy if we could be given a flat rate of 75 per cent. grant for our schools as a further installment towards that complete equality which is denied us."[73]

The Bishop reports that he was asked in a meeting of the Labour Party education committee "specifically about the possibility of pressure being put on candidates in the course of the General Election." His reply hoped for general agreement between the parties so that pressure, to which he was personally opposed, would not be needed. Yet if no assurance of a satisfactory outcome was given he was "not in a position to make any pledge that the Catholic body would not use all legitimate means to ensure that their point of view was understood and considered and accepted."[74]

The Bishop further records that in his conversations with R. A. Butler:

I told him that an increase in the amount of grant merely for re-organization would not be sufficient for our needs. It was imperative to have some assistance for the building of new schools and if we got grant for new schools the question of voluntary schools' finance would be out of politics for twenty years. If it was refused, we should find ourselves obliged to come back again with further requests within five or six years. . . . I pointed out that the problem was one of in-creasing urgency for the Catholic body. Already in one or two dioceses projects had been withdrawn from current programmes or had been delayed. If this were to happen generally, we would be creating a situation in which parental discontent and administrative opposition would provoke blame on the Government. In the new housing areas, particularly, it was for us a question of now or never.[75]

In later interviews with the Labour Party leadership the Bishop reports that "the meeting resolved itself into an attempt by all his colleagues to persuade" one of the members (a member whom David identifies as "a lifelong and influential Welsh noncon-formist" [76]) that "it should be the policy of the Party to support our proposals for a 75 per cent grant." If accepted, "the denomi-national schools' problem would be taken out of politics for the foreseeable future." One of the members ". . . speaking strongly as a Catholic, emphasized that we had up to now proceeded by discussion and persuasion, but that the Catholic community was no longer prepared to be fobbed off with partial concessions. If we did not get what we required the politicians could expect Catholics to 'come up fighting' on this matter at the next general election." [77]

One is impressed in the entire account with the adroit apprais-als of the extent to which power could be used in the achieve-ment of Roman Catholic ends without drawing the 1959 act into the center of religious and political controversy. Bishop Beck says that "it was put to me quite strongly that, if we overplayed our hand, we might end by getting nothing," [78] and he noted the opinion of the *Baptist Times* that the bill was a "betrayal of the 1944 agreement; a betrayal of the rights and views of a consider-able part of the electorate, and a betrayal of our Protestant in-heritance in the face of an unwarranted clamour from a Roman

Catholic minority." [79]   However, two pilot studies had been made of Nonconformist opinion in two areas of the country and as a result it was thought "there was a general exaggeration of the Nonconformist opposition," [80] and "the Nonconformist conscience no longer has the strength to awaken opposition." [81]   The bill was taken as an agreed measure, since in the negotiations it had been agreed between the parties, who were alert, of course, to an approaching general election.

Bishop Beck's account of the strategy of Roman Catholic pressure also contains the argument that even with increased grants the denominational schools were in fact saving public expenditure.   As Roman Catholic diocesan schools are granted "aided" status and their enrollments increase, the local educational authorities stand to gain by having more places at their disposal in the maintained schools.   He concludes by noting an impermanence in the 1959 arrangements since there was no provision in them for public money for new primary denominational schools.

The Agreed Syllabuses

The creation and use of agreed syllabuses for religious teaching in schools provided and maintained by the L.E.A.'s was not in 1944 a totally new invention.   The Cambridgeshire syllabus was first published in 1924, and the preface to the West Riding syllabus says that their committee provided a syllabus as early as 1904.   A survey by the Institute of Christian Education reported that in 1940 practically all of the 317 L.E.A.'s then existing had an agreed syllabus, more than 100 of them using the Cambridgeshire.[82]   The policy laid down in the 1944 act capitalized on a background of experience in the preparation and use of agreed syllabuses.

More than half of the L.E.A.'s have adopted the syllabus of some other authority, though some have added a section dealing with local church history.   The Cambridgeshire, Sunderland, Surrey, and West Riding syllabuses, in that order, seem to be the most commonly adopted ones.   It was thought that as experience with the use of the syllabuses accumulated, more and more the local authorities would produce their own. The Institute's report notes that new ones appeared at the rate of two or three a year in the 1950's. It is uncertain how much piecemeal borrowing has been involved, but it appears to have been very extensive.

Although recent syllabuses show some measure of diversity, the largest part of a syllabus consists of a plan for the content of instruction at different levels — nursery, infant, junior, secondary, and sixth-form levels. Care is taken for the continuity of the student's growth. Topics are provided with biblical and other references. Stories of the Bible, Christian holy days, doctrines, and their appropriate explanations are placed in a plan for developing understanding and appreciation of Christian belief. In many syllabuses this material is introduced after the teacher's attention has been drawn to the relevant sections of the 1944 act and other statutory provisions. Other pages provide articles dealing with the aim or aims of the syllabus, the significance of Christian education today, the nature of worship, the modern approach to the Bible, and the like. A section relating local church history to the fuller sweep of church history is usually provided. A bibliography for teachers and a section on suggested teaching aids are included. In more recent editions more attention is given to the advanced students comprising the sixth form. Considerations about language, myth, art, and the bearing on everyday life of Christian and other religions may be introduced. One can not fail to be impressed with the quality of the work and the care that has been taken with pedagogical considerations in the more modern syllabuses.

Some of the less obvious differences between some of the syllabuses are discussed in various publications of the Institute for Christian Education of which a report of its research committee is typical. It finds that some syllabuses take a psychological approach, arranging materials by noting the developing interests and attitudes of children. Others organize material in biblical order. Still others provide a systematic treatment of biblical doctrine. In addition, more recent syllabuses are said to contain improvements of a practical order in that they (1) are briefer,

(2) use a "concentric" pattern for providing greater depth in renewed study of recurrent themes, and (3) provide alternative courses for different types of students. These considerations point to the plurality of syllabus approaches — "the all purpose syllabus will not do." [83] They also provide the teacher with the means for seeing how his teaching contribution fits into an overall plan.

As the leaders in agreed syllabus instruction see it, their approach is not a single and uniform approach to Christian education. It is characterized by diversity contributed by local control of the design of instruction, and this diversity is itself being studied so that it can lead to better teaching of Christian doctrine. As they see it, differences in agreed syllabus instruction are not denominational but educational. Pluralism within the context of agreed syllabus instruction is of a different order from sectarian pluralism. In English policy, they maintain, diversity in the means by which common Christian doctrine is transmitted is not divisive.

It is clear that the agreed syllabuses place Christian belief and doctrine central in their effort. Knowledge of other religions is postponed until the learner can go more surely along Christian paths and to the sources of Christian belief. The syllabus clearly cannot be said to be "teaching about religion" in the sense in which this term is generally used in the United States. The aim is to lay the ground for conviction and commitment rather than to provide for objective knowledge about man's religious life and experience. With growth in confidence that the teacher can teach undenominational Protestant Christianity without being involved in denominational controversy, the syllabuses have become more sophisticated educational tools for the achievement of this end.

It will be recalled that one of the cornerstones of English policy is the famous Cowper-Temple clause which states that "no religious catechism or religious formulary which is distinctive of any particular denomination shall be taught in the school." This is interpreted to mean that while teachers may not proselytize for a point of view distinctive of a particular denomination, the school shall teach the Apostles' Creed and beliefs common to the churches. That which is common to the churches refers to doctrines affirmed by Anglicans and the main-line Free Churches, that is, Baptists, Congregationalists, Methodists, and Presbyterians. The state through its schools gives a privileged position to ecumenical Protestant doctrine. This means that the views and doctrines of Roman Catholics, of Jewish religious groups, of scientific humanists, to mention a few, do not have the same standing in educational policy with main-line Protestant Christians.

It should be clear that we are here speaking of the basis for distinctions about doctrine; we are not referring to the participation of members of various churches in religious education programs, committees and the like. It is repeatedly pointed out to an observer that Quakers, Unitarians, and Jewish believers might teach Divinity, might serve on the standing advisory councils and otherwise participate; however, scientific humanists would not find this approach to religious education acceptable to their convictions.

The role of the school in teaching ecumenical Protestantism is opposed to secularism and the forces making for secularization of life; moreover, as Margaret Avery, a leading interpreter of the agreed syllabus approach, puts it, "unattached Christianity" or "floating about between the denominations, settling and belonging nowhere" is undesirable. She goes on to say:

> It is a better education to be deeply rooted in one tradition than to have light attachments to several. It is sheer folly to talk about letting children of nine or ten choose their religious allegiance; they do not know what they are choosing nor ought they have the responsibility of choice.[84]

Presumably, on other grounds than their inability to know that between which they are choosing, learners should not be deciding these matters for themselves.

These expressions suggest that the freedom to explore the widest variety of religious beliefs, including dissent from orthodox belief, does not stand on the same educational footing as the freedom to believe in conformity with the main lines of British religious tradition.

Interests in England supporting the policy of the state school's advocacy of Christianity are also concerned that Christian education in all of its component parts should be thoroughly Christian. The Free Church Federal Council, a consultative body contributing to the improvement of religious education, urges that: "History taught by a Christian should be a different experience from history taught by a secularist, a Christian biologist will give a different impression . . . about the significance of biological findings than will a non-Christian." The "way of life" of the school in all of its parts should be "Christ-centered." [85]

This emphasis is given more detailed treatment in a 1960 report of the Institute of Christian Education. In it W. R. Niblett, Dean of the Institute of Education of London University, recognizes that practicing Christians are probably a minority on a school faculty; yet agreement is expressed with T. S. Eliot that the school should be Christian though its personnel be mixed and that this may benefit its intellectual vitality. However, Christian presuppositions, as they differ from secularistic ones, should dominate. The teacher who is a committed Christian should let a hierarchy of values shine through his work as a presupposition of all that he does. "Though there is scarcely a 'Christian' mathematics or a 'Christian' science, the Christian teacher will often find himself placing a different emphasis upon, and — almost without knowing that he does so — giving a different weighting to some parts of the subject than will an agnostic." [86] Hence, the teacher of mathematics will show that there are different kinds of proofs and that one appropriate to mathematics is not appropriate to the study of the Bible or to spiritual experiences of a private or a mystic order. ". . . The teaching of science must cultivate a sense of the continuity of nature on a non-materialistic basis. A persistent creative trend such as the development of the world manifests cannot be accounted for in terms of mere accident." [87]

The ingredients of a particular philosophy of history are central in the Christian's teaching of history.

. . . The Christian's conviction about the true nature of history does impinge very closely on his historical method at one point: it radically affects his view of human nature, which is the real criterion by which he makes historical judgments. He believes that everywhere in history Man is confronted by God and that ultimately history consists of Man's choice or rejection of God. However much the historical situation he analyzes is built up of given circumstances, factors of heredity, environment, contingent event, however much, that is, choice is circumscribed by a real historic situation which it is his work to delineate, there remains for the Christian at the core of every such situation a real, unpredictable, in some sense unmeasurable, choice. The duty of the Christian historian lies in acknowledging this reality. He must make clear in his teaching his conviction that there is this element of spiritual choice embodied in all history, whether officially classified as secular or as ecclesiastical. . . .[88]

This view, the author continues, is not a conclusion proved by the methods of historical study. It is "a conviction about the 'stuff' of history which is brought *to* it," and is hence open to challenge. It must be recognized as one of several possible ways of interpreting history. Although it is not to be passed on in an authoritarian manner, it is a conviction which will be manifest by the way a Christian teacher interprets history.

In this view, Christian education is not only, perhaps not even chiefly, a matter of teaching religious knowledge or the text of the Bible. It is putting the study of any subject within the framework of Christian commitment. Although the truth should be followed wherever it leads, and although young people in school should have increasing opportunities to make their own decisions, the effort of the school in all of its parts should be to make evident the case for Christian presuppositions. As we shall see in later pages, some are not satisfied that the unfettered search for truth and the production of Christian believers are readily compatible educational goals.

Since under British policy, religious education is a subject of study comparable in its academic quality with other subjects, the problems of obtaining instructors adequately prepared for this work has come to the fore. Not only do teachers of the various common subjects need a certain kind of preparation if these subjects are to be taught with a view to their Christian presuppositions, but the teaching of "Divinity," if it is to be accorded academic respectability, requires appropriate specialization. While teachers in infant and junior schools may conduct the school on a Christian basis with minimal preparation in the study of Scripture, in grammar schools and increasingly in secondary modern schools and comprehensive schools specialists are needed.

Students in the higher forms of these schools may be studying for the General Certificate of Education (G.C.E.) examinations in Scripture at the ordinary and the advanced levels, and success in these examinations is the traditional ticket to the university. The recently issued Robbins Report on higher education states that two passes at the advanced level of G.C.E. are the minimum qualification for entry to universities and that over 80 percent of the students have at least three. Furthermore, entry to Teacher Training Colleges is now at the point where 60 percent of those who enter have at least one pass at the advanced level and over a third have two passes or more. In short, as religious education takes its place as an equivalent with other subjects, and this in no small measure by being included in the examination system, there is a need for specialists in the preparatory secondary schools.

"Specialists" in religious education are, generally speaking, clergy or those who have been educated in whole or in part as clergy, or those who have degrees, diplomas, or certificates in theology. Religious education is also taught by semi-specialists, that is, teachers of other subjects who are willing to take a share in religious education and who have had some academic work preparing them to be resources in this aspect of the schools' program. The Department of Education and Science provides short, in-service courses on religious education, and expenses associated with attending these courses are met by local authorities in the cases of teachers from maintained schools. The 1957 edition of the report of the research committee of the Institute of Christian Education, *Religious Education in Schools,* provides interesting information and indicates some of the problems associated with the preparation of specialists in Divinity.

In practice, religious education in maintained schools varies widely both in its educational quality and in its adherence to agreed syllabus plans and materials. In large part, agreed syllabus instruction was designed to bring more concerted plan and order to religious education particularly as it was conducted by nonspecialized teachers. It is difficult to assess the extent to which this more systematic and orderly instruction, as distinct from the teacher's management of religious education as he sees it, has been achieved. Until more thorough study is made, observations lead one to think that what is actually done in the schools departs rather extensively from recommended practices and statements of principle.

In some grammar schools, where instructors are specialists, a stimulating exploration of the meaning of biblical passages goes on. In one school a class was discussing whether the creation of Adam and Eve was to be understood as an act of divine creation of a particular man and woman, or whether it was a Hebrew interpretation of a continuing creative process involving the nature of mankind. The discussion was spirited and was skillfully related by the teacher to the lives of thirteen- and fourteen-year-old grammar school (selected) boys. In contrast, in a grammar school for girls at the same age level, the teacher was concentrating on the facts of the Bible study by asking questions, approving correct answers, and correcting errors in response.

In a secondary modern school (a school enrolling those who have not been creamed off in the selection test at eleven years of age) situated in an extremely rapidly growing suburb of a metropolitan area, no specialists in religious education were on the staff of a school serving more than 900 students. The head of the school remarked that the school conformed with the 1944 act in a minimal way and that it could not do otherwise for lack of plant facilities and trained teachers. However, a few minutes later it was remarked that when he had had an opportunity to expand the staff, he selected a science teacher and let the present staff pick up the classes in religious education. A religious education class consisting of the oldest age group in the school was taught by a chemistry teacher. He presented, somewhat unclearly, what amounted to a distinction between four kinds of evidence and their roles in the substantiation of truth claims. One of these was "by authority" and was exemplified by Roman Catholic belief. When the class was asked for a show of hands, one boy was of this persuasion. It was mentioned that Methodists establish truth differently, but none of the students volunteered to look into this view. The only clear response from the group was to the effect that in this class students could really talk about religion but that in church "you couldn't talk back."

In another grammar school, crowded into an old and inadequate building, the headmaster held the worship service in the school yard. More formal ceremonies, such as the school-leaving exercises, were held in the parish church. The headmaster, as is common in English schools, taught several classes, one in mathematics and the other in sixth-form (most advanced) religious education. For the latter he used a succinctly worded syllabus of his own devising, the county's agreed syllabus being held in the background. The particular course being offered involved independently written papers on Hebrew history and the Gospels, class time being largely taken up with problems in the philosophy of religion. Other classes studied comparative religions, religion and social conditions, and the historical growth of the Christian church. An appreciable number of boys from this school take the General Certificate of Education examinations at both ordinary and advanced levels. The quality of the work of the school as a whole is indicated by the fact that forty-two students among the graduates in 1963 had achieved places in universities, six of them in Oxford and Cambridge. The school enrolled a total of 830 boys. In addition to the considerable leadership of the headmaster in the study of religion, the school had on its faculty two specialists: one, an Anglican cleric; the other, an Oxford graduate who had specialized in the philosophy of religion.

The general impression is that the quality of religious education under the agreed syllabus approach is what the local education authority and particularly the headmaster make it. The policy allows for great latitude in the character and quality of the programs. There are large differences in both the ceremonial and the intellectual aspects of the work, as well as in the general climate of the school.

The influence of inspectors of religious education, whether those of the county authorities or of the Department of Education, appears to have contributed substantially to the quality of agreed syllabus teaching and religious education in general. For example, largely through the efforts of a chief inspector and consultant for religious education, an experienced teacher was appointed to work in an experimental program of religious discussion in London County Council schools. The purpose of the program was to make Christianity meaningful in the context of common faith, to make it relevant to young people's lives today, and to work at this under educational, as distinct from clerical, leadership. The efforts of the inspectorate were to work with all groups to extend the base of Christianity and to feed back the results of conferences to the programs of religious instruction in the schools. One was repeatedly assured that this kind of activity has replaced any tendency to get excited about differences in the interpretation of the essential truth. In short, although the traditional position of the inspector is to serve as the eyes and the ears of an educational authority, some L.E.A.'s are now appointing consultants and curriculum experts to work more closely with the schools in improving the quality of religious education. The inspector is now more commonly described as consultant, source of reference, and carrier of ideas.

Improving Instruction

English policy as laid down by statutory provisions and developed through the efforts of the Department of Education and the local educational authorities provides a variety of means for the improvement of the agreed syllabus approach to religious education. In addition to provision for specialists and for curriculum experts, there is provision for continuously bringing together representatives of the local authority, teachers, and churches. The 1944 act not only directed that the agreed syllabuses should be built, but it provided that standing advisory councils be constituted to advise the authorities on "matters connected with religious instruction to be given in accordance with an agreed syllabus." The policy thus provides a permanent place for constructive cooperation and mutual understanding as difficulties and possibilities are worked out.

In England, many organized channels have been developed for the exchange of views and for participation in the development of national policy. As Sir Ernest Barker has pointed out, "It is an old tradition of Englishmen to do things for themselves, on a voluntary basis, in free association with others; not to expect all things from 'the State' or remit all things to the government. It has shown itself in many fields — education . . ." [89] and many others. The British have not merely achieved a compromise that overcomes much of the religious divisiveness of the past, but in many ways they have provided a forum for the discussion of policy and the refinement, or, perhaps in the future, the fundamental revision, of the patterns by which the religious question is managed in the schools.

Among other important agencies for the realization of national policy in England is the British Broadcasting Corporation (B.B.C.). It provides four series of broadcasts on religion for the schools through the School Broadcasting Council for the United Kingdom. One of these series consists of broadcasts called "A Religious Service for Primary Schools." This series appears to reach about 50 percent of junior and infant schools and 57 percent of junior schools.

Three additional series are designed for the use of secondary schools. One, "An Act of Worship for Secondary Schools," is designed "to unite the schools taking part in an act of worship designed to lead children to offer praise and thanksgiving and to pray for themselves and for others." In January 1965 it was reported that some 40 percent of the potential audience used this series. Another series, "The Bible and Life," seeks "to provide a supplement to religious instruction for children in their last two years at school, taking account of the general scope and content of Agreed Syllabuses for these children." Some 17 percent of the potential audience of grammar schools currently use this series. A third series entitled "The Christian Religion and Its Philosophy" is designed for sixth-form students. About 34 percent of potential grammar school audiences use this series.[90] "A background of settled belief is not assumed in the audience, and the active skepticism, indifference, and bewilderment of some Sixth Form pupils is recognized." The statement of its aims and policy further recognizes "the need to offer sharp challenges to Sixth Formers, and to avoid creating any impression that the premises of the Christian faith can be readily assumed or counter-arguments easily demolished. . . ."

The booklet for these sixth-form broadcasts for 1962–1963 bears the subtitle "Reason and Imagination as Means of Knowing," which is the theme of the broadcasts for the autumn term. The cover of the pamphlet pictures "The Hunt of the Unicorn" from a medieval tapestry in which reason, represented by the spears of the huntsmen, and imaginative power, represented by the unicorn, are locked in a struggle of power. The theme depicted in the tapestry is used to introduce a consideration of the uses and limits of reason, the nature of imagination and myth, and the bearings of these on the understanding and appreciation of Christianity. A variety of volumes such as K. C. Barnes, *The Creative Imagination,* and A. Koestler, *The Sleepwalkers;* selected paintings such as El Greco's "Laocoön and His Sons" and Gauguin's "Where Do We Come From? Who Are We? Where Are We Going?"; and selections from the fields of poetry and music are introduced. Questions for discussion include:

3. Kenneth Barnes wrote of Ethiopian Church ceremonies that they were the most colourful in the world, but had nothing to do with daily life. How far is this true of our own Christian ritual and liturgy?

9. Discuss these well-known lines from Shaw's *St. Joan:*
   Joan: I hear voices telling me what to do. They come from God.
   Robert: They come from your imagination.
   Joan: Of course. That is how the messages of God come to us.[91]

Topics for broadcasts in other school terms include "The Ethics of Power" and "The Book of Daniel." The materials drawn together for these topics appear to be equally challenging.

Over the years a number of studies have been concerned with the improvement of religious education under the agreed syllabus approach. Earlier articles express fears that common Christianity would be only vaguely Christian, that common beliefs would be the least significant beliefs, and that a new orthodoxy would be imposed through agreed syllabus teaching. Apparently, these fears have been dispelled. In general, more recent studies call attention to the need to relate religious education to the actual problems of young people today and the need to bring Christian education under the guidance of psychological considerations, including an educational concern with the integrity of the individual.

This generalization is evidenced by the work of Harold Loukes in his study of teenage attitudes toward the teaching of religion. He finds that two thirds of the children declare themselves dissatisfied with the religious instruction they receive.

> If we read between the lines that our critics write, remembering their cautionary remarks that discussion can be a waste of time, and that discussion needs preliminary knowledge, but remembering too the weight of opinion against repetitiveness and monotony, we begin to see that they are most of them in all seriousness asking for a class in which the teacher is ready to teach, but to teach what they begin to feel the need of learning; to present the message of the Bible in relation to the issues of the present moment, and then to wait, open and friendly — "at ease" — for the class to "have it out" and to try to "get nearer to the truth." . . .
>
> The desire is overwhelming for something that represents an open situation, in which the teacher does not abdicate either his initiative or his authority, but uses them to discover what is going on in the minds of his class, and then to take them demonstrably, palpably, sensibly, "nearer to the truth." [92]

Loukes also makes clear that this does not mean that religion is to be turned into ethics nor does it mean that the school can itself be an organic part of the church, although it should lay the

intellectual foundations for such an affiliation. It does mean
that Christian education should "rest on the same open ground
as that of all our education: it must seek to perform some task
which would be accepted as *healthy*, contributing to wholeness
of the personality, and would not be judged by the conscientious
agnostic to be limiting or hampering." [93] In this view the justification for nondenominational Christian teaching is an educational justification.

> What *can* be objected, by the conscientious agnostic, is that while
> children are too young to judge, they should not be indoctrinated in
> such a way as to reduce their powers of judgment in the years to
> come. But this is no argument against including in the school cur-
> riculum the Christian view of man and his meaning. No one can be
> the worse for having met it: to meet it squarely is an exercise in
> freedom.

It is the continued religious growth of the individual in relationship to his total personality that is drawn into the center of attention as an educational value directing the policy of religious
education.

> This argument does not constitute an attempt to find a highest
> common factor among all shades of opinion in the community, by
> way of producing a harmless, universal syllabus of religious instruc-
> tion that no one can object to. It is an attempt to clear the grounds
> on which a Christian must stand if he is to be honest in his accept-
> ance of the charge laid upon him. This he must do, not merely be-
> cause he lives in an open society, but with no more authority than
> that society confers upon him, but because his duty as a teacher is first
> to the children under his care.[94]

Thus the values directing the program of Christian teaching are
the distinctively educational values of the openness of the knowledge situation, the freedom of the individual to explore the fullness of man's knowledge, and the ability of the individual to continue to develop to the full range of his possibilities. It is in the
education of personality that the teacher finds his authorization
for the teaching of nondenominational Christianity.

In addition to studies done under the auspices of the Institute
of Christian Education, a number of studies have appeared from

the institutes and departments of education of the various universities. A study by the University of Sheffield Institute of Education found a gap between what the teacher was teaching and what the agreed syllabus provided. The chief criticisms of the syllabuses were: (1) they laid down artificial divisions of topics; (2) they gave little help for the teacher's need for simplified schemes of study; (3) they had much material irrelevant to the lives and experiences of students; (4) they did not deal sufficiently with Christian problems in the twentieth century; and (5) they were too idealistic, too pietistic, too ahistorical. These criticisms by a study group were then related to the results of a questionnaire seeking to sample strategically the knowledge, opinions, and religious habits of secondary students in modern secondary, technical, and grammar schools.

Although a summary of the "findings" of the study does not do justice to it, the survey may be represented as essentially critical of present agreed syllabus instruction on the following grounds:

1. The standard of religious knowledge in the schools today . . . is clearly very poor. . . . It is believed that the results obtained are fairly representative of the general state of affairs throughout the country.

2. . . . There is not the wide spread in religious knowledge which one might expect. In many departments of religious knowledge there is little or no difference between the results from the Grammar Schools and those from the Modern Schools. . . . We cannot blame the lack of ability in the children for unsatisfactory results.

3. Although the general standard of the candidates [for teaching certificates] is rising . . . statistics show little increase in the numbers offering religious education as a main subject. . . . The large majority of teachers giving religious education have not received any specialist training in it.

4. [Most of the syllabuses are] elaborate schemes of work rather than syllabuses. This we believe to be a basic fault in the system. . . . To teach most Agreed Syllabuses adequately would demand not only the services of an accomplished theologian but also six or more teaching periods a week.[95]

Studies of religious education in the sixth form indicate the need for open discussion, independence of thought, and the development of tools for a more critical approach to religious knowledge and experience.[96, 97]

Some research seeks to reexamine the assumptions made by the syllabuses concerning the capacities, interests, and levels of insight demanded of students at various maturity levels. The effort is to consider what is known about children's thinking, concept formation, and ability to bring the products of experience to bear upon events in relation to religious thinking. R. J. Goldman states that the aims of his research are "to ascertain the religious concepts central to understanding religious stories, to discover what sequence, if any, exist by which pupils' levels of understanding progress, and to evaluate the logical processes used by pupils in religious thinking."[98] Test procedures involve a standardized interview in which youngsters respond to pictures and recordings eliciting their interpretations. Results are scored and scaled in such a way that sequences of thinking can be identified and shifts to a higher quality noted. Thus, for example, Goldman finds that at about 11:3 M.A. (eleven years and three months, mental age) "pupils begin to see the Church as helping personally, not merely in answering questions in the R.I. [Religious Instruction] lesson (a depressingly frequent answer), but in moral behavior, in achieving peace or confidence, or in supporting belief."

The consequence of these studies is that " we now have a more realistic idea of what children and adolescents can absorb in terms of religious material. There is an interesting agreement by current researchers that religious teaching at all stages should be more pupil-centered and less subject-centered."[99]

The conclusions resulting from these investigations are, typically, that much Bible material suggested for children is unsuited to their instructional level; that pushing beyond the child's limits of understanding may reinforce crudities of thinking and lead to regressive thinking; that indirect methods rather than intellectual presentation by instruction would seem to be profitable; and that intellectual insights into Old Testament material appears to be difficult to achieve before the secondary level of schooling.[100] Further interpretation suggests that: "The content in the first years of secondary schooling should introduce youngsters to a liberal view of the Bible so that they see its grand design. This should not be a chronological history but an exciting discovery of man's eternal problems, about which the Bible speaks supremely.[101] Thus psychological research supports a "liberal" interpretation of the Bible. Religious teaching should avoid being dull, childish, and irrelevant and also beware of creating resistance by treating the child as a mere information receiver.[102]

Goldman's recommendation that the learner's negative attitude to religious teaching be met by a liberal-critical method of treating the Bible is criticized by those who defend "the authority of Biblical teaching."

> . . . It is just this very liberal-critical view of the Bible which undermines the authority of Biblical teaching and tends to evoke a negative attitude on the part of pupils. This view of the Bible bases sweeping subjective judgments upon scanty factual evidence which is too inconclusive to give adequate support to these judgments. "Biblical truth" vanishes behind a smoke-screen of human conceptions which are, after all, those of fallen men. Realizing that this is, in effect, a substitution of authority by which the ideas of men usurp God's revelation, and also that religious truth is not entirely susceptible to subjective human analysis, they [children] treat such teaching with a reserve and even skepticism which is entirely healthy. It is to subjectivism in religion, which the liberal-critical view involves, that the young have built up a resistance. Events in the world around them, of which they are becoming acutely aware, do not lead them to consider as trustworthy the moral and spiritual judgments of men apart from some absolute divine authority.[103]

It is probable that efforts to revise religious teaching in directions that are claimed to follow from psychological inquiry will encounter this kind of opposition particularly from the ranks of the clergy.

The apparent mounting discontent with the agreed syllabus approach to religious education is also expressed by a volume which reports the general verdict of students to be, " You can take it that pretty well the whole of the sixth form is fed up with Christianity." [104] The purpose of the book is to condemn present teaching of religion in schools and to offer in its place a discussion-based course on life in the twentieth century as seen and interpreted by a modernistic but devout Christian. The author, Sir Richard Acland, calls for a fundamental change in Christian teaching which would bring it up to date with what the jacket of the book calls "the egalitarian, science-minded and power-driven age of man." He pleads for a "child-centered and life-centered, rather than a syllabus-centered, approach to religious teaching." The book, written "not perhaps in a white heat, but in at least a pale pink glow, of indignation," has spread much of its glow into the current discussion of the adequacy of present policy.

The position of F. H. Hilliard contrasts but is compatible with the Acland position. Hilliard believes that the study of the Bible should be retained at the center of Christian teaching. Taking into account the studies showing that agreed syllabus instruction has largely failed to achieve its purposes, he seeks to revise the methods in religious education and to promote a distinctively educational approach to religious teaching. State schools should not be an extension of church evangelistic work; they should "seek to teach, rather than to preach, to enlighten rather than to convert." [105] The school should seek to refine its teaching of religion as it has improved the quality of instruction in other fields, by the development of professional educational competence.

A number of criticisms of English policy today are based upon an appeal to educational principles as distinct from questions of faith such as the kind of interpretation of the Bible that should be given to children. The consideration is not whether the Bible should be interpreted liberally or as a unique revelation of the word of God. It is, rather, whether sound understanding of the controlling purposes of education are directing religious education.

Anthony Hartley, promoting the view that the intellectual aims of education should replace aims which are directed to particular beliefs about the reconstruction of the social order, holds:

> . . . it is rather doubtful whether the use of schools and universities to indoctrinate the pupils with a creed, whether religious, nationalist or merely social, can genuinely be called education. This purpose often seems to involve shackling the minds of those under instruction rather than that liberation of them through knowledge and wisdom which should be desired. For it is the essence of such a liberation that any choice of belief should be a free choice with a full knowledge of the possible alternatives.[106]

This criticism confronts most directly those interpretations of policy which hold that religious education should seek to develop committed Christians in the sense that the outcome of teaching should be measured by membership in a church. Since views like that of Hartley are premised on the freedom of informed choice, they open the door to policies which are much broader than those seeking to preserve the main channels of Christianity in English life.

Current dissatisfaction with the terms of the 1944 settlement is expressed in an article on the leader page of the *Times Educational Supplement* for November 13, 1964. H. A. Ree, professor of education at the University of York, a staunch supporter of the grammar school as a separate entity, is disturbed at the "undisguised boredom, indifference, and contempt" which carries over into young people's attitudes toward the church as a consequence of an enforced daily act of worship in school. Teachers and headmasters feel the pressures of conformity. Subtle pressures are exerted against withdrawal. A case is made by Ree for religious service before or after the official school day and for assemblies that might have religious but not specifically Christian character. Integrity rather than conformity to doctrine characterizes Ree's approach to the management of questions of worship in school, and it is probable that a number of churchmen are sympathetic to his view and confirm his argument. Yet the probability of the government and Parliament undertaking legislation to recast the religious requirements of 1944 seems very remote.

Criticisms of English Policy

To be distinguished from criticisms seeking to improve religious education under present policy are those which challenge the policy instituted in 1944 and seek to have it in whole or in part rescinded.

In general, the voices expressing dissent from the policy instituted in 1944 are not highly organized. One does not find societies pressing for fundamental policy changes with the diligence and effectiveness characteristic of organizations seeking to improve religious teaching under present policy. Voices of basic dissent in contemporary England appear to be, for the most part, individual voices speaking through channels that are not organized primarily to effect changes in present policy. Perhaps the clearest exception to this generalization is to be found in the National Secular Society which conducted a Secular Education Month during November 1964. This activist group campaigns against state aid for religion in state-controlled and in denominational schools. Although the group reports that the "Month" was widely reported in the national and provincial press, on radio and television, it is doubtful that a widely shared national interest in secular education is in the offing. However, the fact that this effort was made and was well reported constitutes an item in a growing list of dissatisfactions with the 1944 settlement.

It may be that, as Tudor David has observed, "The secularist dragon is dormant at present," and has been slumbering since the first decade of the century when the Secular Education League and a number of secularistic journals were influential.

> But it would be a mistake to suppose that secularism has no fire left in its belly. What is more, a revived secular movement might well have a more influential and cohesive leadership than it had in the 1900's. Humanism now has powerful adherents in the most surprising quarters and not least important among the teachers.[107]

Humanists may be found in important places, and the voice of humanism may be heard in such works as *The Humanist*

Frame,[108] but there is little coordinated movement comparable to that of the organized voices of the Christian churches.

Rumblings of discontent with present policy are made somewhat more explicit in some activities sponsored by the Ethical Union. In general, these activities express dissatisfaction with the existing provisions for moral education in schools and challenge the assumption that this is settled through present patterns of religious instruction. Although direct moral instruction — telling the young how they ought to behave — may be neither desirable nor effective, according to this view, education in ethical thinking and the critical forming of ethical judgments is another matter. H. J. Blackham, secretary of the Ethical Union, suggests four general common aims to guide the rethinking of present policy:

1. the child should be enabled and encouraged to think for himself;
2. the perplexing diversity of beliefs and convictions, and lack of belief and conviction, which is characteristic of the world about him, should not be concealed nor exaggerated, but should be taken as the situation in which the child has to choose his way;
3. he should be helped to sort out his ideas and to resolve his difficulties and conflicts;
4. he should be taught to appreciate that ideas have a history, and change and develop, rise and fall, in ways of their own.[109]

Blackham feels that these aims would help develop what it is claimed "most parents the world over want for their children in school, religion without dogma and without prejudice." This effort would involve treating the Bible more imaginatively as " literature of a religious faith and experience" rather than as "sacred scripture, a book apart, divinely inspired, being revealed truth essential to salvation." The Ethical Union's view is also critical of a compulsory daily ritual which may stultify, rather than express and inspire, a higher quality of religious experience.

Criticism of this humanistic view, or at least disagreement with some of its ingredients, has been expressed over the years through the journals seeking to implement the 1944 settlement.

The content of a British Broadcasting Corporation program by a scientific humanist who regarded "orthodox Christianity as no longer intellectually tenable" [110] may also be cited as an example of the continued discussion of the fundamental assumptions of present policy. In the early months of 1955, Margaret Knight, a psychologist, stirred up a hornet's nest of indignation as well as critical discussions by stating the case for morality independent of religious doctrine and sanction. The ensuing discussions show the highly controversial assumptions involved in present policy, the continued debate in English life about the grounds of this policy, and the considerable willingness to entertain these considerations without upsetting the educational efforts of the nation under the framework of the 1944 act.

One of the key ingredients of the state of the religious settlement in English schools is the attitude of the largest teachers' professional association, the National Union of Teachers. It seems clear that its cooperation in the development of national policy about religion and schooling has been an important contributing factor in the present settlement.

Asher Tropp, in his social history of the teaching profession, reviews the role of the N.U.T. in the negotiations leading to the 1944 act. Sir Frederick Mander, general secretary of the N.U.T. in this period, stated that the teachers realized that a general educational advance could come only with a national system of schools. In it local authorities should effectively control all the schools and their faculties. The clergy should not continue to call the tune either in church schools or in those provided and maintained by public funds. The teachers and the representatives of the churches "clashed violently" in the negotiations since the union strongly upheld the Cowper-Temple clause. "It was resolved to maintain that basis and to fight against any increased control by the clergy or any attempt to impose religious tests on teachers. For its own part it demanded that any further public aid to the non-provided schools should involve an extension of public control." [111]

The attitude of the N.U.T. in the early years of the operation of the 1944 act is well expressed in the following several paragraphs from the "Notes of the Week" column in *The School-master:*

> For the purpose of obtaining a unified system of education and as a means of providing a greater measure of equality of educational opportunity for all children many educationists — though not without hesitation — accepted the clauses in the Education Act which deal with religious instruction in County Schools. Only with reluctance did the teachers accept them. One reason frequently advanced for that reluctance was a lack of confidence that all the representatives of the Churches would abide by the terms of the compromise reached by national representatives of the various interests.
>
> But having accepted the arrangements the teachers sought loyally to carry them out both in the spirit and in the letter. The National Union of Teachers collaborated with representative men of the various Churches and representatives of the L.E.A.'s to formulate *The Basic Outline of Religious Instruction.* In the various areas representative teachers have cooperated with Church representatives and others in the preparation of *Agreed Syllabuses.* They have, therefore, given every proof of their intention to make religious instruction an integral part of the curriculum and of school training. H.M.I.'s have reported that they are doing so with success.[112]

Within the context of this cooperation the N.U.T. appears to have been sensitive to what it took to be unwarranted criticisms of the efforts of the teachers and to attempts as it saw it to reinstitute control by the clergy in religious instruction in county schools.

For instance, six months later in the same column the spokesman for the teachers chastises a bishop who had "impugned the professional honour of members of the teaching profession" by saying, "In many cases, as some of you know, time that is allotted for religious teaching is used for other purposes, simply because the teacher is a little bit embarrassed about these things or, again, perhaps does not believe in the Christian faith." [113] The N.U.T. points out that no teacher needs to use subterfuge if he does not believe in the Christian faith or if he prefers not to participate in religious instruction. It observes that the criticism does not contribute to the cooperation which characterized the

1944 act, the subsequent efforts of teachers, and the relations between clergy and teachers. In large part, this incident epitomizes the position of the N.U.T. in the first twenty years of the policies enacted in 1944.

A number of articles in *The Schoolmaster* in this period indicate the receptive attitude of the N.U.T. to undenominational religious education, and the authors attempt to deal helpfully with how the job should be done.

By the 1960's Robert Londin, chairman of the education department of the British Council of Churches, could observe, "the whole atmosphere of school-church relationships has changed quietly but effectively in the past ten years." [114] Suspicion and misunderstanding were giving way to frank discussion of problems and a wider range of cooperation. The pamphlet reporting this change in outlook is the outcome of more than two years of meetings between the N.U.T. and representatives of the education department of the British Council of Churches. Two things are done in the pamphlet: (1) procedural rules are laid down; (2) some examples of cooperation are given. The latter are mostly in the form of church services and school-leavers' conferences. The former refer mainly to cooperative action, particularly in the form of representative local committees. Emphasis is given to "an ecumenical approach," and the schools are warned against "bodies and groups which lack the ecumenical approach and which tend to set up new groups divorced from the Church as it exists, and which are often strongly critical of the religious education offered by the schools." [115] On the whole, the pamphlet is modest and cautious in what it has to say and manifests a spirit of amity between school and church.

Recent issues of *The Teacher,* the current title of the N.U.T.'s weekly, reveal that more space is being given to the discussion of religion in education, and its columns reveal a mounting wave of criticism of the character of religious instruction and particularly of collective worship in the schools.

An article entitled "Captive Congregations" [116] points out that although "We pride ourselves on the freedom of English education, yet in one case, and in one case only, the content of education is laid down." It is suggested that daily doses may have been thought to remedy "the increasing insecurity of the Christian religion." The conscience clause is ineffective since many parents are ignorant of it and are usually indifferent. The piece argues for putting worship "back where it belongs, in the home, the church, and the chapel" and for instruction in other great religions which would be more appropriate in our present world of closer contact between nations. It is time that Christianity abandon its position of entrenched privilege and that the consciences of many teachers be liberated.

In another article a young teacher is worried about the "automatic inevitable pattern of all schools" where teachers are "to keep order" and "make sure that The Lord's Prayer is not mumbled," and to see that "some reverence, even if only simulated" is enforced.[117] The character of the author's objections are worth noting in detail.

> What worries me is that I am required to do this every morning in defiance of any conscience I might have. Maybe it is because I am new that I chafe at the hypocrisy required of me. I must police children and mumble hymns and prayers, without believing at all in either the ceremony itself or the wider implications of it. Nobody seems to care that there is any hypocrisy.
>
> Presumably the laws allowing liberty of religious conscience to the teacher were framed to protect the unbeliever as well as the many sects. Yet is it assumed, as a matter of course, that this duty, like playground patrols and dinner duties, will be done by all the staff, whatever their views.
>
> . . . .
>
> . . . if we really wanted, we could create enough trouble to get out of it.
>
> But in how many schools has this freedom to contract out any substance? Does it not mean extra duties, begrudged written permissions and other humiliations heaped on these odd teachers who refuse to help?
>
> And we have our references to think of.

These remarks seem to hit a responsive chord in the experience of twenty-four members of a school staff who

. . . believe, unequivocally, that the enforcement by the 1944 Act of a religious assembly is immoral, and would urge all teachers who feel as we do to exert what pressure they can for an amendment.

Many Christians, we find, are as worried as atheists and agnostics by the enforcement of a religion supposed to be grounded in a doctrine of free will.

Meanwhile, we can and should make sure that the existing "rights" are vigorously protected both for ourselves and for our pupils. . . .[118]

Other letters to *The Teacher* reveal further difficulties with present policy. For instance, a letter bearing the heading "Morning Blackmail" says:

. . . Many students on teaching practice must also have found difficulties.

While some schools acknowledge differences of belief and are prepared to excuse atheists and agnostics from the morning religious observance, other schools exercise a kind of blackmail. Students who would prefer to miss the morning service are apprehensive of unfavourable reports from the school to their college. Those who attempt to miss it may be requested by the college authorities to attend "for appearance's sake."

Nor does the fact that few children opt out of the religious service indicate that parents as a whole approve of compulsory religious teaching. Few parents give the matter any thought.

Those who do are often reluctant to make their children appear "different" from their fellows by withdrawing them from the religious assembly, so that many children must receive religious instruction with which their parents are fundamentally in disagreement.[119]

Another letter points out that the government that passed the act of 1944 did not have

. . . a mandate from the people to decide questions of religious observance. Its job was to win the war and we accepted that it must have dictatorial powers for that purpose.

Under cover of necessary educational planning, the religious clauses were pushed through at a time when most of the men and many of the women who should have decided these issues were busy all over the globe with more urgent matters. Certainly the teachers among them were out of touch with educational development and with one another.

. . . .

It is time an effort was made to assess the real views of parents and teachers on the question of religion in schools. Too many teachers have kept silent from a mistaken view that it is their duty to carry out the provisions of the Act regardless of their personal opinion or because their promotion prospects are likely to be affected.

Conformity pays, there is no doubt about that, whatever the theoretical safeguards, as long as the Christian religion is compulsory in the schools run by local authorities and the Church controls numbers of appointments in schools and training colleges.

The tragedy is that there are large numbers of sincere teachers who would like to make a positive contribution to the moral and social training of their pupils if it were not tied to religion.[120]

Another difficulty which current English policy encounters is raised by an incident in which "a fifteen-year-old boy due to read the lesson at morning assembly walked to the front of the stage and declared: 'This morning, I will not read.' This somewhat dramatic incident, which led to his immediate suspension and subsequent resignation" happened at a college of further education, and the 1944 act does not provide a conscience clause at this level. The incident, according to the report in *The Teacher,* was reported in *The Birmingham Post* on June 22, 1964. The student had asked to be excused from the morning assembly on the grounds that he objected to the compulsory religious assembly. He had been refused on the grounds that this was a matter of discipline and that he must accept the rules. The Birmingham paper points out that the purpose of worship is religious, not disciplinary, and that a student ought not to have to choose between dropping his study for the general matriculation exam (G.C.E.) and religious conformity. The incident "spotlighted an anomaly which will have to be settled one way or the other: either no act of worship in institutions of further education, or, if there is to be an act of worship, there must be a 'conscience clause' like that in schools if it is not to degenerate into a hollow mockery." [121]

According to another recent article in *The Teacher,* playwright Harold Pinter enters the lists against compulsory religious instruction in schools, finding it "ill-taught, ill-considered, and ill-understood." The article reports that "a growing body of public opinion, rapidly becoming more articulate," including many intelligent Christians, were "depressed by the 'rigidity and atrophy' of what had become a ritual ridiculing something that should be a living idea." Mr. Pinter had himself reacted to school assembly with "undisguised boredom, indifference and contempt." He "asked if the history of doubt and unbelief was ever referred to in the schools." [122]

In the "Notes on the News" section of *The Teacher* the objections of Pinter were used to raise a question concerning the significance of an established church in this matter. "There is an inevitable confusion between the purely secular authority of the school on the one hand, and the authority of moral law on the other. If we believe in religion, we do not tell children that they must be good because the school rules say they must be good, but because God says they must be good." It is interesting to observe that other alternative views about the authority of moral law, considerably more secular than the assumed authority here, have not entered the picture. However, the article continues by pointing out that the confusion here is more obviously at stake in "statutorily-ordained" worship than in classroom work in religious education.

It is significant that the criticisms which have recently been voiced in the N.U.T.'s weekly have also been expressed in other sources. *The Observer* recently printed an article by John Grigg, a well-known critic of the establishment, in which he argued that "the time has come to review the relationship between the State and religious schools. The State should no longer subsidize sectarian forms of education." The arguments put forward are directed to the policy in support of Roman Catholic aided schools, but as the author intends, they apply also to the support of any denominational schools.

Should we not try to have schools which are themselves miniature open societies (in the intellectual sense), and should it not be the function of our State to provide such schools, and such schools only, while leaving parents free to have their children indoctrinated at their own expense?

. . . .

Our State ought to stand for an open, non-sectarian (and, of course, non-political) education: its philosophy ought to be a philosophy of free choice for *each individual* — not just for parents. It ought to have no special relationship with any religion or any church, and it ought in future to give no financial support to any schools other than its own.[123]

Grigg concludes by warning that unless this problem is dealt with honestly, unflinchingly, and without delay, the fact that about 15 percent of all babies the country over are baptized into the Roman Catholic Church enables one to predict the future spiritual complexion of Britain. The correspondence elicited by the article seems to indicate considerable concern with teaching which prejudges religious issues too early in the life of the child and policies which separate children at an early, impressionable age and thus may easily mature into instinctive prejudices. The article in *The Observer* appears to bring the question of the educational values in current policy into the broader area of common discussion.

One further point remains to be made in this survey of British opinions and appraisals of church-school policy. As one ranges through the materials representative of the various interests seeking to have their values and preferences more fully realized in English policy, one finds from a variety of sources the opinion that the religious clauses of the 1944 act would not be achieved today.

As far back as 1949, *The Schoolmaster* recognized that no party to the agreement was wholly satisfied but that it was a working arrangement which, taken as a whole, was not unjust or unfair to any. "The conflicting interests were finely balanced. Even so, it is very questionable if the Act would have been accepted had not national and international circumstances created the climate favorable to its passage." The particular combination of circumstances promoting the settlement of 1944 was not likely to recur and "the climate those circumstances created has completely changed. He would be a bold man who affirmed that the Act passed in 1944 would have been passed in 1950." [124]

The Roman Catholics have always regarded the 1944 act as provisional. The Archbishop of Liverpool, formerly Bishop of Salford, who is chairman of the Catholic Education Council, has referred to "the myth of the '1944 settlement,' " [125] and has made it clear "that the Catholic Hierarchy had never accepted the 1944 Act as a 'settlement.' " [126]

We have noted that representatives of the Anglican Church express views which would make the 1944 act unacceptable today. The more recent view is that nothing short of a school which is a part of the worshipping family of the church will do.

A report of a recent address by Dr. F. Lincoln Ralphs, chief education officer for Norfolk and a stalwart upholder of the Christian basis of the state schools, expresses his concern with the growing disenchantment with the spirit of the 1944 act.[127] As he sees it, today's affluent society with its ready acceptance of a realistic, quantitative concept of normality is not appealed to by the perfectionism demanded by Christianity. The intellectual and moral atmosphere today is not compatible with the achievement of policies enacted in 1944.

Significance for American Policy

In the light of our investigation of English policy three questions about the effort to model American policy upon that of the British appear relevant: (1) Are the historic and social conditions of the two countries sufficiently similar that an analogy in their policies is appropriate? (2) In what sense are the claims about the protection of individual rights in England fulfilled? (3) To what extent are the consequences of English policy desirable in America?

Despite America's considerable inheritance from British life and culture, the historical conditions of policies about religion and schooling are significantly different in the two countries. In the first place, the United States has no history of an established church. In England, as in other European countries, historic institutions and church-state relations were Catholic and involved the reformation of Catholic traditions and the consequences of the Reformation. Second, education in England was, as we have seen, the business of the church until well into the nineteenth century. It was not until 1870 that a national system of elementary schools was established side by side with the church schools. Third, not only does England inherit the pattern of an established church but, as Sir Ernest Barker has pointed out about its national character,[128] religion has been a primary organizing fact and condition of English political and social life. A number of other conditions of policy in England, some pertaining to the structure and organization of education, do not apply to the United States. In view of these differences it is difficult to see the force of the argument that America should develop policies modeled on those of England.

In regard to the second question, if what we have observed about the protection of rights of conscience and of religious freedom is a reasonably faithful and balanced account of English experience, the American people might well consider the character of their commitments to these civil liberties. We have seen that English efforts to continue and revitalize the Christian basis of national life have not led unequivocally to the fullest measure of self-determination for all.

There is no question of the attention of the molders of English policy to the principles of religious freedom and freedom of thought. For example, R. A. Butler's concern with religious freedom was echoed repeatedly in the Parliamentary debates over the 1944 act. "There is another element which should never be banished from our system of education. Here we have freedom of thought as well as freedom of conscience. Here we have been the pioneers of religious toleration. . . ." In his next sentences Butler introduced the grounds of the problem. "But side by side with all this there has been the fact that religion has been the rock in the life and character of the British people upon which they have built their hope and cast their cares. This fundamental element must never be taken from our schools. . . ."[129] Religious freedom and the freedom of conscience are qualified by or exist in the context of Christian belief. Nonbelief or belief which falls outside of the main-line English churches does not have the same standing in English life or education. This seems to be a root condition of English policy as it relates to the meaning of freedom of conscience and freedom of religion.

The consequences of this presupposition are manifold. A "compulsory freedom" mandates Christian education and worship in schools, and if this violates the conscience of the parents, they are expected to seek the withdrawal of their children. But together with the compulsory character of religious instruction and worship we find evidences of parental apathy and of meaningless formalism in the schools. Although denominational doctrine is excluded from schools, students should achieve "membership in a worshipping community." It is one thing to see to it that students know their Judaic-Christian heritage, quite another to promote commitment to a particular faith. Nonbelieving teachers are not to be discriminated against, but insincerity and hypocrisy is found in their ranks. Although "the conscience clause is at the teachers' disposal, . . . it is most inexpedient for the primary teacher to take advantage of it." [130] Although the kinds of criticism of orthodox belief found in the Bishop of Woolwich's *Honest to God* [131] and the Cambridge Divinity Faculty's *Objections to Christian Belief* [132] — criticisms within the mainstream of English church life — are commonly referred to in religious education, humanist and other than main-line Christian forms of religious belief are less commonly encountered. The freedom of parents to send their children to the school of their choice is supported by public subsidy, but it is not clear that the freedom of the learner to come critically to grips with his own determination of his beliefs and values is effectively provided for.

These tensions involved in English policy are not noted in an effort to make a sweeping criticism of English efforts to balance freedom of thought with the preservation of Christian belief. However, they do serve to alert Americans to differences in the context of the meaning of religious freedom and to the view that the English approach is a suitable model for problems that confront American policy.

Although we are already dealing with some of the consequences of English policy for the meaning of religious freedom, we are concerned in the third question with some of the other consequences of English policy that portend certain outcomes in American life if we are to adopt English policy as our paradigm.

We have in mind here the lesson that Americans might learn from the way in which religious differences and controversies in England have been woven into the fabric of political and social life. We have seen that the history of English education is replete with the conflict of religious interests and that religious differences and controversies were interwoven in the political and social system of the country. The extension of educational opportunity was dependent upon a religious settlement. In large part the 1944 act represents a compromise between Roman Catholics, Anglicans, and Free Churchmen. Furthermore, the revisions entailed in the 1959 act reveal the skillful appraisal of the political strength of church interests and the adroit use of techniques of persuasion and pressure in the interest of particular church groups. Although a democratic society is one in which interests should freely interact in the pursuit of common policy, it might be well for Americans to consider whether they want to encourage the kind of political action represented by certain church leaders in the 1959 Parliamentary negotiations.

We have also seen that there is much dissatisfaction in England with the agreed syllabus approach and its outcomes. If our interpretations are at all correct, there are rising voices both within the denominations and without which find neither corporate worship nor Christian instruction producing desirable outcomes. Dissatisfaction with the Cowper-Temple philosophy is expressed not only by Roman Catholics but by Anglicans and influential representatives of the Free Churches. From the point of view of many educators, the settlement of 1944, including the solution provided by the agreed syllabuses, is seen as a denominational compromise rather than an educational solution. Despite ecumenical movements, differences between major religious groups find expression in the struggle for financial support. Since it is questioned in England whether the 1944 agreement could again be achieved today, Americans would need to be cautious about their enthusiasm for a common doctrinal Christianity in the public schools.

Although Americans can profit from considering the difficulties encountered in England, they can also learn from the strengths of English policy and its applications. Without attempting any balance sheet between negative and positive factors, and refraining from any effort to suggest a program derived from British experience, we can suggest some directions suggested by the substantial achievements of British policy.

Americans could profitably attend to some English achievements in the art of compromise. While this matter merits much more thorough study if Americans are to understand their own situation in the light of experiences of another nation particularly at the level of public policy, we can sense that very considerable achievements in English education since 1944 are the result of diligent efforts to overcome the effects of earlier intransigencies. What is meant by "compromise" demands clarification and refinement. Presumably it is far more than a common stereotype of muddling through; and it is not a matter of giving up one's principles. It appears to involve a persistent and carefully negotiated search for the basis of what people can do together in the achievement of some, but not all, of their values, with the minimum of distortion and surrender of their ideals and commitments.

English achievement of a compromise in this sense of the term in the church-school area in 1944 enabled constructive steps to be taken in the development of their schools. These achievements may in turn promote an eventual return of the church-school problems to the arena of compromise at a more advanced level of policy development. We might learn from the English experience, not by adopting their policy as a model for our own, but by considering the processes, including liabilities as well as assets, by which a determinate and positive policy was forged.

At least a few steps have been taken to identify these ingredients in the present study, although further inquiry should search out more fully and carefully the full range of considerations. For example, we have noted the significant role of negotiation and informed leadership both by government and by participating interests in the achievement of a policy with which all can live for at least an extended period of time. The English example of statesmanship in this matter in the years following the war should teach us something about responsible utterances and the democratic development of social policy.

The value of reports by deliberative bodies assessing the directions of desirable policy in the context of contemporary conditions, exemplified by the reports of educational commissions of the Department of Education has been noted. This does not mean that there is no dissatisfaction expressed in England with what is considered to be the inadequate scientific background of the work of advisory committees.[133] But, as the extensive materials of the Robbins Report indicate, this deficiency is not irremediable and does not recommend the rejection of this aspect of policy formation. Furthermore, planned efforts to cultivate an enlightened public opinion are a significant aspect of British achievements. The policy whereby local authorities acting under the directives of the Ministry set up standing advisory councils to investigate and develop practical agreements and arrangements brings various interests in the community to bear upon significant aspects of educational planning. To bring basic differences to the conference table where an adequate regard for the values of opposing interests can be developed is to take one of the steps toward greater toleration and understanding of conflicting points of view on matters of educational policy. To take a page from English experience in this regard might reduce the kind of political use of religious differences, fears, and tolerances sometimes reported in the press in this country. For example, during a recent election campaign a candidate for national office charged that "enemies of religion" were attempting to reinterpret the constitutional doctrine of church and state to mean establishment of atheism as the official religious position of the government. It seems clear that this kind of talk is not conducive to the responsible development of policy in this country.

Efforts in England to have questions about religious education dealt with in terms of educational values and principles rather than exclusively those of a political or sectarian religious nature suggest an appropriate movement in this direction in the United States. The English have not excluded the interests of specialists in the various areas of study in religion, including the educational contribution of those educated as clergy. However, they have shown that these specialists may well deal with problems of policy in the teaching of religion under the guidance of educational rather than denominational principles. This suggests that a new dimension in the education of teachers in the United States might well be entertained as a step toward a more considered solution of our problems. The study of the philosophy of religion and of an educational philosophy attuned to the policy problems of American education would offer a greater background of wisdom in helping teachers and other leaders of community life to come to grips with problems of handling religious questions.

Furthermore, English experience reveals a way in which they have conceived, and in some measure achieved, a relationship between diversity and unity in the function of education. This matter also merits fuller study which might lead to applications in the American situation. Apart from the structure of English education, such as the balance between the Ministry and the local authorities, there is the matter of seeking a substantive balance in the life of a culture between that which pulls people apart and that which unites them in their commitments. One may find that the particular policies of a nation are inappropriate as a model for another and yet find that policies meshing diversities with unity are of considerable worth for other societies. Sir Ernest Barker has said the English have "learned from the religious experience of their national life, that it was possible to be united and divided at one and the same time." [134] In no small measure this has been exemplified in, and perhaps considerably achieved through, their efforts in education.

One senses that the experiences of the war years together with the dissolution of the empire and the challenges to at least the older forms of the establishment have led to efforts to achieve a new sense of unity in a quest for national significance. One hears rumblings of an effort to become the equivalent of a new Switzerland in Europe. In the confusion of efforts to attain a new orientation to world affairs, the conception of a unified people takes on new meaning. The unifying factors in a national system of education are drawn into the center of national effort. If Americans were to look at British policy in such a perspective, they might discover much of what is hidden from their view of their own situation. What is frequently obscured in the American self-image is the concerted effort to find a more enduring unity that derives from our historic roots and moves toward the fulfillment of the creative potentials of our form of a free society. Although in our quest for unity we may not be able to turn in the direction taken by other peoples, yet we could profit from the experiences and efforts in which they engage.

Closely related to the matters already mentioned is the observation that freedom in English policy is given a positive meaning. It has been understood to open the door to what should be done in the public school rather than to indicate what should be prohibited from entering there. English policy not only enables but facilitates in large measure the parents' choice of a school appropriate for their children. It provides a way for the state-controlled school to study the religious aspects of the national life. In contrast, in America we have been so caught up with the problems of the nurture of freedom in the midst of diversity that we have underestimated the values carried by a knowledge of religious life and by commitment to something more than immediate practical and material gains.

Although space does not permit the development of a more positive meaning of religious freedom appropriate to American traditions, it may be noted that the lack of a more positive sense of freedom tends to choke off the development of a fuller religious growth in the student's life. This by no means subscribes to the charge that American schools promote an antireligious doctrine of secularism by omitting the study of religion. Nor does it accept the stance of those who reason that "if you're not with us, you must be against us." It does mean that it may well be time for an affluent America to seek a more positive conception of religious freedom. We need to cultivate what we are free to engage in as well as to clarify our freedom from various restrictive conditions.

However, conceptions of freedom which provide that the door to a particular profession of faith should be freely open to all and conceptions which involve paying the costs of schools devoted in their distinctive *raison d'être* to perpetuation of a particular faith are two different things. British policy affirms that the function of the state includes the responsibility of subsidizing the improvement of existing church schools and paying their operating costs and appears to move in the direction of providing what approaches total financial support for new church schools. This policy, if pursued to its logical conclusion, including the generalization of the principle of distributive justice, leads to the total support of all denominational schools. Hence, it encounters the consequences of policies in such countries as the Netherlands, and particularly the problems of equality of treatment of religious groups and of groups which prefer either no religious faith at all or some deviation from main-line churches and theologies. It appears that when the state gets into the business of subsidizing the citizen's religious choice in this sense, it becomes the arbitrator of religious beliefs and thought in a sense which Americans, surveying mankind's total experience with this role of the state, have rejected.

We have also seen that teaching a common doctrinal Christianity in state-controlled schools involves in England such distinctions between churches that some are not accorded the equality of others. It appears that the positive contribution of the American school to religious freedom should develop from considerations of freedom and equality more appropriate to the diversity of American faiths and the desirability of compatible and mutually supporting conceptions of freedom and equality.

These considerations also suggest, following a certain aspect of English experience, that the school's attention to religious aspects of the education of the young should be studied as an educational problem rather than ignored or reduced to a power struggle between organized religious interests.

In the main the greatest value of English policy and experience for Americans consists in the detailed development of a positive policy which has been studied and appraised in terms of its applications and consequences. Americans could profit from studying the materials involved in the agreed-syllabus approach, the accounts of the influences brought to bear upon the determination of policy, the efforts of voluntary associations of many kinds to contribute to a national purpose, and the studies that have been made of the student's responses to the school's efforts in religious education. Although English policy and the practices developed from it, in their totality, are not desirably applicable to American conditions or appropriate for the fulfillment of educational values in the United States, there are many aspects of English experience which provide significant clues for the development of American policy.

NOTES

1. Educational policies in Scotland and in North Ireland are regulated by acts other than those pertaining to England and Wales. Scotland and North Ireland have separate educational systems with their own administrative systems.
2. In practice, in many voluntary controlled schools a form is distributed to parents in which they, through their signature, approve the religious teaching of the school. The technical request becomes simply a signature of approval.
3. James G. Laidler, *Voluntary Schools* (London: National Society and Society for Promoting Christian Knowledge, n. d.), p. 31.
4. *Ibid.*, pp. 46–47.
5. Detailed in Sir William Alexander and F. Barraclough, *County and Voluntary Schools* (3rd. ed.; London: Councils and Education Press, 1963), chap. 3.
6. Detailed in Marjorie Cruickshank, *Church and State in English Education* (London: MacMillan & Co., Ltd., St. Martin's Press, Inc., 1963), pp. 132–135.
7. W. O. Lester Smith, *Education in Great Britain* (3rd. ed.; London: Oxford University Press, 1958), p. 123.

8. Cruickshank, *Church and State,* p. 176 *n.*

9. According to Isidore Fishman, Director of Education, London Board of Jewish Religious Education, about 9,000 children (in 1964) in Great Britain and Ireland attend Jewish Day Schools.

10. Tudor David, *Church and School* (London: Councils and Education Press, 1961), p. 14.

11. Smith, *Education,* p. 129.

12. Institute of Christian Education, *Religious Education in Schools* (London: National Society and Society for Promotion of Christian Knowledge, 1957), pp. 28–29.

13. Institute of Christian Education, *Agreed Syllabuses and Their Revision* (Wallington, Surrey: The Religious Education Press, n. d.), p. 17.

14. Gordon C. Lee, "Church, State, and School in England," *Teachers College Record, LVI* (January 1955), p. 211. Here he points to the policy of the British Broadcasting Corporation that the air waves are available only to those churches which are "in the mainstream of the Christian tradition."

15. Ministry of Education, *Citizens Growing Up* (London: Her Majesty's Stationery Office, 1949), p. 11.

16. *Ibid.,* p. 42.

17. Institute of Christian Education, *Religious Education in Schools,* pp. 108–109.

18. Michael Argyle, *Religious Behavior* (London: Routledge and Kegan Paul, 1958), p. 38.

19. *The Teacher,* January 10 and July 10, 1964.

20. Diana Dewar, *Backward Christian Soldiers* (London: Hutchinson & Co., 1964), p. 167.

21. Institute of Christian Education, *Religious Education in Schools,* p. 27.

22. Smith, *Education,* p. 26.

23. Asher Tropp, *The School Teachers* (London: William Heinemann, 1957), p. 6 *n.*

24. *Ibid.,* p. 29.

25. *Ibid.,* p. 39.

26. *Ibid.,* p. 41.

27. M. Travis, "The Dual System in English Education," *Researches and Studies,* University of Leeds Institute of Education (May 1952), p. 82.

28. James Murphy, *The Religious Problem in English Education* (Liverpool: Liverpool University Press, 1959), p. 34.

29. *Ibid.,* p. 19.

30. *Ibid.,* p. 139.

31. *Ibid.,* pp. 251–252.

32. Commentator quoted in Murphy, *The Religious Problem,* p. 267.

33. The Elementary Education Act of 1870, 33 & 34 Victoria, C. 75, Section 14 (2).

34. Tropp, *The School Teachers,* p. 172.

35. Board of Education, *Secondary Education with special reference to Grammar Schools and Technical High Schools* (London. Her Majesty's Stationery Office, 1938), p. 208.

36. *Parliamentary Debates* (House of Commons), 5th Series, Vol. *396* (January 20, 1944), p. 433.

37. Institute of Christian Education, *Religious Education in Schools,* p. 27.

38. F. H. Hilliard, *The Teacher and Religion* (London: James Clarke & Co., 1963), p. 19.

39. *Parliamentary Debates* (House of Commons), 5th Series, Vol. *396* (January 19, 1944), p. 414.

40. *Ibid.,* p. 277.

41. *Ibid.,* p. 227.

42. Board of Education, *Educational Reconstruction* (London: Her Majesty's Stationery Office, 1943), p. 15.

43. *Parliamentary Debates* (January 19, 1944), p. 228.

44. *Ibid.,* p. 226.

45. *Ibid.,* p. 229.

46. Cruickshank, *Church and State,* p. 153.

47. *Ibid.,* p. 163.

48. *Ibid.,* p. 178.

49. David, *Church and School,* p. 20.

50. "From 1906 to 1911 denominational schools came up at every single Labour Party Conference and Trade Union Congress. In 1911 it was excluded from future Labour agendas and in 1912 the TUC took the same decision. The issue — which invariably became a battle between the Roman Catholics and the secularists — caused such disruption as to threaten the unity of both the party and the TUC on matters quite other than education." *Ibid.,* p. 4.

51. *Ibid.,* p. 4.

52. *Ibid.,* p. 16.

53. *Ibid.,* p. 6.

54. According to A. C. F. Beales, outstanding authority on Catholic teacher education:

"There are two Catholic teacher training colleges for men, and ten for women. Several others are being created at this moment, as part of the national plan for educational expansion. These denominational teacher colleges receive 75 per cent State-grant towards their building expansion, and a full 100 per cent grant for maintenance. But Catholics who are university graduates, training for work in secondary grammar schools (U.S. senior high schools) are for the most part trained in the (secular) Education Departments of the universities. There is no Catholic university in England, and Catholic opinion is sharply divided on the desirability of one." See "Appendix" in Daniel Callahan (ed.), *Federal Aid and Catholic Schools* (Baltimore: Helicon, 1964), p. 145.

In this connection it should also be noted that according to the Robbins Report, "Local education authorities entered this field [the establishment of teacher training colleges] in 1902 and are now responsible for ninety-eight of the present total of 146 colleges." See Committee on Higher Education, *Higher Education* (London: Her Majesty's Stationery Office, 1963), p. 27. Although the Robbins Report recommended that Catholic training colleges along with local authority training colleges be incorporated into University Schools of Education and so become degree-granting institutions, the Government has apparently sought to leave the administrative control of the training colleges much as it is but to encourage the universities to accept certain students as candidates for university degrees.

55. David, *Church and School,* p. 11.

56. *Ibid.,* pp. 13–14.

57. *Ibid.,* p. 14.

58. Free Church Federal Council, *Annual Report and Directory: 1963* (London: The Free Church Federal Council, 1963), p. 14.

59. Myer Dominitz, "Religious Education and Schools in the United Kingdom — Some Jewish Aspects," Religious Education, *41* (March–April, 1961), p. 137.

60. David, *Church and School,* p. 15.

61. Diana Dewar, *Backward Christian Soldiers,* p. 26.

62. David, *Church and School,* pp. 16–17.

63. *Ibid.,* p. 17.

64. " 'Church-State Landmark,' " *The Teacher,* November 8, 1963.

65. David, *Church and School*, p. 5.

66. *Ibid.*, p. 7.

67. See A. C. F. Beales, *Education Under Penalty* (London: Oxford University Press, 1963), 306 pages.

68. See H. O. Evenett, *The Catholic Schools of England and Wales* (London: Cambridge University Press, 1944), p. 141. Also Philip Whitaker, "The Roman Catholics and the Education Act of 1944," *Political Studies, 4* (June 1956), pp. 186–190.

69. George Andrew Beck, "The Cost of Schools," *The Clergy Review, 40* (January 1955), pp. 1–22; Beck, "School Costs and School Plans," *The Clergy Review, 43* (January 1958), pp. 1–11; Beck, "The Cost of Schools," *The Clergy Review, 44* (February 1959), pp. 65–77; Beck, "Counting the Cost," *The Clergy Review, 45* (March 1960), pp. 129–144.

70. George Andrew Beck, "How the 1953 Education Act Took Shape," *Catholic Education, 3* (December 1957), pp. 1–31; Beck, "Background to the Education Act, 1959," *Catholic Education, 7* (December 1959), pp. 1–26.

71. Beck, "Background to the Education Act, 1959," p. 4 n.

72. *Ibid.*, p. 26.

73. *Ibid.*, p. 5.

74. *Ibid.*, pp. 10–11.

75. *Ibid.*, p. 11.

76. David, *Church and School*, p. 8.

77. Beck, "Background to the Education Act, 1959," p. 16.

78. *Ibid.*, p. 20.

79. *Ibid.*, p. 24.

80. *Ibid.*, p. 12.

81. *Ibid.*, p. 25.

82. Institute of Christian Education, *Religious Education in Schools*, p. 23.

83. *Ibid.*, p. 49.

84. Margaret Avery, *Teaching Scripture* (Wallington, Surrey: The Religious Education Press, 1967), p. 26.

85. The Free Church Federal Council, *Church, Child and School* (London: The Free Church Federal Council, 1960), p. 31.

86. W. R. Niblett, *Christian Education in a Secular Society* (London: Oxford University Press, 1960), pp. 40–41.

87. *Ibid.*, pp. 43–44.

88. *Ibid.*, pp. 70–71.

89. Sir Ernest Barker, "An Attempt at Perspective," in Sir Ernest Barker (ed.), *The Character of England* (Oxford: Clarendon Press, 1947), p. 567.

90. A recent survey by the British Broadcasting Corporation reports that some 78 percent of secondary modern schools in England, Wales, and Northern Ireland and some 58 percent of secondary grammar schools use school radio broadcasts.

91. Margaret E. Rose and Robert C. Walton (eds.), *The Christian Religion and Its Philosophy* (London: British Broadcasting Company, 1962), p. 23.

92. Harold Loukes, *Teenage Religion* (London: Student Christian Movement Press, 1962), p. 83.

93. *Ibid.,* p. 96.

94. *Ibid.,* p. 97.

95. Hugh M. Pollard, *et al., Religious Education in Secondary Schools* (London: Thomas Nelson & Sons, 1961), pp. 44–47.

96. D. S. Wright, "Study of Religious Belief in Sixth Form Boys," *Researches and Studies,* University of Leeds, Institute of Education (October, 1962), pp. 19–27.

97. J. W. Daines, *An Enquiry into the Methods and Effects of Religious Education in Sixth Forms* (Nottingham: University of Nottingham Institute of Education, 1962), p. 36.

98. R. J. Goldman, "The Development of Religious Thinking," *Learning for Living, 2* (May 1963), p. 7.

99. R. J. Goldman, "The Agreed Syllabus: A Guide for Reformers," *The Times Education Supplement,* October 4, 1963, p. 439.

100. R. J. Goldman, "The Development of Religious Thinking," p. 9.

101. R. J. Goldman, "The Agreed Syllabus," p. 439.

102. R. J. Goldman's more recent *Religious Thinking from Childhood to Adolescence* (London: Routledge and Kegan Paul, 1964) incorporates material from the earlier articles and has become a standard reference in the field. Three more general implications for religious education (Chap. 15) are: (1) the need to examine the concepts involved in understanding material chosen for any given age group; (2) the limits of understanding imposed by the levels of operational thinking; (3) the need for a more child-centered religious education.

103. *The Times Educational Supplement,* October 11, 1963, p. 488.

104. Richard Acland, *We Teach Them Wrong* (London: Victor Gollanez, 1963), p. 17.

105. F. H. Hilliard, *The Teacher and Religion* (London: James Clarke & Co., 1963), p. 47.

106. Anthony Hartley, *A State of England* (London: Hutchinson & Co., 1963), p. 196.

107. David, *Church and School*, p. 19.

108. Julian Huxley (ed.), *The Humanist Frame* (London: George Allen & Unwin, 1961).

109. H. J. Blackham, "Religion in Schools," *The Hibbert Journal, 61* (July 1963), p. 181.

110. Margaret Knight, "Morals Without Religion," *The Listener,* January 20, 1955, p. 109.

111. Asher Tropp, *The School Teachers*, p. 231.

112. "Notes of the Week," *The Schoolmaster,* March 24, 1949, p. 362.

113. *The Schoolmaster,* September 8, 1949, p. 234.

114. National Union of Teachers, *School-Church Relationships* (Pamphlet No. 238, n. d.), p. 3.

115. *Ibid.,* pp. 8–9.

116. *The Teacher,* November 15, 1963.

117. *The Teacher,* February 28, 1964.

118. *The Teacher,* March 13, 1964.

119. *The Teacher,* March 27, 1964.

120. *Ibid.*

121. *The Teacher,* July 10, 1964.

122. *The Teacher,* July 17, 1964.

123. John Grigg, "State, Religion and School," *The Observer,* June 28, 1964.

124. *The Schoolmaster,* December 1, 1949.

125. Beck, "Background to the Education Act, 1959," p. 5.

126. Beck, "How the 1953 Act Took Shape," p. 2.

127. *The Times Educational Supplement,* August 28, 1964, p. 281.

128. Barker, *Character of England*, p. 570–571.

129. *Parliamentary Debates* (House of Commons) 5th Series, Vol. *396,* (January 19, 1944), p. 267.

130. Dewar, *Backward Christian Soldiers*, p. 167.

131. John A. T. Robinson, *Honest to God* (Student Christian Movement Press, 1963), p. 143.

132. A. R. Vidler, *et. al., Objections to Christian Belief* (London: Constable & Co., 1963), p. 111.

133. See C. H. Dobinson, *Schooling: 1963–1970* (London: George G. Harrap & Co., 1963), pp. 20–29.

134. Sir Ernest Barker, *Britain and the British People* (London: Oxford University Press, 1942), p. 96.

CHAPTER 3

Religion and Schooling in the Netherlands

The Netherlands is frequently referred to as an example of a staunchly democratic country that provides full financial support for denominational schools. Although other countries completely subsidize church schools, the Netherlands is considered a most appropriate example for the consideration of a more equitable policy in the United States. In Scotland the dominance of Presbyterianism and in Ireland the dominance of Catholicism have produced settlements which are in keeping with their historical conditions, but are less appropriate to the religious pluralism of the United States. In the Netherlands religious pluralism and religious freedom have developed together with full financial support of church schools as well as of schools which are religiously neutral. It is frequently argued that countries which have not achieved this full material freedom for education under the control of the church, or which have arranged only for partial support of denominational schools, should seek the equalization epitomized in the Netherlands.

To present an adequate picture of Dutch policy is a complex undertaking. Not only is educational policy centrally embedded in the political and social structure of the Netherlands, but the subtleties of its operation in the life of the people are many and may not be fully revealed in the written word. A full understanding calls for considerable penetration into the idiosyncratic experience of members of the culture. Furthermore, so much is typically taken for granted by a Dutch citizen that one needs to have in mind a considerable range of distinctions and qualifications.

Not only is there a wide variety of schools in the Netherlands, but distinctions are made between various aspects of what is included in the United States under the term "education." For instance, in the Netherlands, as in other countries of Western Europe, "upbringing" is distinguished from "education," the former relating to the entire process of bringing up the young, the control of which rests primarily with the family. *Onderwijs,* as distinct from *opvoeding* (upbringing), refers to the instructional aspects of education, that for which the school is primarily responsible. The difference is not identical with what Americans refer to as formal and informal educational influences, although there are certain similarities. Upbringing refers more particularly to the character molding processes and beliefs at work in the circle of one's family. There is a sense of responsibility associated with its meaning which is lacking in the American meaning of informal educational processes.

In primary education in the Netherlands the two concepts are distinguished, but they are not separated. The school bears certain responsibilities for upbringing. However, there is disagreement in the Netherlands about the place of upbringing and education in secondary education, particularly in pre-university schools. Although traditionally and in theory, upbringing is not the responsibility of this level of schooling, some urge that it should be. They are opposed by more conservative interests seeking to limit pre-university schooling to education.

One also needs to recognize the changing character of the organization of education, particularly secondary schooling, in the Netherlands in the 1960's. Secondary education, called " continued education," has developed under a variety of conditions and enactments and is currently in the process of being reorganized into an inclusive national pattern.

Statutory Provisions

The law of February 14, 1963 (generally referred to as the Mammoth Law [1]), was designed to regulate continued education and outlined a set of changes long considered desirable by various ministers of education and other educational and political leaders. It is part of an effort to divide the educational system into four groups: infants' education (for ages four to six plus), primary education (six plus to twelve plus), continued education (twelve plus onwards), and scientific (university) education. Various enactments had already dealt with infant, primary, and university education. The Mammoth Law is an effort to provide a "balanced whole of educational provisions" — [2] to synthesize earlier legislation about secondary education and to extend educational opportunity at the secondary level to more students who will not go on to the university. Although we are not concerned with the full complexities of the Mammoth Law, we must be attentive to its general purpose and to the situation which it was designed to improve.

Continued (secondary) education in the Netherlands had grown up without coordination. In various periods different kinds of schools had been developed without synthesis; the elements worked separately, each in its own province, and sometimes the various parts worked against each other. The 1963 law seeks to create a systematic order in the diversity of Dutch secondary schools. It continues the constitutional provisions for education and preserves the tradition of cultural, and especially religious, pluralism but in an effort to organize schooling into a whole that is more than individually operating parts.

Secondary education in the Netherlands is divided, in general, into three types: pre-university, general continued, and vocational, although there are also comprehensive schools and other special purpose schools. The gymnasium and the *hogereburgerschool* (higher civilian school) , before the 1963 law, provided preparation for the universities and technical universities. Formerly the gymnasium was included under the law on higher education. The *hogereburgerschool* was initially conceived as providing general education to prepare students for the outside world but more recently had provided also for entrance to universities. The gymnasium and *hogereburgerschool* offered six-year and five-year courses of study in two sides or streams, one centering in the classical humanities and languages, the other, in mathematics and science. The classical gymnasium continues to have high status. Curriculum and teaching in pre-university schools in general are dominated by the interests and disciplines of the university.

In the 1963 act the *hogereburgerschool* in so far as it offers pre-university education is to be called the atheneum. The lyceum is a combination of gymnasium and atheneum. The first years in all these schools is regarded as a "substructure" or "transitional" year in order to provide horizontal movement between schools and courses of study.

Higher general continued education, under the 1963 act, is to be provided in a school which replaces what the *hogereburgerschool* was initially to do and in part continued to do. A modern grammar school for higher general continued education will have a five-year course giving a general education which may also serve as a basis for higher vocational training. Its first-year course should contain the same subjects as university preparatory education, thus providing for a transitional year. In addition to these schools there are commercial day and evening schools and secondary schools for girls.

The 1963 bill also seeks to replace the present school for advanced primary education with "secondary general continued education." This is a school providing entry to vocational schools as well as to working positions which do not require further schooling. It offers a three- or four-year course. Its four-year course provides entry to the teachers' training colleges for primary school teachers. General continued education is offered not only in a "higher" and in a "secondary" school but there is also "elementary general continued education" which leads more directly into vocational education at levels which demand less academic study.

In general, vocational education in the Netherlands is highly differentiated and is commonly recognized as a well-developed branch of Dutch education. In home economics, agricultural education, education for trade and commerce, for industry, fisheries, transport, and service occupations, schools in the Netherlands are carefully and thoroughly at work providing a basis for the hard-working Dutch economy.

The 1963 bill endeavors to bring order into these types and levels of secondary education, to direct the selective process involved, to establish a planning procedure for creating schools, and to work out financing regulations. Through comprehensive enactment in these matters, there will be room for differences in the ideological character of the school and more opportunity for variation in curriculum planning. It may be viewed as a manifestation of a pervasive tendency in the Netherlands to order and organize things so that they run effectively and by lawfully established means. Although much of what is involved in the reorganization of secondary education awaits continued study and conference before it is put into practice, the bill enacts changes which will be in line with traditional values that are highly cherished.

The character of these values, which focus directly upon policies concerning religion and schooling, is seen in the section of the Constitution dealing with education. We quote the entire article.

> Education shall be an object of constant solicitude on the part of the government.
> The imparting of education shall be free, saving superintendence by the authorities, and moreover, in so far as general education, primary as well as secondary, is concerned, saving the examination with

regard to the ability and morality of the teacher, the whole to be regulated by law.

Public education shall be regulated by law, every person's religious views being duly respected.

In each municipality the authorities shall impart sufficient public general primary education in an adequate number of schools. According to the rules to be laid down by law, deviation from this provision may be permitted, provided that opportunity is given for such education to be received.

The standards of efficiency to be prescribed for education to be defrayed wholly or in part from public funds shall be regulated by law, with due observance in so far as private education is concerned, of freedom of direction.

These standards shall be regulated for general primary education in such a manner as to guarantee equally well the efficiency of the private education defrayed entirely from public funds and public education. In these regulations the freedom of private education concerning the choice of means of instruction and the appointment of teachers shall, particularly be respected.

Private general primary education fulfilling conditions to be imposed by law shall be defrayed from public funds according to the same standards as public education. The conditions upon which private general secondary education and preparatory university education shall be granted contributions from public funds shall be fixed by law.

The King shall cause a report on the condition of education to be made annually to the States-General.[3]

The Constitution was initially accepted in 1848 and has been amended in certain respects some seven times since. The revision of 1917 established the present article providing for the support of private as well as public primary education from public revenues.

The Constitution established the government's constant concern and care for education; the Ministry of Education in cooperation with the municipal councils should take care to nurture schools whether established by public or by private agencies. The authorities must make provisions so that the preference of the parents as to the spiritual or religious way of life of their children shall be supported financially. Both public or private schooling should be of an equal quality. Public education is fully regulated by law, but government has a different role in regard to private education. Here the Ministry is responsible for seeing that it is effective and of good quality in order to be subsidized, but its direction as interpreted by its basic values, whether of a religious or educational nature, is left to the determination of the group sponsoring the school. The Ministry exercises very extensive direction in public schools, but for the private sector it keeps "only a watchful eye on the observance of the conditions governing the subsidy and abstain[s] from any direct interference." [4] In later sections we shall be concerned with some of the problems involved in these provisions.

In infant education about 80 percent of schools are private; in primary or elementary education about 70 percent are private; in secondary and preparatory higher education over 60 percent are private; in vocational education more than 90 percent of the schools are private; four out of eleven universities and technical universities are private.[5]

Private education in the Netherlands consists of Roman Catholic, Protestant, and nondenominational or neutral schools. Protestant schools are founded and controlled by private organizations of a religious character; Roman Catholic schools are, of course, under the more direct influence of the church; neutral schools are established by associations which prefer no religious orientation in the schools.

The extent of state financial support of church schools is indicated by several examples. In Roman Catholic schools ecclesiastical authorities exercise the right of inspection of all subjects, and the cost of this inspection is paid from public funds. The cost of maintaining the Catholic Central Bureau, which is charged with the overall care of Catholic education, is financed by payments from each Catholic school which are repaid in the state subsidy for Catholic schools.[6] Since this bureau works with the Catholic State Council, which speaks for Catholic interests in matters of national policy and legislation, and with Catholic parents' committees, which have among other functions that of propagandizing for Catholic schools, the state subsidizes at least indirectly the efforts of the Church to promote its educational views and interests.

The conditions regulating the establishment of these schools at the primary level are different from those at the secondary level. The conditions were furthermore different for two kinds of primary education: ordinary primary education and complementary primary education, the latter now included within the regulations of the Mammoth Law for secondary education. Ordinary primary schools are six-year elementary schools. Complementary primary education provided for at least two more years and emphasized social subjects and manual skills. Primary schools are said to place their emphasis in the order head-heart-hand; in complementary primary education the order is said to be hand-heart-head. The kind of schooling represented by complementary primary education may be found in independent schools or in sections or departments associated with ordinary primary schools.

An association wishing to found an ordinary primary school should show a minimum student enrollment dependent on the size of the town. Enrollments should number 125 for a town with more than 100,000 inhabitants, 100 in towns of 50,000 to 100,000 inhabitants, 75 for towns of 25,000 to 50,000, and 50 for smaller municipalities. A somewhat similar minimal enrollment condition was set up for complementary primary education. When the required number of pupils is available, the applying organization automatically receives the cost of the building if it has raised 15 percent of the cost. This sum is repaid after the school has been in operation for a certain number of years. Special arrangements can be made in the case of smaller numbers of students.

Provisions for private secondary schools do not grant funds for schools automatically. The founding of a school must be included in a planning procedure of the Ministry, and the state of the country's finances must be such that the cost can be included in the nation's resources for subsidization. We shall return to some problems in this regard in a later section.

The provisions for elementary schools were enacted in the Primary Education Act of 1920; because it provided for equal support of private as well as public primary education, this act is spoken of as providing the "pacification" of the historic "school struggle."

In order to sense the significance of the division of primary education into public and private sectors and the latter into Protestant, Roman Catholic, and neutral school associations, in

TABLE 2   *Percentage of Ordinary and Complementary Primary Education in Public and Private Schools in the Netherlands* *

YEAR	PERCENT PUBLIC SCHOOLS	PERCENT PRIVATE SCHOOLS		
		Protestant	*Roman Catholic*	*Other*
1921	56	22	21	1
1936	38	27	33	2
1946	35	27	36	2
1959	32	29	37	2

* Adapted from Ministry of Education, *Dutch School System* (The Hague: Netherlands Government Information Service, 1960), p. 25.

Table 2 we note some figures showing the percentage of ordinary and complementary primary schools for various years since 1920. Thus an increasing proportion of common schooling in the Netherlands has since 1920 been controlled as to its spiritual and religious direction by private societies and institutions.

In addition to the types of primary schools listed in Table 2 there are a number of specialized primary schools for handicapped children and for those who present unusual educational problems, such as the children of barge crews and those of itinerant workers. During 1959, of the children who attended specialized primary schools, about 30 percent attended public, 22 percent attended Protestant, 41 percent attended Roman Catholic, and 7 percent attended various specialized schools.[7]

The extent of the divisions in secondary education is suggested by some figures reporting the number of day schools for preparatory university and secondary education in September, 1960. The Ministry reports a total of 447 schools enrolling a total of 170,253 students. They were distributed as to type of school as shown in Table 3.

Of the total number, 169 were public schools, 53 run by central authorities, and 116 run by municipalities. These schools enrolled 60,371 students. Of the 447 schools, 84 were Protestant, 160 Ro-

TABLE 3   *Number of Day Schools and Various Types for*
Preparatory University and Secondary Education
in the Netherlands, September 1960 *

TYPE OF SCHOOL	NUMBER OF SCHOOLS
Gymnasium	82
Hogereburgerschool	150
Lyceum	162
Secondary Schools for Girls	39
Commercial Day School	14
Total	447

* Adapted from *Digest of the Kingdom of the Netherlands: Education, Arts, and Sciences* (The Hague, Netherlands Government Information Service, n. d.), p. 23.

man Catholic, and 34 were other private, that is, neutral, schools. They enrolled 109,882 students.[8]   Thus, in 1960, of the total number of pupils, approximately 35 percent attended public schools, 22 percent attended Protestant schools, 35 percent attended Roman Catholic schools, and 7 percent attended neutral day schools.

Public and private schools pay the same salaries to teachers, thus avoiding any competition between them in this respect. Further, the pupil-teacher ratio is the same in both types of schools. Teachers must have the same qualifications and satisfy the same moral standards. The curriculum of the schools, apart from religious instruction, must be shown to be of the same quality. State inspectors supervise schools of both types. In the event that the inspector is not satisfied that the curriculum comes up to the requirements of "adequate and regularly progressing"[9] instruction, the matter is decided by the Educational Council, a body of educational experts appointed by the Queen and thereby independent of the Ministry. Thus great care is taken that the general conditions of education — the buildings, the quality of instruction, the competence and good character of teachers, the salaries — are the same for both public and private schools.

In summary, in the Netherlands the freedom of education, specifically laid down in the Constitution, is the central characteristic of national policy. Education is free in the sense that parents can choose the form of schooling which accords with their religious preference, and this freedom is implemented by full financial support by the state. The basic principle upon which this policy is grounded is that the parents have the "natural right and duty" [10] to determine the schooling which is appropriate to the upbringing of their children. In this conception of freedom it is the state's responsibility to promote full material opportunity for the parents to exercise this choice. We shall return in later sections to a consideration of this policy in its more concrete manifestations.

Turning now to statutory provisions relating to the teaching of religion in public schools, the Primary Education Act of 1920 provides that the public schools are to be "open to all children irrespective of religious convictions or affiliations, although they respect all religious beliefs." Furthermore, "the law expressly lays it down that the teachers shall abstain from teaching, doing or permitting anything that is contrary to the respect demanded by religious convictions." [11] This means that the teaching of religion is done by special teachers of religion rather than by classroom teachers; however, biblical materials may be used incidentally as part of the teaching of language, reading, and history. Otherwise, religious instruction is provided in the timetable and in the classrooms but on an optional basis and is taught by members of church communities or societies or by teachers selected by the church community for this purpose. This instruction is given by a large number of primary schools, and apparently only a few parents exempt their children from it. It is given for the most part at the level of the fifth class and higher. In 1929, 60 percent of the public elementary schools provided this religious instruction; in 1954, 88 percent of these schools did so.[12] The largest part of this religious education is provided by the Netherlands Reformed Church.

The situation in regard to religious education at the secondary school level is more complicated. Not only are the changes in the organization of secondary education in the Mammoth Law involved, but enactments make provisions for different kinds of religious education. There are different provisions for public and for private schools and differences as to whether religious instruction is controlled by the church or by societies with a religious interest.[13]

In the Netherlands a subject called "Knowledge of the Bible and Cultural History of Christian Religion" is, in law and in school practice, a cultural subject and may not be called "religious education." It is an optional subject in both public and private secondary schools. The selection of its teachers falls under the jurisdiction of the government or the school board, not under the control of the church. The government or school board is not obligated to provide this instruction. Those who are trained as ministers may be appointed to teach this subject, but if they do so, they speak as educators rather than as clergy. If the student becomes interested not only culturally but also spiritually in the subject, this interest is to be managed outside the school. Thus, knowledge of the Bible and of religion is marked off from religious instruction by the church or by religious societies. It is what Americans would recognize as "teaching about religion," and is found to a rather limited extent in the more metropolitan and industrial sections in the central part of the country.

Religious instruction, as distinct from this cultural subject, may be given in pre-university or in continued public secondary education where certain hours and facilities are provided free for teachers appointed by the church or by religious societies. Religious education in public schools is ecclesiastical; it stems from the church. It is an optional subject. It may be given by

ministers; it may have the character of preaching; it may be catechetical. In 1929, 37 percent of public continued secondary
schools offered religious education; in 1954, 65 percent did so.[14]

Other provisions regulate religious instruction in private
schools. By enactment some subjects taught in private schools
are obligatory, but in addition there are four hours a week that
may be used for other subjects. Among these may be religious
instruction. This is given in Protestant Christian schools under
the auspices of school foundations composed of representatives
of different churches — the Dutch Reformed Church, the Neo-
Calvinistic Free Church, and some others. It works out so that
in Protestant Christian schools, where some students are enrolled
from families which are not particularly religious, the church
reaches indirectly a number of nonreligious or vaguely religious
families.

Thus a range of possibilities is provided for religious instruction, and it may be provided in public schools by the church or by
religious societies. The situation is a curious one. In the public
school sector, religious education is managed by the church. In
the Protestant Christian sector catechetical religious education is
provided by religious societies but not churches. In both public and private schools the study of the Bible and the cultural
history of religion may be offered by specialists whose authority
stems from educational rather than ecclesiastical sources. It is
difficult to say how fully these distinctions provided in enactments are followed in practice, but one obtains the impression
that the lines often blur depending on the situation and the
person engaged in the teaching.

The subject, "Knowledge of the Bible and Cultural History of
Christian Religion" is for our purposes of special interest. In
providing for knowledge of the Bible as a cultural product and
for an awareness of different interpretations of religion, the subject is more satisfactory to the more liberal religious interests.
Typically these are found within the less dogmatic and more inclusive outlook of the Netherlands Reformed Church as well as
in humanist circles. Other groups take religious education and
Bible history to be intrinsically instruction in religious doctrine.

To "let the Bible speak for itself," that is, to regard it as a source for religious experience and insight appropriate to confronting the various problems of the modern world appeals to the more thoughtfully liberal components in Netherlands religious life. The specialists who are employed as teachers are drawn from this segment rather than from those representing a strict adherence to Calvinistic doctrine.

This is reflected in the materials provided for use in these classes. A textbook called *Seeking the Way in the Varied World of Belief and Thought* [15] presents the various religions of the world today and the historical development of Christian churches. It provides a factual description of the churches of the Netherlands, the number of members, the liturgy of the churches, the general characteristics of their beliefs. It also contains brief characterizations of the thought of great "seekers of the way" ranging from Augustine, Erasmus, Luther, and Spinoza to Tolstoi, Nietzsche, Barth, and Sartre.

When one visits a class in Bible history and the cultural history of religion, he is impressed with the objective treatment of the subject and with the teacher's effort to cultivate a thoughtful understanding of a considerable range of religious experience. At the level of the first class of a municipal lyceum, instruction centered in giving information about the Psalms and in interpreting the meaning of the Psalms as an aspect of the religious life of a people. After informal discussion in which the teacher obtained expressions from the members of the class of their ways of perceiving the function of the psalmist, the teacher's summation of the main points of the lesson were taken down in the students' copybooks. Although there was no evidence of group work or of any activity to supplement the rather academic and bookish character of the instruction, one could sense the effort to place talk about religion on a thoughtful and nondogmatic basis.

Columnizing

To understand policy about religion and schooling in the Netherlands, one needs to see it in the light of some of the salient conditions of national life. We have already noted that the private sector of education is divided into Roman Catholic, Protestant Christian, and neutral schools and that statistical data on Dutch schools are reported in terms of these categories. If we are to understand the meaning of Dutch educational policy and particularly what it may mean for American problems, we need to see this division of Dutch schools in its cultural and historical setting. These conditions are enormously complex; hence we shall only suggest some of the conditions bearing on the nature of policy and then explore more fully three aspects of national life that are particularly crucial to our purposes. After suggesting some general characteristics of Dutch life, we shall want to look more fully into the phenomenon of "columns" or "pillars" as an aspect of the social structure of the Netherlands, the character of political parties in their relationship to religious groups and educational policies, and the historic school struggle leading to the pacification expressed in the Constitution of 1917 and the Primary Education Act of 1920.

The land is indeed the low country, large sections of it reclaimed from the sea, and the continued struggle against the waters of the sea and the rivers has influenced the way the people have gone about their affairs and thought of themselves as a people with a distinctive way of life. A visitor is frequently reminded of how the Dutch have literally made the land on which their culture rests and adapted their institutions to its conditions. Furthermore, the country is small, consisting of some 13,700 square miles, an area about equal to that of Massachusetts, Connecticut, and Rhode Island. Its population numbers more than 11.5 million. The density of population is 850 to the square mile as compared with 537 in the United Kingdom and 52 in the United States. The birthrate, about 180,000 in 1939, is now about 240,000 a year.[16] Moreover, the Netherlands is a well-developed country in the sense that agricultural, service, and industrial activities are highly refined and efficient. These conditions call for a pattern of national life that does not leave policies to chance. They demand a kind of control and common effort if the freedom so centrally treasured in Dutch life is to endure.

The Netherlands has in many ways and for a long period of time been at the crossroads of European and world affairs. Its geographic position, its tradition of world trade and commerce, the international activities centering at The Hague, and the dependence which limited resources impose upon an economy produce a cosmopolitan setting and a concern for affairs that lie beyond national boundaries. Historically, the tides of belief of the Roman Church, of Calvinism, of the Enlightenment, and of reactions to each of these have left their mark upon national policy. In various periods the Netherlands has been brought under the rule of other nations: the Spanish, the French, and the Germans, and cultural residue of these periods of foreign domination remain. These factors make for the development of policies that are responsive to historical influences and movements of thought and yet have the distinctive traits of Dutch experience.

It is of central importance to our purposes to recognize the diversity of Dutch life and culture. The Netherlands is far from a homogeneous society although certain forces contribute to its unity. The Dutch people do not derive from a single stock. Historically, they are composed of Frisians in the north, Saxons in the east, Franks in the south, and a still more different group in the Zeeland islands of the southern delta. Further, profound cultural differences are found in close proximity. One has only to travel very limited distances to encounter very fundamental social and cultural differences. For example, within the city limits of Amsterdam one enters a different world and culture as he travels across the harbor and into the waterlands adjacent to the Zuiderzee. Here a historic pastoral life is found just a few miles from one of the major commercial and shipping centers of Europe.

This diversity is particularly noticeable in the variety of churches and religious societies in the Netherlands. Official statistics on religious affiliation report a list of some twenty denominations and in addition a number of smaller groups and sects. According to the census of 1947, about 38 percent of the population were Roman Catholics; about 31 percent were Netherland Reformed; about 10 percent were affiliated with the Neo-Calvinist Free Church (*Gereformeerde*) and smaller related groups; about 4 percent were members of smaller churches and sects; about 17 percent had no religious memberships. These figures have not changed appreciably in subsequent years. Historically, the main changes in the percentage of members of the religious groups are associated with the relative decline of Netherlands Reformed Church membership. In 1850 about 38 percent of the total population were Roman Catholic, 55 percent Netherlands Reformed, 1 percent Neo-Calvinist, 6 percent other, and none without religious identification. The membership of the Roman Catholic Church has thus remained relatively constant.[17]

These populations are not distributed evenly over the country. In general, Roman Catholics are predominant in the south; Protestants, in the north. The provinces of Limburg and North Brabant, in the south, are 94 and 89 percent Roman Catholic, respectively. Provinces in the extreme north have the largest proportions of Neo-Calvinist Free Church members, although Zeeland is 20 percent of this persuasion. The proportion of those without church membership is largest in the vicinity of Amsterdam. However, there is also a general distribution of all major church groups in all sections of the country.[18]

For more detailed consideration of the characteristics of Netherland culture, a particular aspect of the social structure is especially important for our purposes; the Dutch term is *verzuiling,* derived from the word *zuil* which means a column or pillar. The term refers to a vertical pattern of social differentiation as distinct from the horizontal pattern of social classes or an oblique line of demarcation into caste or ethnic groups. Although there are marks of differentiation in the Netherlands in terms of socio-economic levels of well-being, position, or status, and some recognition of racial or ethnic origins, the outstanding pattern of social organization pertains to religious ideologies or columns.

In the Netherlands the organization of social life is dominated by membership in and distinctions between Roman Catholic, Protestant Christian, and general or neutral associations. Not only do private schools fall into these categories, but the organizations and institutions of social life are marked off so that people of the same religious group interact with each other rather than with members of other religious ideologies. A pillar is a block of social organizations encompassing the entire range of group activity — church, school, employment, trade unions, professional and occupational organizations, stores, hospitals, sports and leisure time activities, newspapers, radio and television, political and civic activities — so that an individual may spend almost his whole life in contacts with members of his own religious group. His contacts with persons of other religious faiths are purely tertiary — they ride in the same trams, attend certain community celebrations, may have a few business and community contacts apart from organized religious demarcations, but basically the entire range of group life is organized on a denominational basis. The columns cut across almost all of the areas of group life so that "to each his own" in the sense of loyalty to members of his own religious orientation characterizes the entire range of institutions and associations.

This pattern of social differentiation has become so embedded in Dutch life that it is commonly taken for granted. Despite certain efforts, largely in the intellectual and higher cultural levels of the society, to break away from differentiation by columns, the pattern is so entrenched in the way of life of the people that its operation is seldom in the center of attention. Despite the pervasive character of this pattern of social organization and control, there is remarkably little study of it. Most of the articles that deal with it point out the paucity of research into the matter.

One study, in English, by a refugee from Czechoslovakia, describes the social structure and culture of a Dutch community.[19] This sociological study provides a wealth of descriptive information about Sassenheim, a community of 7,470 inhabitants (1947) midway between Amsterdam and The Hague and just a few miles from the well-known park and display garden, Keukenhof. The study reveals that the community of Sassenheim is split up into more than five religious communities — the Roman Catholic Church, the Dutch Reformed Church, the Calvinist Church (*Gereformeerde Kerken*), the Christian Calvinist Church (*Christelijk Gereformeerde Kerk*), a group of free-thinking Protestants belonging to various unorthodox denominations (*Protestantenbond*) — and a group without denomination consisting of about 2.4 percent of the population.

"The Roman Catholic Church is undoubtedly the largest and most influential organization in the community. In the latest directory no less than forty-four different clubs, committees, and associations of the Roman Catholics are mentioned." [20] In addition to committees more directly associated with the worshipping life of the church, there are the school board, the youth organizations of the church, a Roman Catholic theater club, a Roman Catholic sport association, a Roman Catholic athletic association, a girl scout group, a Roman Catholic workers movement, a Roman Catholic middle-class association, two religious educational and nursing orders, two retreat groups, a Sunday afternoon club, a group which organizes pilgrimages, the Catholic People's Party, a Roman Catholic organization of laborers, an association of farmers and gardeners, an employer's association, a Roman Catholic family care group, a Roman Catholic children's colony association, a Roman Catholic burial association, and a Roman Catholic travel association.

The Protestant churches also control a number of subgroups cutting across a wide range of public life. In addition to political parties, which we shall treat in a later section, there are trade and employment associations such as a Protestant Christian trade union, a Protestant association of employers, and a middle-class association. The Calvinist Church and the Dutch Reformed Church have their separate school boards. In some sectors of public life the Protestant churches coordinate their policies in common Christian organizations. There is a Protestant public library, a Protestant kindergarten, a Protestant music club, a

Protestant hospital association, a Protestant nursing association, and a Green Cross functioning side by side with a Roman Catholic White and Yellow Cross and a neutral Red Cross.

"Most churches urge their young members only to marry persons of the same denomination. This pressure is somewhat less if it concerns the relationship between the members of the akin Protestant churches." [21] Although it is particularly strong in the Roman Catholic group, most churches are opposed to a weakening of belief or a loosening of ties. The Dutch Reformed and other "modernist" churches rely more heavily on the inner sense of identity rather than on explicit public forms of control. In most sport associations and clubs "the people of other denominations are not only unwelcome but often openly refused membership. . . . Tennis and dancing parties are strictly denominational affairs." [22]

The study by I. Gadourek included the use of a questionnaire in which an item was modeled on Bogardus' and Dodd's social distance scale. "Do you object to your children or brothers and sisters: (a) being married to; (b) being acquainted by friendship; (c) working with a person of different religious denomination?" The study reports that 81.9 percent opposed interdenominational marriage; 40.6 percent objected to mixed friendship; 11.4 percent opposed working with people of other faiths; 15.8 percent accepted all three forms of contact. "Church affiliation divides the whole community into distinct, separate, social segments," [23] the Roman Catholic group avoiding interfaith contacts the most, the Calvinists approaching them in this respect. The Dutch Reformed, the minor churches, and the unchurched hold greater tolerance for people of different religious views.

In speaking of the schools and cultural institutions of Sassenheim, Gadourek notes that the function of cultural integration is not observed, but that institutions help to divide the population into distinct denominational groups.

The differentiation sets in at a very early age. In the kindergartens, for instance, children learn to choose their friends from the Roman Catholic or the Protestant *milieu;* the songs they sing, the verses they learn, differ in both groups. The differences are accentuated in the system of elementary education. A considerable time is spent on religious teaching in each grade. The classes on religion as well as "singing" (consisting of singing psalms and religious hymns) foster the denominational differences that are not counterbalanced by an exhortation to national unity in other classes. In the courses of the "Dutch Language" stress is laid more on the lessons in grammar than on the stimulation of a consciousness of national cultural inheritance and unity. An insignificant part of the curriculum is spent on teaching Dutch History. . . . In these short lessons, the pupils are not taught to interpret history from a common national standpoint but rather from the standpoint of their own denominational group. Even a superficial analysis of the textbooks reveals the conflict of values that is rooted in the different interpretations of the history.[24]

In an appendix Gadourek reports the evidence gathered from his inspection of the history textbooks used in the various elementary schools of Sassenheim. Paragraphs were selected from the texts used in the Roman Catholic, the Calvinist, and the Dutch Reformed schools. The paragraphs deal with one of the most important periods in the origin of the Netherlands as a nation. Following some passages showing considerably less than fair and balanced treatment of the Reformation and Martin Luther's place in it, some briefer passages present comparative treatments of Philip II and the Inquisition.

On Philip II:

The Roman Catholic text:

Philip II was a religious sovereign. To him the Catholic cause was beyond anything else. In those days the apostasy was generally considered as a crime and had to be punished. Very many sovereigns did not bother about it too much. But Philip did. He was not too popular in the Netherlands. He was a proud Spaniard, and did not feel at home in the Netherlands.

The Calvinist text:

Philip did not like the Dutchmen and the Dutchmen did not like him. He was a typical Spaniard: proud, ambitious, unfriendly, and a merciless persecutor of heretics. People understood quite well why the Spanish soldiers received orders to stay here. It was to wipe out heresy from the country, to rob the Dutchmen of their freedom, in the long run.

The Dutch Reformed text:

Philip II was by far not such a clever sovereign as his father. He was a typical Spaniard, and had nothing in common with the Dutchmen. He could not even understand their language. The purpose of his rule is as follows: the extirpation of the reformed religion in the Netherlands. Everybody had to be a Catholic!

On the Inquisition:

The Roman Catholic text:

This was a tribunal of the Church. Its members were wise and pious bishops and priests.

The Calvinist text:

Each day, now here then there, especially in the Southern Netherlands, innocent people were tortured and murdered. The inquisition was merciless. . . .

The Dutch Reformed text:

Everybody hated the Inquisition. William of Orange, while still being a Catholic, hated it too, together with many other Catholics . . . .

Thus the books used in the schools of the denominations interpret historic events in terms of the values of the particular religious groups at the expense of the values of an integrated national culture.[25]

The bearing of the establishment of denominational schools on the maintenance of a public school in Sassenheim is an interesting story. Following the settlement of the "school struggle" by the adoption of Article 208 of the Constitution in 1917 and the Primary Education Act of 1920, the public school in Sassenheim had no chance to survive and was abolished in the early 1920's. Since, according to law, the amount of subsidy provided private schools is based on the number of attending pupils, the existence of a public school was in direct competition with the denominational schools.

More recently a local neutral group petitioned the Community Council for the establishment of a public school. The petition was sponsored by a local socialist group of more recent immigrants which was a small minority and was represented by only one of the thirteen seats in the Community Council. Its petition, however, was signed by other influential townspeople, some belonging to the more liberal Protestant church and others without denominational affiliation. The petition was repeatedly outvoted in the Council since the denominational interests were united in opposing an action which would diminish the subsidies granted to their schools. However, although the Council could delay the petition for the public school, it could not prevent the founding of a neutral school when the group had fulfilled the legal requirements which we have earlier noted. Although a footnote in Gadourek's study points to this outcome as evidence of the protection of minority rights in this freedom-loving country, we note that the effect of columnization is to force those who do not find a place within existing columns to form a neutral column to secure their own interests.[26]

Although Gadourek's study of a Dutch community reveals the centrality of columns in Netherlands' social structure, other detailed studies of Dutch community life are not available. In 1956 a special issue of *Sociological Guide* contained four articles dealing with columns. One of these in discussing the process of forming columns suggested that socialism was the source of the tendency to form columns since it involved a range of organizations such as: political party, labor union, youth movement, adult education, radio, sports clubs, vocational centers, press, scientific research, and the like. Later on, especially after World War II, the socialist column disintegrated and became less rigid in ideology. It sought to include more people of other persuasions who could unite on the level of political organization. Consequently, the socialist column became weaker.[27]

Other writers do not agree with this placing of the socialist movement as a condition giving rise to pillarization, although they agree that the third — the general or neutral — column has a different character from the Protestant and Roman Catholic columns. In a subsequent issue of the *Sociological Guide,* D. I. Schöffer held that socialist organizations were quite different from columns and that the "neutral" column was formed later as a reaction to the religious character of the others.[28] Furthermore, he was concerned with how columns developed in the Netherlands and not elsewhere.

Schöffer offered seven tentative hypotheses to account for the appearance of columns as a uniquely Dutch phenomenon: (1) A tradition of particularism (regional autonomy and diversity of authority) in the Old Republic (before 1795) and a continuing spirit of federalism in later periods, in contrast with French centralism, left room for the development of columns. (2) The tradition of Protestant individualism and Calvinistic ethics emphasized the primacy of the family. It affirmed the sovereignty of the primary group indicated in such expressions as: "My home is my castle" and "Each must take care of his own." (3) Calvinism encouraged typically a dogmatic attitude with rigorous moral codes of behavior, and this attitude is also shared by Dutch Roman Catholics. (4) Historically, Protestant and Roman Catholic groups, composed of "little people," were discriminated against by the middle class of the province of Holland, and were emancipated largely under the leadership of priest and minister. (5) The industrial revolution was late in the Netherlands and the movement of people away from the church was not experienced. The churches achieved a social conscience in time to hold the big majority of Protestant and Roman Catholic laborers from the appeal of socialism. (6) The comparative isolation of Roman Catholics below the great rivers and of Protestants in other provinces tended to make columnizing easy. (7) The two religious groups stimulated each other to build strong organizations and yet to form a coalition against liberal and socialistic movements, first in the school struggle and later in other problems of social policy. Schöffer indicates the need for more careful research concerning the continuance of columns in modern times.

In an article appearing in 1957 H. Verwey-Jonker stresses the view that the columns are not, except for the Roman Catholic one, monolithic structures.[29] They are, rather, built up of bits and pieces that run more or less into each other. She suggests that it might be better to speak less of columns and more of a thicket of little trees that are tangled up together. Involved in this thicket are choices as to denomination, political party, and type of school. In trying to find out what percentage of the Dutch people belongs to each of the columns she finds it very difficult to obtain numbers yielding comparable statistical data. There is no adequate index, for no column contains a complete cross section of the Dutch people; one cannot find a criterion that applies to all Dutchmen and gives an indication about the column to which they belong. Probably the best index concerns the numbers of children in various primary schools, for all parents have to make a choice at this point. Even this index has to be corrected because, for example, Roman Catholic families have more children than families without religious affiliation.

After a complex and somewhat obscure process of correcting for various variables, and using the choice of school as the criterion, Verwey-Jonker concludes that 34 percent of parents belong to the Roman Catholic column, 28 percent to the Protestant Christian, and 38 percent to the neutral. The Roman Catholic column is monolithic because most people that belong to the Roman Catholic Church vote for the Roman Catholic party, although 3 percent of Dutch voters are Catholics who vote for the Labor Party and 1 percent send children to public schools. In contrast, the Protestant Christian column is composed of Netherlands Reformed, Calvinist, and other denominations. Although most members vote for Protestant political parties, 18 percent of Dutch voters are Protestants who vote for the Labor Party. Of those without religion, most vote for the Labor Party although an appreciable number vote for liberal and for Communist candidates. Labor Party members send their children to Roman Catholic and to Protestant Christian as well as to public and to private neutral schools. In short, the columns other than the Roman Catholic are not monolithic, and it is doubtful that one can speak of the neutral-socialist-humanist remainder of the Dutch population as a column. Verwey-Jonker concludes that the picture one gets of the column system depends upon the perspective with which one looks at it.

In several articles J. P. Kruijt has made more extended analyses of the columnizing of Dutch society. In one of these he offers a definition which seeks to mark columns off from other varieties of social structure.[30] "Columns are blocks of social organizations and forms of living together which are based on spiritual foundations, equal before the law, and existing within a larger spiritually mixed, but predominately racially and ethnically homogeneous, democratic nation." [31] Columns are implicitly equal before the law because the law never mentions columns; there are no legally defined privileges. The definition enables us to distinguish columns from other related phenomena such as ethnic groups, religious sects, and social classes. Ethnic groups are not treated as socially equal; they are strangers who are attached to their own language and culture. Classes lack the common spiritual basis of columns. Churches and their religious tasks are not to be identified with columns. Denominationalism itself does not necessarily produce separate organizations of social life to keep spiritually like-minded people in contact with their own rather than with other-thinking people. Columns appear in a democratic society because the isolation of the group is freely chosen, voluntarily enforced, and can only voluntarily be weakened.

Kruijt suggests drawing a number of circles around the church. The first circle would contain the essentially religious functions; the second, the educational and philanthropic tasks — schools, hospitals, old people's homes and the like; the third, economic and general cultural activities — sporting societies, labor unions, political parties, insurance companies, corporations, radio, technical schools, music societies, building societies, farmer societies, commercial organizations, teetotalers organizations, libraries. One can speak of columns only when the third area is included.

In addition to this way of looking at the organization of columns, Kruijt suggests that one can also consider another range of social forms: the *intranubium* (intermarriage), the *intravivium* (associating together), the *intracaritas* (mutual assistance), and — although, as he says, it is no fine term — the *intraeconomie* (mutual economic relationships). We have already seen that columnizing involves the preference of people to marry within their own denominational group. Kruijt's main point is that the range of interaction between people of different columns is drastically reduced by the dominance of patterns of interaction between people of the same column. Although 14 percent of Roman Catholic voters did not vote for the Roman Catholic party in the last election, and although 50 to 75 percent of radio listeners who subscribe to a columnized program magazine listen to other broadcasts than that of their own column, and although some unions are not columnized, the range of associations between members of different spiritual perspectives is severely limited. Village and neighborhood associating has lost to an ideological principle of interrelationship.

In areas where there is a marked majority of one column and a small minority of another, there may be much cooperation between them. However, in situations where a Roman Catholic minority has recently grown into a majority or will shortly achieve a majority, there is such a struggle day in and day out that one can hardly speak any more of a local community. The struggle manifests itself everywhere: in appointments and elections; in renting, buying, and selling of farms and houses; in buying in shops; in the playing of children; in pressure against mixed marriages. Protestant boys are not allowed to come into Roman Catholic cafes and football clubs. One village even had columnized celebrations of the anniversary of the ending of the war.

. . . Here in such areas — and these areas are not alone — what is so often denied comes clearly to the fore, the element of power in the struggle between columns. We who watch the course of development of our country must fear that in spite of the reflections of intellectual leaders, the height of the struggle is not yet reached. The column organizations are busy conquering the last peaceful areas. Therewith the daily intervivium for our people becomes smaller and smaller. We live separately as at least three people.[32]

Kruijt points out that Christian charity in the Netherlands rather than taking after the example of the good Samaritan, accentuates the latter part of Paul's letter to the Galatians where it says, "Where we have opportunity, let us do good unto all men, especially unto them who are of our own belief." Since much specialization and many kinds of experts are involved in modern Christian charity, each column must see to it that it has its share of the national effort. Every denomination should have so many beds in hospitals, so many doctors, specialists, nurses, psychiatrists, psychologists, dentists, social case workers and so on, all of the same denomination and supported by their proportionate part in the provided subsidies. He feels that this is not just a matter of justice and equal opportunity for charitable work, but that there are elements of power and influence coming into play.

Kruijt calls attention to economic discrimination as the worst aspect of columnization, especially the preference to appoint in employment situations members of one's own denomination. The process is automatically reinforced since if one denomination does so, others are inclined in defending themselves to do the same thing. In employment advertisements one can find small letters indicating the preferred column: *r.k.* for Roman Catholic; *p.g.* for Calvinist; *n.h.* for Dutch Reformed; *g.g.* for no religion.

In a study of advertisements in general and denominational papers he found four groups or kinds of advertisements where discrimination was present. The first group consisted of non-economic advertisements — advertisements for marriage, correspondence, dancing clubs, choirs, tennis clubs, and the like. The second group concerned personal services — maids, baby-sitters, and so on. The third group advertised for people to work in institutions — hospitals, rest homes, and schools. These three groups contained by far the largest amount of discriminatory advertisements. The fourth group dealt with positions in trade and industry — salesmen, shop girls and secretaries. Much less discrimination was found here especially if a firm was mentioned by name or was a large firm. The phenomenon of economic discrimination by columns is certainly present, but research in the matter is insufficient to yield a clear picture.

According to Kruijt, economic discrimination between columns is found in the selling and leasing of farm land and houses. In some villages a wide variety of measures exist to keep property in the hands of coreligionists.

It is interesting in this regard that an article in *Delta* mentions the religious factor in the selection of farmers and other occupations to become members of communities settled on the new polders (reclaimed land) of the Zuiderzee.

> . . . Farmers wishing to settle on the new land are required to give proof of competence, financial resources, and good reputation, and on this basis the most suitable applicants are selected. It is rather typically Dutch that the religious beliefs of the applicants are also to some extent taken into consideration, the aim being to ensure that the religious composition of the new communities will correspond to that of the country as a whole. The conditions for acceptance of farmers also apply to shopkeepers and tradesmen. . . .[33]

In another article, written in English, Kruijt observes that the columns may perform the function of binding members to the various churches, but for the nation as a whole they work dysfunctionally.[34] Since people in different columns do not meet in such a way that they come really to know each other, the formation and spread of stereotypes about people in other columns than one's own may readily occur. Furthermore, since in the Netherlands the confessional columns are related to political affairs, the churches may be drawn into a situation in which they apply pressure and sanctions in regard to the political choices of their members.

An instance occurred in 1954 when a comprehensive pastoral letter signed by the Archbishop of Utrecht and six Roman Catholic bishops was issued.[35] In the last sections of the Mandate dealing with membership of Roman Catholics in socialistic associa-

tions, the bishops observe that although they appreciate that socialists in the Netherlands are not pushing for the class struggle
any more, their principles are not safe anchorages for Christian
belief and morals. There are Catholic organizations in all areas
so that Catholics can belong to them. There is no reason to belong to socialist societies; this brings serious dangers to the
preservation of the faith and the Christian character of society.
Hence, Catholics are not permitted to be members of socialistic
organizations, to visit socialist meetings regularly, to read the
socialist press regularly, or to listen to VARA, the socialist broadcasting station.

> . . . We maintain the rule that the holy sacraments must be refused
> — and, in the case of death without conversion, also the ecclesiastical
> funeral — to any Catholic, who is a known member of a socialist asso-
> ciation, or who without being a member, still regularly attends
> Socialist meetings, or is a regular reader of Socialist periodicals or
> papers.[36]

This statement stirred up much comment at the time it appeared,
and Kruijt says, "It was a declaration of war from the R.C. church
against the idea of breaking through the antithetical lines of
demarcation set up by the Neo-Calvinists and their Catholic
allies." [37]

By way of explanation here, although we shall deal with the
matter in a later section, a movement known as the *doorbraak*
(breakthrough or bursting of a dyke) had sought to break with
the tradition of columns at least on the political side, and with
the "antithesis" set up by strict Calvinists against liberalism and
modernistic religious outlooks. The bishops were explicitly re-
pudiating the *doorbraak* movement. Kruijt points out that the
Dutch Reformed Church in a Protestant pastoral letter rejected
this pressure evident in the bishops' mandate. One of the Protestant political parties, the Anti-Revolutionary Party, which derives directly from the "antithesis," heartily agreed with the
Catholic hierarchy's position.[38] The Neo-Calvinist Church
(*Gereformeered*) at first disagreed with the position of the Catholic bishops, then had a number of petitions filed against this

position, and have more recently appointed a committee to study the issue and recommend their position to the general synod. The incident illustrates the complexity of the Dutch system of columns, the character of the churches' involvement in the ideological and spiritual basis of the columns, and the extent of the churches' influence in the political life of the Netherlands.

Kruijt and Goddijn have also tried to analyze columns more quantitatively through the identification of factors contributing to their growth in some dimensions and their decline in others.[39] They concluded that the Dutch population is not evenly columnized; the Roman Catholics are more clearly a column. The difference between the Roman Catholics and the more dogmatic Calvinists as compared to the nonaffiliated is such that the term column does not have the same meaning for each. The Dutch Reformed Church, containing more varied points of view falls between the Neo-Calvinists and the neutralists. The selection of primary school is the area of maximum structural pillarization. The religiously unaffiliated and the liberal wing of the confessional churches seem to have much more in common than either of them have with the more conservative Calvinists or with the Roman Catholics. In terms of Ralph Linton's analysis of cultures into universal, specialist, and alternative dimensions, the cultural universals serving to unite the Dutch people are difficult to find.

In another aspect of his analysis, Kruijt reports that the degree of pillarization is highest for "free youth education" and social work, respectively. It is lowest for sports, press, cultural organizations, and trade unions, in that order.[40]

The degree of pillarization in organizations, especially Roman Catholic ones, is increasing; [41] however, a reversing tendency is present, pertaining primarily to a small group of intellectuals and especially those within the Netherlands Reformed Church.[42] Cooperation between members of different groups has not led to a revision of fundamental policies of columns but only to some understanding of other groups which may in the long run be a condition for new developments to come.

Political Parties

Since much of the history of Dutch politics concerns differences of religious beliefs and interests, and the function of the state in the support of them, the parties reflect these basic religious differences.[43] The struggle over the schools established the main lines of the Dutch party system, lines which continue today in the rift between confessional and nonconfessional parties and a division between conservatives and progressives in both confessional and nonconfessional parties. The history of Dutch politics is largely that of compromise or establishing of a temporary truce between confessional and public interests.

The chief outlines of the political situation at the national level is shown in Table 4 summarizing election results for the composition of the Second Chamber in the last four elections. As a result of the 1963 election a coalition of the Catholic People's Party, the Anti-Revolutionary Party, the Christian Historical Union, and the liberal party or People's Party for Freedom and Democracy formed the Cabinet. The Labor Party or socialists formed the opposition. Before 1959 the Cabinet consisted of a coalition of the Labor Party, the Catholic People's Party, the Anti-Revolutionary Party, and the Christian Historical Union.

In a study by the Netherlands Institute of Public Opinion in 1954, a cross tabulation shows the percentage of the total party vote contributed by the major church groups. A representative sample of 1,908 voters was interviewed. Table 5 summarizes the findings.

We shall now consider the general positions of the parties from the point of view of their influence on educational policies particularly as they deal with religion and the schools.

The Catholic People's Party (K.V.P.) is not a clerical party and is in principle open to non-Catholics, though it expresses the political philosophy of the Roman church and is the political spokesman for Catholics in the Netherlands. Its purpose is to bring the principles derived from the revelation of God as interpreted by church authorities into the natural order. In the natural order there is a hierarchy; every lower form has its own

TABLE 4   *Summary Table of Election Results, Second Chamber, 1952–1963**

	1952		1956		1959		1963	
Number of valid votes cast	5,335,754		5,727,742		5,999,531		6,258,521	
Percent of valid votes cast for each party followed by number of seats obtained	*Percent*	*Seats*	*Percent*	*Seats*	*Percent*	*Seats*	*Percent*	*Seats*
RELIGIOUS PARTIES								
(a) *Protestant Parties*								
Staatkundig Gereformeerde Partij (Calvinist Reformed Party)	2.4	2	2.3	3	2.2	3	2.3	3
Anti-Revolutionaire Partij (Anti-Revolutionary Party)	11.3	12	9.9	15	9.4	14	8.7	13
Christelijk-Historische Unie (Christian-Historical Union)	8.9	9	8.4	13	8.1	12	8.6	13
(b) *Roman Catholic Parties*								
Katholieke Nationale Partij (Roman Catholic National Party)	2.7	2						
Katholieke Volkspartij (Roman Catholic People's Party)	28.7	30	31.7	49	31.6	49	31.9	50

	1952		1956		1959		1963	
	Percent	*Seats*	*Percent*	*Seats*	*Percent*	*Seats*	*Percent*	*Seats*
LIBERAL PARTIES								
Volkspartij voor Vrijheid en Democratie (People's Party for Freedom and Democracy)	8.8	9	8.8	13	12.2	19	10.3	16
SOCIALIST PARTIES								
Partij van de Arbeid (Labor Party)	29.0	30	32.7	50	30.3	48	28.0	43
Pacifistisch-Socialistische Partij (Pacifist Socialist Party)					1.8	2	3.0	4
Communistische Partij van Nederland (Communist Party of the Netherlands)	6.2	6	4.8	7	2.4	3	2.8	4
OTHER PARTIES								
Those with seats obtained	2.0				2.0		2.9	4
Those with no seats obtained			1.4				1.5	
Total	100.0	100	100.0	150	100.0	150	100.0	150

* Adapted from G. H. Scholten and G. Ringnalda, "Summary Table of Election Results, Second Chamber Elections, 1918–1963" (unpublished manuscript); data from Central Bureau of Statistics, The Hague.

TABLE 5   *Percentage of Political Party Vote by Religious Affiliation**

	Roman Catholic	Dutch Reformed	Neo-Calvinist	No Church Affiliation	No Answer	Total Percent
Labor Party	7	45	1	41	4	100[sic]
Catholic People's Party	96	1	—	1	2	100
Anti-Revolutionary Party	1	35	58	3	3	100
Christian Historical Union	—	94	2	2	2	100
Liberal Party	2	58	2	28	10	100
Communist Party	5	19	—	71	5	100
Remaining Parties	39	25	23	7	6	100
No Answer	32	36	3	25	4	100

* Adapted from Netherlands Institute of Public Opinion, *De Nederlandse Kiezer* (*The Dutch Voter*) (The Hague: State Printing House and Publishing Service, 1956), p. 86.

function and is a step to the higher. Just as the church rules in spiritual matters, so the state rules in the natural area, save that the state is restricted by the law of nature. The state must promote total well-being; the lower societies taking care of human wants and necessities according to their distinctive character. Only that may be done by the state which the lower societies or communities cannot do for themselves, and the state is to help individuals and lesser societies do what they cannot do effectively for themselves. This is the principle of subsidiarity. Hence, the state should not interfere with schools run by private groups, and it should aid them in providing a suitable level of schooling.

The K.V.P. was formed after the war, in 1946, replacing an earlier party. In general, it represents progressive policies in regard to socio-economic matters. From 1946 to 1959 there was a coalition between the K.V.P. and the Labor Party. This coalition was thus in effect during the passage of the 1958 secondary education bill, the so-called Mammoth Law. After the 1959 election this coalition was replaced by one with the Calvinist and liberal parties. The Labor Party is the present opposition party.

The Anti-Revloutionary Party emerged from a nineteenth-century movement led by Groen van Prinsterer against the secular tendencies of the French Revolution. By "revolution" van Prinsterer meant, not overthrow of political authority and substitution of another as exemplified in the American Revolution, but a total conversion of ideas and transformation of attitude in which Christian principles are done away with. In his view, the theory of the sovereignty of the people was based on anti-religious views. God, not the people, should be recognized as sovereign. The true Christian was in this sense an anti-revolutionist.

The party developed in 1878 from a petition against an education act which sought to improve public schools and did not provide subsidy for private schools. Under the leadership of Dr. Abraham Kuyper, who became Prime Minister in 1901, a petition for "the school with the Bible" was within a few days signed by more than 300,000 people, although this did not keep the act from being passed. In formulating the principles of the party, which remain its principles today, Kuyper held that in the word of God — the Bible — are the eternal principles which direct political life. The various areas of life, including the state, are directly responsible to God. The state cannot be sovereign over all the spheres of life. Such spheres as the family, church, and school are "sovereign in their own right" directly under the sovereignty of God. Government has to do away with everything which impedes the free influence of the Gospels on the life of the people. An antithesis to the rationalism of the eighteenth century is set up. Christian principles should penetrate every area of life; Christians should organize in every respect apart from and against other-thinking, non-Christian people. Under this doctrine, a free school — the school freely chosen by the parents — should be the dominant type of school and the public school should be the supplement.

The Christian Historical Union derives from a break with the Anti-Revolutionary Party in 1894. Its leaders were convinced that a party should have a religious foundation, but they were not willing to carry the antithesis to the extreme advocated by Kuyper. The antithesis is restricted to inner religious life rather than extended to all the areas of life. Although God is the source of all authority, more room should be left for independent human choice. Practical political matters should not stem directly from Calvinistic interpretations of the Bible. Although what the church says is important for political life, government should be independent of the church. Thus the Christian Historical Union is less strictly Calvinistic than the Anti-Revolutionary Party. Its members come mostly from the Dutch Reformed Church, rather than from the more dogmatic Calvinist Church whose members usually belong to the Anti-Revolutionary Party. After the forming of the Labor Party in 1945, several leaders in the Christian Historical Union went over to the Labor Party, thus contributing to the *doorbraak* movement previously mentioned.

The Labor Party was founded after the war as a new socialist party. An earlier Social Democratic Laborers Party had been much more Marxist. The new party was formed with the aim of being a progressive people's party. Its socialism was only a view of social policy, not a spiritual view of life. It aimed to do away with political parties on a denominational basis and hence is a *doorbraak* party. Believers and nonbelievers should unite on a common program about economic, social, and political matters.

The Labor Party's program proposes an economic order without opposition between classes. The most important means of production in the areas of industry, banking, and transportation are to be brought under public control and the remaining means of production regulated in the public interest. Consultation and planning to this end is to take place not only within existing political bodies but also in new organizations in the industrial and economic fields. Democratic socialism is to be promoted by lawfully established bodies, below the level of governmental agencies, which plan and control an area of production or economic activity and in which both labor and management are represented. This creation of new, largely autonomous, regulatory organizations is an important aspect of the socialist program in the policy area, for in the Mammoth Law an effort was made to extend this kind of planning and control to the area of education.

The Labor Party is mainly supported by the more progressive wing of the Dutch Reformed Church and by those without church affiliation. However, the party has within it societies of Protestant Christian, Roman Catholic, and Humanist League members. The formation and work of these societies within the party make possible a common responsibility for forming opinion and decision. The need for such societies again demonstrates the difficulty of attaining an integrated movement in the context of the columnizing of Dutch society.

The present liberal party, the People's Party for Freedom and Democracy (V.V.D.), was formed in 1948 of several groups which had existed before the war and a number of people who were inclined toward the new Labor Party but who for one reason or another were unable to accept its program. The V.V.D. holds that the essential moral elements of Christian belief — freedom, responsibility, and social justice — are the foundations of Dutch life and are accepted by many who do not confess the Christian religion. The essential moral attitude is sufficient to provide a common view on political principles and policies. How to combine religious conviction and political principle is left to the individual. Freedom of fellowman is as important as one's own freedom; tolerance for the spiritual beliefs of others is a first demand of democracy.

The liberals are opposed to the extension of the powers of the state which in the socialist movement leave too little room for the development of independent power and responsibility. Although the liberals deny a laissez-faire position, they oppose the socialist policy of increasing nationalization of industry because it concentrates too much power in the state and endangers individual freedom.

In regard to relations between the government and the Chambers, the liberal party is opposed to the process whereby in the appointment of Ministers agreements are made between Prime Minister and party leaders. These agreements, sometimes taking a protracted period to work out, produce legislative decisions that are not the product of public discussion. Decisions are closed before debate. Furthermore, representatives in the States-General should vote their own freely taken decisions rather than be bound by party doctrine.

Because these three confessional parties and two nonconfessional ones account for the main distribution of power in the States-General, we shall not attempt to delineate the various minor parties on either side of the religious-nonconfessional division. Perhaps it is sufficient to say that there are even more fundamentalist religious parties as well as a more radical socialistic party interested primarily in antimilitarism. There is also a communist party which is Marxist but independent of international communism and is characterized by one review of its record as "a study in futility." [44]

Key Elements in the Historic Growth of Current Policy

The historic roots of present policy concerning religion and the schools are entwined in the complex story of the emergence and growth of the Dutch nation. Only highly selected historical conditions contributing to an understanding of the present situation will be presented here.

Some of the ingredients of present policy derive from the time of the Reformation. The influence of Calvinism began particularly in the southern provinces about 1540 and spread rapidly to the north. It was a revolutionary doctrine both on the side of religious belief, in which it supported the view of man's direct relationship with God, and on the political and economic side, in which it supported a strict regime of life based on personal conviction and conscience. Its stress on Bible reading led to an emphasis on schools for all children regardless of rank or wealth in which each could learn to be directly accountable to God. It gave spiritual backing to movements that were already asserting the independence and autonomy of the people.

One of the results of the Eighty Years War (1568–1648) was the establishment of Calvinism in the form of the Dutch Reformed Church of the Old Republic. A school regulation of 1655 brought the schools under the direction of the Calvinist Church, placing the emphasis on the honor of God, the prosperity of the church, the welfare of the commonwealth, and the well-being of citizens in this order. Teachers had to be pious, godly men, members, with their wives, of the Calvinist Church. On their appointment as teachers they had to subscribe to the profession of faith and the catechism. Books contradictory to the Calvinist religion were banned, and the church was to supervise the observance of this regulation. Teachers were to enforce children's regular attendance at church and urge parents to attend. These measures pertained also to private schools. In addition to them, the teacher was very often the sexton of the church. The regulations were issued in a more stringent form in 1725.

However, the conception of man's place as a personally called servant of God, directly and entirely responsible to him, tended also to mitigate against the acceptance of church doctrine. The formula for administering holy baptism to children made it the responsibility of the parents to bring up children so that they could read the Bible and understand the Christian faith for themselves. Although "the school of the parents" is a later conception, the roots of this policy are found in this expression of Calvinist principles. It has been appraised as "one of the most important and influencial pedagogical documents produced in the Netherlands." [45]

The forces of the Enlightenment, following the period of French domination, gradually began to undermine the hold of the religious convictions of the earlier Calvinist period. Tolerance became recognized as a central Christian virtue. Discrimination against Roman Catholics and Protestants outside the Calvinist Church was more and more seen as injustice. The close cooperation of the Calvinist Church with the state came to an end. A Dutch declaration of the rights of man in 1795 provided that no one could be excluded from public office on religious grounds. The teacher no longer had to conform to the profession of faith; he submitted testimony of his civic loyalty. A conception of the separation of church and state became dominant.

The Education Act of 1806, opening the schools to the historical and moral part of Christianity but not to the dogmatic aspects of religion, initiated a national state system of schools. The control of schools was highly centralistic. The appointment of teachers, the content of schooling, the selection of books were in the hands of supervisors appointed by the state. Although the policies of 1806 raised the quality of primary education and provided a unity that transcended earlier provincialism, they resulted in a reaction against an autocratic central authority and thus began the long school struggle against a monolithic school system. Gradually the provisions of 1806 were modified under the influence of various movements opposed to the centralization of power in the state.

In general, in the early decades of the nineteenth century a relatively weak state authority built a national system of primary education of a Christian character. In the later decades of the first half of the century a more dominant central authority provided a religiously unoffensive curriculum supplemented by church teaching. In the last half of the century a third position was dominant in which cultural unity was provided by state schools, but the right to found private schools not controlled or financed by the state was recognized. This third position, involving the redirection of educational policy according to the Constitution of 1848, was achieved under the direction of the liberalism of the period and especially the leadership of the great Dutch statesman Thorbecke.

In the last half of the nineteenth century the public school became increasingly neutralized. The movement in this direction was primarily that of the new generation of liberals. They began more and more to express an active cultural policy favoring an increasing trust in rational deliberation rather than an appeal to religious doctrine in coming to grips with human problems — an optimistic view of man's ability to control the direction of human affairs and a new and more critical morality. They sought to use the state as an instrument for raising the level of public understanding. Roman Catholics, who had supported the neutralization of the school in order to remove its Protestant bias, and the anti-revolutionaries — the more orthodox Calvinists — now broke openly with the liberals.

The Education Act of 1878 aimed at the improvement of public education at public expense and laid down higher requirements for private education while denying support to confessional schools. This reinforced the growing opposition coalition of the Catholic and conservative Calvinist forces. This was brought to a head in the People's Petition in response to the act of 1878. The movement for state support of the school of the parents' choice, the "school with the Bible," was clearly articulated. Since the Roman Catholics, who had become increasingly powerful politically in the second half of the nineteenth century, also joined the People's Petition, an alignment of forces was created that would overcome the liberals' support for the public school. More and more the power was shifting from those who affirmed the public school to be the rule and the private school the complement to those who affirmed the private school the rule and the public school the complement.

After the elections of 1888 the Catholic-Protestant coalition had a majority of 54 of the 100 seats in the Second Chamber. The coalition lasted until 1925. In 1889, an act introduced the principle of equalization of public and private schools by providing subsidy for the salaries of the obligatory teaching staff in the private school.

The growth of an anti-revolutionary movement, from the early period of the Revival, through the election of Groen van Prinsterer to the States-General in 1840, and into the period of the forming of the Anti-Revolutionary Party under Abraham Kuyper's leadership in 1878, comprises a highly significant ingredient in the growth of Dutch educational policy. Beginning as a vigorously personal and evangelistic movement, it emphasized, in addition to personal faith and piety, the divine authority of the Bible and an unconditional submission to God's word. The movement became under Kuyper not only a party but an entire political-religious-educational way of life.

This movement placed the campaign for the state-supported religious school, as the Dutch say, "under the token of the antithesis." That is, the choice is ultimate; there are no middle grounds. One is either for Christianity or against it. In demanding "Are you going to vote for or against Christ?" Kuyper was laying down the doctrine that if one did not favor state support of religious schools, he must be anti-Christ. This way of thinking remains a powerful ingredient in the forming of Dutch policy particularly when joined with the anti-revolutionary doctrine of sovereignty within one's own circle, which has been sketched in the preceding pages characterizing political parties in the Netherlands today.

Although the position of the Anti-Revolutionary Party was of considerable importance in the development of Dutch educational policy, it was not the only form of Calvinism bearing upon educational policy. The Dutch Reform Church has contained a range of views relating Calvinism to political life in different ways.

Some, rejecting the extreme form of the antithesis as developed by Kuyper, sought the Christianization of public institutions rather than the dual system of public and private schools. Others have considered dogma less important than the inner expression of identity with the spirit of Christ. An ethical-irenic school was more concerned with the development of a conciliatory attitude within the denomination. The general consequence was to search for an educational policy geared to the ethical dimensions of Christian belief rather than a policy flowing from creedal doctrines.

Toward the closing years of the nineteenth century the attitude of the liberals began to change in the direction of providing subsidies for the private schools on the grounds of fairness of treatment rather than rights established by ecclesiastical doctrine. They wanted an end to the school struggle. Although there was still considerable opposition to subsidizing private education on the grounds that it would endanger national unity, subsidies were no longer seen as contrary to the Constitution. The government's continual care for education was given a more generous interpretation. The consequence of these changes, including the culmination of the move to equalization in 1920, is indicated in the statistics in Table 6.

TABLE 6   *Percentage of Students in Public and Private Primary Schools from 1850 to 1958 in the Netherlands**

Year	Public	Private	Year	Public	Private
1850	77	23	1910	62	38
1860	79	21	1920	55	45
1870	77	23	1930	38	62
1880	75	25	1950	27	73
1890	71	29	1957	28	72
1900	69	31	1958	28	72

* Reproduced from P. J. Idenburg, *Schets van het Nederlandse Schoolwezen*, (Groningen: J. B. Wolters, 1964), p. 114.

Philip J. Idenburg, director-general of statistics, has supplied a graphic picture of the enrollments in public and private schools

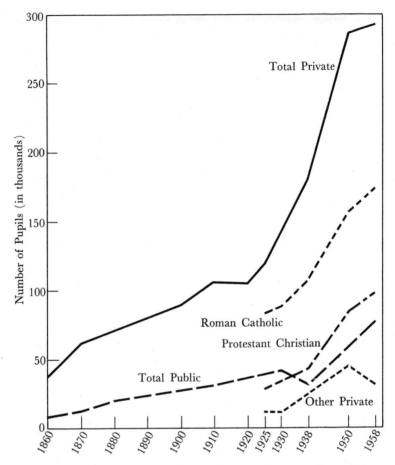

FIGURE 3. Enrollments in Dutch infants' education 1860–1958. Pupils in public and private schools. (From Phillip J. Idenburg, *Schets van het Nederlandse Schoolwezen* [Groningen: J. B. Wolters, 1964], p. 121.)

in the years before and after the "pacification." We observe the very rapid increase in private education at all levels — primary, elementary, and secondary — following the equalization of 1920. Idenburg enters an important consideration in the interpreta-

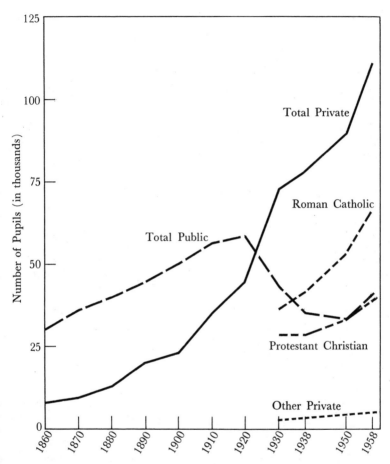

FIGURE 4. Enrollments in Dutch primary education, 1860–1958. Pupils in public and private schools. Until 1920, this figure includes advanced primary education; after that, ordinary and complementary primary education. (From Idenburg, *Schets van het Nederlandse Schoolwezen*, p. 121.)

tion of the significance of these figures. The distribution of student enrollments in public and private schools, and in the latter in Roman Catholic, Protestant Christian, and neutral schools,

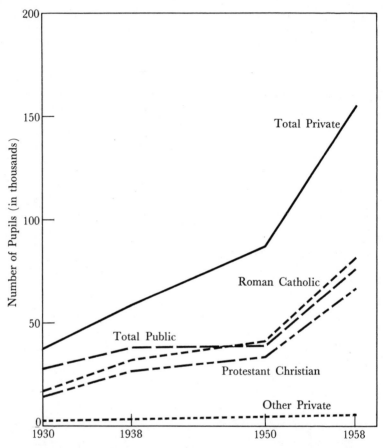

FIGURE 5. Enrollments in Dutch secondary schools, not pre-university (that is, continued secondary education), 1930–1958. Pupils in public and private schools. (From Idenburg, *Schets van het Nederlandse Schoolwezen*, p. 122.)

is not identical with what it would be if parents always chose schools only in accordance with the religious belief of the family. But other considerations do in fact enter. Some children from families which live according to a Christian tradition attend public and neutral private schools. Some children are enrolled

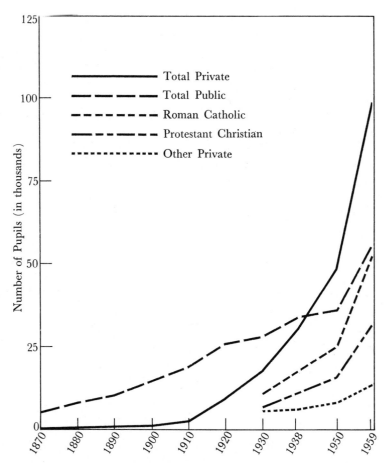

FIGURE 6. Enrollments in Dutch secondary schools leading to the university, 1870–1959. Pupils in public and private schools. (From Idenburg, *Schets van het Nederlandse Schoolwezen,* p. 122.)

in denominational schools who come from families that do not share the religious conviction expressed in that school. Some teachers in public and neutral private schools profess a Christian religion.

Idenburg argues that the choice of one columnized school or

another is associated with "definite pedagogical opinions" of the parents. In many other cases the parents will select a school which suits best their particular situation and which is not markedly different from their denominational beliefs. Within their margin of choice thus created, some parents choose the school which is geographically or socially advantageous or which has a reputation for quality or which follows a favored method of teaching (Montessori, Dalton) or which has the most attractive building. In Idenburg's opinion, the parent's choice of a school is arrived at from a mixture of motives, of which considerations of religious principles are one factor.[46]

Although Idenburg does not say so, presumably this wider matrix of the grounds for choice is more typically found in more sophisticated and more metropolitan populations. Despite the qualification which he enters, the graphs indicate a reliable view of the relative growth of different kinds of schools in the Netherlands.

A study completed in 1959 reports the proportionate growth of public and confessional schools since the end of World War II. If the totals of enrollment figures for various types of schools are looked at:

> . . . It appears that the religious schools have had the greatest growth since the war, with the Protestants a bit ahead of the Catholics. The greatest denominational aims are in vocational and secondary education, over-balancing the public school gains at the elementary levels.[47]

The study thus confirms the view that in Dutch policy religious schools are the norm and public schools the complement.

Parliamentary Debate on the Mammoth Law

The Mammoth Law went through an extended process of discussion before it came to the Second Chamber, which has the power to amend bills proposed by the Ministry. The First Chamber has only to accept or reject the bill on the basis of what had been involved in all discussion of it. The legislative process was not completed until February 1963. Many of the changes involved in the enactment have not yet been carried out, but the policies have been established so that their implementation is now being studied and worked out.

Even before the parliamentary debate, certain Protestant Christian circles reacted vigorously to the proposed new structure of secondary education. The primary objection was that the fundamental difference between public and private education was not sufficiently stressed in the bill. The tasks and responsibilities of the state, according to this view, are fundamentally different for public and for private schools. In public education the government should regulate, supervise, and direct the work of the schools. However, for private education the state has only the task of seeing to it that the conditions needed to get public subsidy are fulfilled.

This difference has relevance in the discussion of the government's relation with public and private schools.[48] The representatives of the Anti-Revolutionary Party urged that because there was not an adequate difference in the bill between public and private schools, the bill was unconstitutional and endangered the freedom of education. They held that education is primarily the task and vocation of the parents. Schools established and run by free societies — voluntary confessional associations of parents — should develop and be controlled under their own principles. The state has only the function of taking care of their general well-being and, aside from this, of providing schools for children of those parents who are not sufficiently interested in their educational responsibility. In regard to free — private — schools, the government finances them but can only require that they be of good standard. It may provide rules for the qualifications of teachers, for their ethical character, for hygienic buildings, for equal salaries in all schools, but beyond these conditions of good quality the control of the state should not interfere.

Reference was made in the debate in the Second Chamber to a

paper prepared by a professor of the anti-revolutionary school of thought who surveyed the historical development of the pacification in relation to the present bill.[49] Financial equalization, according to this paper, had made possible the realization of the freedom of education. Every word of the Constitution was a guarantee of freedom, freedom bought with blood and tears, freedom for adherents of public education and of private education. In the effort to get a systematic total educational system under one law for secondary education, the bill violated the constitutional limitations placed on the state in regard to private education. For example, the bill provided that only with the permission of the Minister can lessons be given in other compulsory subjects. It also prescribed the founding of a committee of parents, the use of experts in administration, the introduction of courses of certain kinds, and many other things that have nothing to do with good quality. If subsidy depends on all these things, the freedom of the private school is jeopardized. The professor feels that for the sake of administrative neatness, the core idea of pluriformity in education is sacrificed. He concludes by expressing a fear of dictatorship in education.

The discussion in the Second Chamber further reveals that different conceptions of freedom were at stake. The Anti-Revolutionarians and Christian Historians were thinking of freedom in terms of sphere sovereignty. They wanted to be free from the state in order to be able to practice their conception of internal freedom, freedom in their own circle. The bill, presented by a Roman Catholic minister, was couched in terms of a more general conception of freedom. He saw that educating children is by nature the duty of parents, but from this he drew another conclusion. The law should provide for the freedom of all education in the way the parents want it. Government should give as much freedom as possible, not only for private education, for education within one's own circle, but for all education, public as well as private.

Numerous amendments were introduced seeking to limit the conception of freedom to sovereignty in one's own sphere and to lessen the controls of the government over private schools. The socialists were opposed to them on the grounds that if private education was to accept a 100 percent subsidy, then they should be prepared to accept a greater measure of state control.

Roman Catholics were interested in the broader conception of freedom because they had in mind, according to the principle of subsidiarity, the establishment of public lawful social organizations in the field of education. These organizations would be able to direct educational policy, not by involving all the steps in the enactment of bills but by a "general measure of decision," a way of taking action in accordance with law but passed much more quickly. The social organizations would be able to confer and agree on issues so that action could be more readily taken. The Roman Catholics and some socialists were in partial agreement, or close to agreement, about the desirability of this move and were hence opposed to the Anti-Revolutionary amendments to limit the role of the state in effecting educational decisions and policies. Hence, the Anti-Revolutionary amendments were defeated.

In the matter of the establishment of lawful organizations for the establishment of educational policy and decisions — organizations which could plan and develop policies without involving full legislative procedure — the preference of the Roman Catholic party and the minister encountered opposition from various sources. A spokesman of the Christian Historical Union could not understand how it would work and was supported by a leader of the liberal party. A socialist member observed that these free social organizations with the status of lawful decision-making bodies would in reality be government. However, since such bodies would not be directly responsible to parliament, they would violate the principles of democratic responsibility. Yet the socialists approved the general notion. They would like to see the already existing Educational Council serve in the suggested capacity. Other Protestant Christian members approved of this suggestion rather than taking a jump into an unknown future, as they expressed it. Consequently, amendments in this direction were accepted.

The Roman Catholic party and the minister expressed deep disappointment at this development for they had taken the efficient development of new organizations as an essential condition of the bill. Rather than endanger the whole bill, however, they conceded that some change was better than nothing at all. This compensated in a way for the disappointment of the Protestant advocates of private education in their effort to have a clear separate treatment of public and private education.

We have already noted that provisions for state subsidy of private secondary schools are different from those for elementary schools. State support for the founding of elementary schools is automatic; but secondary schools must fall within the Ministry's plan for wise use of available funds. There is a provision in the Mammoth Law whereby public secondary schools may not be established apart from the plans of the Ministry. But the provisions are not the same for private secondary schools. The freedom of education means that founding schools by private groups cannot be forbidden, if they pay for them. Privately financed private schools can be founded if they are not within the Ministry's plan.

In the parliamentary debate the socialist leader called attention to this situation, pointing out an inequality in the chances of establishing public and private secondary schools.[50] Private school interests can start to found a school if they can find some way to finance it; they can then ask each year to be taken into the planning procedure. Once founded, it is clear that the schools chances of being included in the plan, and thus subsidized, are much better. The socialist leader proposed an amendment whereby a school which is founded apart from the plan could not get support for a certain number of years and whereby this would pertain to both public and private schools. In this way they would both be on an equal basis.

The left wing of the Second Chamber including the liberal party warmly approved. The communist leader observed that if the amendment were not approved, he would vote against the entire law, for in the specification of the planning procedure the true character of the bill — its preferential treatment of the private school over the public school — came to light. The Roman Catholic and Protestant parties had a completely different view. They could not approve of measures making private sources finance their own schools for a period of years.

The minister was in a difficult situation since he needed the support of the socialists in the passage of the bill. He acknowledged a certain privileged position for the private school, but he thought this was offset by the opportunities that growing towns had to make preparations for founding public schools. The vote went against the socialist's amendment. The socialists' response was that they took this matter very seriously and would find it difficult to support the bill. Consequently, the minister made an effort to do something to make the bill more acceptable to the socialists' position. He submitted the matter to a committee. As a matter of fact, the committee has reported subsequent to the passage of the bill, but the report has met with much opposition. One of the consequences of this entire matter is that the adherents of public education are in the process of organizing for a more positive and spirited defense of public schools.

A further point is of considerable interest in the debate about the Mammoth Law. We have seen that the law on elementary education gave the churches the right to give religious instruction in public schools. The same provision existed in the old law on secondary education. The minister wanted to preserve this provision in the Mammoth Law.

In general, everyone agreed. However, a member of a very orthodox Protestant party thought that the government should not give this right to churches of all kinds. His view was that the government as the servant of God should only permit that kind of religious instruction which is in agreement with the Holy Scriptures.[51] But this view was not general. Most thought that the government should not decide what should be the content and norm of religious education.

Here a problem arose through an amendment proposed by the socialists and supported by many liberals. The amendment proposed that this right be given not only to churches but to "societies on a spiritual foundation." Concretely this refers to the Humanist League.

The Humanist League had met with some success in the Chamber on previous occasions when questions arose concerning their place side by side with Protestants and Roman Catholics in providing services in military centers and in prisons. In debates about these matters, the tolerant and understanding attitude of a Roman Catholic spokesman, Father Stokman, had drawn much attention. Now the question concerned the place of the Humanist League in providing spiritual instruction in the public schools. The socialist leader, although not a Humanist League member, thought that the League should have the same opportunity that the churches had in such instruction.

The Dutch Reformed Church had expressed its view that the government should leave enough room for people to be humanists. This tolerance, the socialist leader said, derives from the church, not on the grounds of formal constitutional law, but because it is the task of the church to be tolerant to people of different persuasions. But an Anti-Revolutionarian said that the matter was under consideration in the churches. To be obedient to the Gospels meant that the church has the task of educating people according to the Gospels, and this does not mean giving the humanists the opportunity to have their kind of instruction in schools. A Christian Historian took the view that provisions for soldiers and prisoners, who are grown-ups, were quite different from those that should pertain to children. In general, the Protestant Christian parties were divided on the matter.

This put the Roman Catholic representatives in a difficult situation. They would like to show their tolerance toward the Humanist League, and in so doing support the view of the socialists. However, this might imply that humanist organizations were to be treated on an equal basis with the churches, and there should be no doubt that these organizations when compared with the churches were of a lower order.

The socialists wanted to be in agreement with the Roman

Catholics because that would mean that they could obtain the opportunity for the humanists to participate in the spiritual upbringing presented in the school. The socialist leader suggested forming two articles, one for religious education by the churches and the other to cover that of the humanists. The Chamber approved this arrangement and the law now provides that "In public school pupils whose parents wish it so can have *vorming-sonderwijs* (spiritual instruction) in school rooms by teachers who are appointed by the societies which are admitted for this purpose by the government." [52] Thus the Humanist League, a society with a rather small membership, was able to have its demand for equal opportunity for religious instruction in public schools fulfilled through the cooperation of the Roman Catholic and the socialist parties.

It is interesting to note that in the acceptance of the Mammoth Law none of the major parties achieved all that they desired. The socialists and the liberals did not achieve the equal treatment of public and private education in regard to the founding of schools. Public school supporters were not able to establish schools apart from the Ministry's planning procedure. The Roman Catholics did not obtain the new social organizations for the determination of educational policy below the level of full parliamentary processes. Their principle of subsidiarity was not adequately provided for in the bill. The Christian Historians and the Anti-Revolutionarians were not pleased with treating private and public education alike as far as the freedom of education was concerned. To them, a Thomistic meaning of freedom was employed rather than the meaning of sphere sovereignty which they found in the Constitution of 1848. Thus each relinquished some demands for the sake of the general advances made possible by the bill. Further compromises may be involved as the practical applications of the new enactment are worked out.

Dutch Criticism of Their Policy

Although the probability of any substantial change in present policy for the support of private education is extremely remote, considerable uneasiness over the full range of consequences associated with this policy is manifest. The dissatisfaction typically focuses upon the columnizing of Dutch society and the educational problems associated with the columns. Yet these difficulties are thought to be the price that one pays for the complete freedom of the parent to send his children to the school of his preference.

> . . . Our country has renounced the attractions of the common school. Our children go to one of several segregated schools. It is possible, in the Netherlands, to start one's life in a Roman Catholic family, to go to a Roman Catholic nursery school, and to spend one's entire school career, including the university, in Roman Catholic institutions. The same is possible for a Protestant child. It is not improbable that during this entire period he never meets a single person who has different convictions. This is the consequence of a principle of freedom consistently applied. But few would for that reason abandon a system which they conceive as a consequence of democracy. . . .[53]

Apparently, those who are thinking about the highly segregated pattern of school life are not willing to reopen the door to the conflict between public and private school interests settled by the pacification of 1920. Although some are critical of the effects of columnizing, this criticism is tempered by a respect for freedom of education as it has been understood and achieved in the Netherlands.

It is clear to the Netherlanders as well as to the visitor that the cost of education is considerably higher in a system of many diverse schools side by side than it would be for a single system of larger schools. At first glance it may seem curious to a visitor that a country with such a high regard for thrift should prefer to maintain a large number of small schools. But the Dutch regard for religious diversity, expressed in the freedom to found the school of one's choice, outweighs the economic consideration.

Apart from the question of columns, the Dutch sometimes say that they do not prefer large schools. This claim is difficult to assess, for some schools in the Netherlands are fairly large and average school size alone is a questionable index. It is more commonly acknowledged that the small school is a consequence of the religious settlement and that this is part of the price of Dutch devotion to commitments.

Some are critical of these policies on the grounds that they contribute to extensive state control and the present low level of local interest and incentive. They see education in the Netherlands as under tension between forces that tend to centralized authority and those that move toward greater responsibility for individual and local diversity. Idenburg devotes considerable attention to this matter, both historically and in connection with contemporary expansion of state controls. In this matter many other factors than those directly associated with policies governing religion and schooling are involved. Practices concerning the admission of students to the next higher level of their education, particularly the policy of uniform final examinations, promote the dominant role of centralized authority. For example, it is laid down in central directives exactly which formulas in chemistry should be mastered and what should be taught before the next step is to be taken. However, it seems clear that part of what contributes to the domination of centralized authority flows from policy concerning religion and the schools.

We have seen that considerable criticism of the Mammoth Law developed from its extended interpretation of the qualities of good standing and excellence that a private school should have in order to receive subsidy. In short, if the state is to subsidize private schools, Dutch experience indicates a large measure of central control in seeing to it that the nonreligious aspects of the school are of high quality.

Idenburg notes that this centralized control is needed to avoid disparities between public and private schools, between urban and rural schools, and between schools in prosperous and less prosperous communities, particularly at the higher levels of education.

The result is that, despite the democratic structure of the municipal administration and the imposing number of schools founded by local church and other organizations, the communities can no longer feel that they possess and direct their own schools. State supervision is so all-embracing that local control is no longer possible. The state provides the necessary finances, and the state decides very largely what will be taught. The disconcerting feature is that this situation has come to be accepted so unquestioningly by the majority of the people that there is no likelihood of a revolt against the system. Many teachers fear that the standards of education would decline should the state slacken the reins, and parents are wary of experiments that might possibly endanger the future of their children.[54]

In the Netherlands there is a lack of participation by citizens in educational decision and policy in spite of the slogan of "the school of the parents' choice," and some feel that this results in part from readily available state funds for private schools.

There is also some dissatisfaction with patterns of teacher education particularly as they relate to policy about religion and schooling and the influence of the columns on Dutch education. Here one must have in mind the difference between two kinds of secondary education: elaborated or continued primary education and pre-university secondary education. Teachers for the latter are trained in the disciplines of the university with a minimal attention to the study of professional education. Teachers of continued elementary education as well as of elementary schools are trained at *kweekschoolen,* teacher training colleges. Each of these two separate kinds of teachers, functioning in different kinds of schools, has its own professional organization, its own journal, its different status in society. The teachers prepared at the *kweekschoolen* attend public or nonconfessional, or Roman Catholic, or Protestant training colleges. The work of these colleges and the educational research associated with it is promoted by pedagogical centers which are also divided into Roman Catholic, Protestant, and neutral centers. These centers have not yet clearly defined the way in which they relate to pre-university secondary education.

It has apparently been very difficult to achieve educational research as we know it in the United States. The sharp separations between teachers of elementary and of pre-university secondary education and of training colleges into columns have tended to prevent opportunities for research. Inquiry into educational problems within the columnized patterns of teacher education is limited because if one institution is to be granted funds for a research project, the corresponding institutions of the other columns must also be funded. Duplication rather than cooperation of effort predominates. Thus the influence of Dutch policy about religion and schooling extends deeply into the patterns of teacher education and into efforts to promote research in education.

It is also of interest that the failure in the legislature to provide an equal opportunity for the founding of public schools has resulted in an effort to organize a society to articulate and promote the interests of the public school. It will be recalled that in the Mammoth Law the Ministry's annual plan for the establishment of secondary schools is a means of establishing the priorities for the building of schools. Apart from the planning procedure, a group of parents may take the initiative in building a private secondary school, but this opportunity to take initiative is not provided for adherents of public schools. The planning procedure exists in large part to provide preference in initiative to confessional school interests. This use of the planning procedure met with considerable criticism from the friends of public education.

As a result of what was considered to be an inadequate attention to the interests of the public school, an organization called "The Foundation for Promoting Public Education" was formed. On December 19, 1963, it founded in Amsterdam a "Center of Contacts" for considering the situation in which public education finds itself under the new law, for coordinating and planning the activities of groups interested in public education, and for expressing to the Ministry the interests of supporters of the public school as the provisions of the Mammoth Law are gradually put into practice.[55]

A number of articles are appearing in professional magazines and also in the papers protesting what is thought to be discrimination against public education. One such article appeared in a socialist weekly paper called *Vrij Nederlands* (*Free Netherlands*) for April 18, 1964, and was reprinted in the magazine of the society of neutral teachers. Since the piece reveals rather clearly the current challenge to some aspects of Dutch policy, we offer a free but detailed translation of its content.

An article appearing in 1963 raised the question of who should administer the Educational Ministry. It expressed the view that it should be an advocate of public education.

Unfortunately, this remained only a wish. Again for four years the Educational Ministry is headed by a Roman Catholic unless there is a cabinet crisis. Thus the largest Dutch enterprise with the largest part of the national budget will have been administered for sixteen years by a Roman Catholic. Can one expect that he will do more than serve the interest of public education at a technical level? Such a minister cannot have any idea about the importance of public education. Clearly Protestant Christian schools are closer to his heart than schools of the third column. We do not doubt the integrity of the present or of the former minister, but how will public education ever go well when for one period after another the policy of this important ministry is defined by a convinced advocate of denominational education? A former prime minister, a socialist, has written, "We could not maintain all of our seats in the cabinet and the Catholic Party wanted in any case the department of education."

It is a political secret that with any cabinet formation, denominational parties demand the Ministry of Education. Why? Because this is the most important ministry. Always it is true that he who has youth has the future. Since 1920 the department of education has been nearly without interruption in the hands of denominational ministers. Recently we have heard the question raised whether a Roman Catholic could be permitted to become a queen. It is much more important to ask whether the throne of education could be taken for a certain period by a socialist or a liberal.[56]

The article continues by asking whether the liberal and the labor parties are sufficiently alert to this concern and whether the new law on secondary education did not discriminate against public education.

The article expresses alarm that in the discussion of the education budget of 1964 it was clear that no adequate attention was given to the public school in those areas where only one school can be provided. In its character it ought to be open to children of different denominational views. The article is concerned that the annual Royal Report of the Ministry is one-sided in reporting only the work of the Roman Catholic pedagogical center. It points out that the governmental statistics for 1962–63 concerning the number of pupils in elaborated primary education show a decrease of 1.2 percent in public education, a decrease of 0.3 percent in Protestant Christian education, and an advance of 1.4 percent in Roman Catholic schools. Reference is made to an instance in which public school interests thought that inadequate illumination had been provided in the construction of a public school and was corrected only after considerable protest. These details are mentioned to show the active concern for what is considered to be a pattern of many-sided discrimination against the public school.

Another movement of considerable interest is one of Roman Catholic circles in which basic questions are raised concerning the reason for the Roman Catholic school. In 1963 five volumes appeared expressing a Catholic view of Dutch society. They were issued under the auspices of a Roman Catholic council for considering social and economic issues. The council consisted of representatives of a number of Catholic trade unions. The editors were prominent Roman Catholic laymen and specialists; the constituent parts of the work were under their responsibility rather than signed by particular authors. We are particularly interested in a chapter entitled "Core Problems of Progressive Educational Management." [57]

The chapter places the discussion of the Roman Catholic school within the context of the total range of considerations of public policy. It discusses questions concerning the place of education in modern society in general, in the Dutch constitutional system, and in relation to the Church. It discusses first the social function of present-day education.

According to this view, it does not make sense to talk of *the* aim of *the* school in abstract terms. There are only concrete schools in situations of time and place. School systems develop in response to the culture. Schools in the middle ages were completely different from Dutch schools today. One should take a dynamic view toward education which does not see it as always the same. The school should be responsive to the conditions and needs of the day.

For the Netherlands this means educating people for the kind of life they live today. The authors are challenging the view, extremely common in Dutch pre-university secondary education, that education is the cultivation of the individual and has nothing to do with social conditions. They decry what they call "the myth of disinterested education," the view that education is merely individual improvement — typically, in its highest form through the study of the classics — unrelated to the needs of society. They criticize the view of culture involved in this attitude, a view which sees it as a thin upper veneer, a status symbol. The authors are urging a social or cultural interpretation of education which brings it into relationship with the social realities of the day. And they argue that the Mammoth Law makes a serious attempt to move in this direction.

As they see it, the core of these considerations is found in how the Dutch people think of the freedom of education. Traditionally free education was identified with denominational education; education was free because it was denominational. To the contrary, they think education by nature and by the Dutch constitution is free, and because of this it may be denominational. Education derives from the social nature of man and is in its nature a social good. The freedom of education is a deeper value than the more limited historical identification of freedom with confessional education. Public education is also within this deeper meaning free.

Furthermore, according to the Dutch constitution, government has an active role to play in caring for education and this means that it should not wait for private initiative but should take the lead in judging what should be done for the whole society. Today it must include what is best for all. The premise of starting with one's "own circle" (sphere sovereignty) is an anachronism. Education is now a part of general human culture and one must break with those aspects of the past which paralyze the kind of cooperation needed today.

According to this view, the historic principle of financial equalization promoted an equality of opportunity appropriate to its time. But now, with the dominance of private education, one must accept responsibility not only for education of one's "own circle" but for the education of all the Dutch people. This is other and more than the sum total of each group's responsibility to its own circle. The principle of financial equalization means that each circle bears responsibility for the totality of the Dutch people. Complete subsidy means that all take an interest in the way the money is used. It is no longer the old business of everyone getting as much subsidy as possible in order to go his own unrestricted way. Private education is semipublic education.

Thus, the questions of the relations between the school and the state come down to problems about freedom. Freedom is not just a matter of providing money to private groups and leaving them alone to spend it as they wish. It concerns the nature of the total management of a school in the public interest, equally a concern in private as well as public education. The old notion of the antithesis of private education and the government with its public school is no longer relevant or tenable.

Moreover, the authors are saying that the older conception about the control of education is no longer tenable. No longer realistic or practical is the idea that the state controls public education but only provides money for private schools which — aside from a few matters concerning adequate sanitation, good moral character of teachers, equal pay and the like — are controlled by private groups. The main point is that "the requirements of good quality," which private schools must meet to qualify for subsidy, refer purely to educational conditions and arrangements which are identical for private and public education. The idea that private education has a highly individualistic freedom from the interference of the state is no longer an adequate policy. That everyone should only be interested in his own (denominational) school and not interested in the others is as anachronistic as the conception of freedom of education in one's own circle and of the antithesis between state or public and "own circle" or private. A new conception of cooperation is called for, and the state is a thorough partner in it.

According to this view, the Catholic Church as an institution — the ecclesiastical hierarchy embodied in the Dutch Episcopacy — should be distinguished from the educational tasks of Catholic laymen. The activities of the Church — preaching, the sacraments, worship, the care of the spirit and the saving of souls — do not derive from sources in this world but from another, although they occur *in* this world. The school, however, is *of* as well as *in* this world. The two orders should not be interchanged. The Church should Christianize the school, but that does not mean that it should confuse the work of the school with the activities of the Church. Conditions may be such that a country needs denominational schools; they may also be such that such schools should not be present. Even if separate Roman Catholic schools are necessary and desirable they should be managed and taught by laymen. This viewpoint questions whether circumstances in former periods that justified church schools in the Netherlands continue to exist today; it suggests that times and conditions have changed so that the hierarchy should withdraw from the school business and leave it to Roman Catholic believers as their own social work.

This position, while respecting the Church, does not devolve from *argumentum ex auctoritate,* from exegesis of the encyclicals or ecclesiastical law, or from judgments of the bishops in these matters. Not only do these ecclesiastical documents not have a completely binding force, but they all must be interpreted in terms of the times and conditions within which they appeared. What may be appropriate in one time may not be so in another.

It may be that when the public school in the Netherlands had a marked liberal Protestant character, Roman Catholics as well as orthodox Protestants needed their own denominational schools. There was not sufficient tolerance in certain periods and this led to the columnizing of patterns of life commitments. But should we have a denominational school today?

The analysis continues by calling attention to two traditional motivations or arguments for the denominational school. One has a positive character. It urges that religious conviction should be evident in all parts of education; the school should be pervaded with this view of life. The other is negative as well as positive. It holds that a closed or protected milieu, steeped in one's own religious conviction, should isolate the pupil from other views and that this is necessary to teaching that maintains the faith.

But the acceptance of conviction may be as well or perhaps better reached by confrontation, even collision and conflict with other views. Further, firsthand confrontation is both more real and more effective than secondhand representation of it and hence pedagogically recommended. Furthermore, questions about securing conviction are not answerable from abstract premises but from pedagogical experience; they are pedagogical problems. Concerning the argument about pervading the school with a religious faith, it is much more important that the rest of life, especially the family and the church, provide and support real religious conviction.

But, this position continues, what do we mean by a Catholic school and what makes a school Catholic? The answer moves in the direction that we have no clear normative and empirical basis in public policy for the distinctive basis for a Catholic school; in short, that a good Catholic school would hardly be distinguishable from a good (public) school. The discussion of the response to the question is rather long and involved, but comes down to something like the following.

It cannot be the presence of rituals and ceremonies which identifies a Catholic school. If this were the case, the pupil, identifying them with schooling, would do an injustice to their sacred character. It cannot be the teaching of religion as a subject, for this matter is full of problems, and a school can be Catholic without the subject religion in its curriculum. It cannot be a general atmosphere of good human relations for this does not distinguish between Catholic and other schools. Is it then the way considerations about outlook toward life (*levensbeschouwelijk*) are brought into the other and especially the less secular subjects?

Should a Catholic Luther be different from a Protestant Luther? But this is a matter of the educational control of value judgments. In these matters the child should not be handicapped by a lack of confrontation with differences in ways of thinking. Matters of life conviction are personal decisions; one cannot enforce them; the school can only provide leads to thinking that result in personal choice. The isolation and the protective insulation of the columnized school is disadvantageous for the modern society of pluriformity.

In this view, these considerations mean that the problem of the Catholic school is an educational and sociological problem rather than a matter of Catholic principle. A non-Catholic school is an important possibility for a Catholic child. Such a school is not devoid of opportunity to reach conviction, but it should provide this fullness of opportunity in the context of diverse thinking. Its teachers should with honesty, respect, and intellectual integrity promote the understanding of convictions. The new times call for what might be called an ecumenic school.

The above account is much abbreviated and is presented in a more direct statement than that of the original. The attitude described is a minority view in Roman Catholic circles. However, the position received attention in the legislative debate about the budget of education. One of the leaders of the socialist party observed that the point of view expressed in the volume had impressed him very much because it opened the possibility for a discussion with people of differing religious persuasions. Representatives of the Catholic Party were not uniformly confident of the grounds for opening this new dimension of discussion about the denominational schools. A former Roman Catholic member of the Second Chamber stated publicly his opinion that both public and private schools served the public interest and that the time had come for advocates of both to cooperate instead of struggling. This cooperation should be based on a public policy offering equal chances for development to the public school.

It might be well to recall that Professor Wielenga, representing the Calvinist point of view, wrote a few years ago that Christian schools and teachers in them tend to be conservative. Further, the board of the school association, which is the controlling group, is made up of those who are not professional educators and who tend to be tradition-minded. They are likely to be suspicious and to have reservations about modern trends which depart from prevailing practices.[58] This observation seems to pertain to the general range of religiously oriented schools in the Netherlands.

The position expressed in the volume by the Catholic laymen has also been expressed elsewhere. A paper presented before a Catholic schoolmasters' society, consisting of pre-university secondary school people, raised some questions of the same order.

> . . . You find yourselves in a country whose strong liberal school legislation stands out as an object of jealousy — of holy jealousy to be sure — on the part of those responsible for Catholic education in other countries.[59]

After observing that the Dutch have achieved a famous financial equality, he observes that "some come to ask themselves whether this situation is really ideal."

The author observes that the encyclical *Divini Illius Magistri* of Pius XI (1929) was placed by the Archbishop of Utrecht in its historic setting, a period of "a fascist state all powerful and monopolistic, which hoarded all of its youth in order to enslave it to its political system." [60] Church law of the period emphasized the educational responsibility of the Church as the only institution capable of acting as a countervailing force to the totalitarianism of Mussolini's state. The encyclical restated the text of Canon 1374 of the Code of Canon Law which provided that the diocesan bishop is invested with the right to decide whether attendance at a mixed school may be tolerated after observing precautions against the danger of corruption that attendance at these schools involves. The author observes that the common component of the words "danger," "corruption," and "to tolerate" is the idea of defense, of fear, of a "citadel" church protecting those inside her walls.

It is pointed out by André de Beurs that the sense of the words of the encyclical and the Code of Canon Law may have been appropriate in the defense against totalitarianisms of their day, but may be inappropriate to the tasks of the Church in the 1960's. He quotes from the letter of June 10, 1963, by Pope John XXIII to the bishops of the world:

> To have remained faithful to the purity of the Gospel, to Tradition, to the Fathers of the Church, and to the Roman Popes, is assuredly a great grace, a title of merit and honor. But this is not sufficient for the accomplishment of our Lord's precept, when he said to us: "Go and teach all the nations," or again a similar passage in the Old Testament: "he has entrusted to each the care of his neighbor." [61]

The Church today is speaking less of "dangers," "corruption," and of "tolerance" of others and engaging more in a fraternal dialogue with "men who are all on the road that leads to Christ." With the modern Vatican Council the Church has been seeking new routes, demolishing the walls of separatism, reflecting upon the faults that human weakness has been able to commit in her name. Catholic schools will not remain outside this movement.

The author broadly describes the financial problems facing Catholic education particularly in view of the population explosion, the increasing need for higher education and technical education, the probable limits of state financial support, and the problems Catholic education will have in deciding a just basis for trying, as it must, to fulfill selectively its educational tasks. He urges facing these realities realizing that the Catholic school will be cornered by expenditures surpassing by far what it now demands from its families.

But when the financial problems are solved by 100 percent subsidy as they are in the Netherlands, how does one assess the consequences? He is particularly concerned with two. (1) The close bond between the family and the school is no longer there. "The family has forgotten to get itself interested in an institution which it hardly considers its affair. . . ." [62] (2) The school does not lead to a deeper experience and knowledge of God. The system is an obstacle to this achievement; it is self-defeating. The process profanes the objective.

Finally, the question was put to a group of thoughtful, convinced Catholics: "If one were to fight again this fight over education, do you think the result would be the same: Catholic schools for Catholics, Protestant schools for Protestants, and pubic schools for the rest?" The answer of all those present was: "No, no more such separation." Several thought that the present system in the Netherlands would probably be transformed in a few decades.

The author thinks that the day will come when "we no longer fear one another, where the old separation and mistrusts will be surpassed, where we shall make the happy discovery of all that men have in common." This predicts that the concept of neutrality will no longer be what it has been in the past. "It will no longer be a notion of a vacuum, a misinterpretation which amounts to emptiness, the negation of all positive faith, of all religious conviction. The idea of neutrality is in the process of evolving toward a positive conception of respect for the equality of all religious or philosophic convictions. One hopes then that a change of climate will take place in public schools." [63]

Movements of thought within liberal circles in the Netherlands express seriously considered dissatisfaction with some of the consequences of present Dutch policy. That these criticisms will result in any marked change in the immediate future in the policy of full subsidization, however, seems doubtful.

Significance for American Policy

One of the fundamental questions to be confronted in the designing of American policy concerns the extent to which American conditions and the direction of national policy encourage the columnizing of our society. An American sociologist, David O. Moberg, who was a Fulbright lecturer in 1957–1958 at the University of Groningen reports that he and others are of the opinion that the forming of columns could become the future pattern of our country.

Certain forces in American society appear either to be planned intentionally to establish vertical pluralism in America or to have latent consequences that may result in it. The historical events and social forces that led to Dutch vertical pluralism and certain analogous trends in contemporary American society support this conclusion.[64]

Moberg indicates that he is using the term, "vertical pluralism" following the precedent of Michael P. Fogarty in his *Christian Democracy in Western Europe*.[65] However, Fogarty's interpretation and appraisal of vertical pluralism, expressing the point of view of a Roman Catholic Christian Democrat, is very different from that of Moberg and other sociologists, discussed earlier in this report. Moberg believes that, although differences exist between the two countries, we are now experiencing a period of social trends analogous to those of the Netherlands in the period of the forming of the columns.

He points to an increasing identification of the American people in terms of their membership in Protestant, Catholic, and Jewish subcultures as evidence that vertical pluralism is growing in this country. Religious subcultural identifications are replacing earlier identifications by nationality. The growth of these identifications is aided by favorable attitudes toward cultural pluralism. Sharp differences between religious groups tend to dominate the way in which problems of public policy are considered and managed. Religious groups are achieving more solidarity and with it more exclusiveness. As groups become tighter, their members tend to perceive their world and to think in terms of denominational differences. Their concerns tend to limit their interactions with others.

Furthermore, when political preferences and religious ideologies are closely correlated, as is increasingly the case in controversies over public funds for church institutions, one of the basic conditions of the forming of columns is fulfilled. In addition, the percentage of the nation's children in religious schools has been increasing. Efforts to provide public funds for church-controlled schools tend to establish a dual system of education. Emergent vertical pluralism is evident on the local level in community fund-raising activities which recognize Catholic, Protestant, and Jewish welfare agencies. Sphere sovereignty theology among conservative Protestants and the principle of subsidiarity among Catholics are receiving more attention. "The ideological basis for vertical pluralism, even though it is not labeled as such, is thus promoted." [66] Divisions between secularists and religionists are commonly drawn; the public schools are called "Godless"; labels encouraging the columnizing of organizations and institutions are commonly in use.

It may be that countervailing conditions and tendencies may be strong enough to reduce the effect of these tendencies toward the columnizing of American life. Moberg suggests that the two-party system, the lack of confessional political parties, the relative strength and diversity of the churches, and the influence of the tradition of separation of church and state may counteract tendencies toward the growth of columns.

It would be highly desirable to have more empirically detailed studies of the extent and character of the growth of vertical pluralism in America. The hypothesis that some kind of columnizing is likely in America might be refined so that a more precise assessment of forces acting for and against it could be made. The study of these conditions and forces could be largely independent of judgments as to the desirability of vertical pluralism as a pattern of social structure and of social control in a democratic society. Yet the need for studies of the defensibility of vertical pluralism as a pattern to be approved and encouraged are also indicated. Such studies might carefully appraise the relatively determinate consequences of this pattern of life for the achievement of the values of a free and open society.

In another article Moberg summarizes what he considers the manifest and latent consequences of Dutch vertical pluralism.[67] It seems clear that the consequences which he lists develop from the characteristics of columns which we have earlier noted.

Columns increase the spatial and ideological isolation of religious groups. They extend an interlocking network of control over most of the areas of life, a control which limits the interactions of people and prevents the full interplay of ideas. They compel conformity to the pattern of life and thought of a confessional column or, alternatively, force one against his free choice into a column of neutrality. When the consideration of political questions and questions of public policy is limited to applications of religious doctrine, a specious use of principles blankets the weighing of values.

Vertical pluralism requires much duplication of effort in education and also in the use of specialists in columnized institutions. Efficiency may be reduced; problems of maintaining equal levels of quality are increased. The exchange of views with those of other columns is prevented; a concerted attack upon common problems is difficult to achieve.

Misunderstandings and tensions between groups can readily develop. The grounds for national unity are diminished. Difficulties arise in understanding the points of view of others. Ethnocentrisms and latent hostilities are encouraged.[68]

Moberg also points to the instance of the pastoral letter the *Mandement* as an example of the way vertical pluralism carries ecclesiastical dogmatism into political life. Religious doctrines and ideologies, which may be incompatible with democratic conceptions, are superordinate to the values of a free society. Considerations of religious ideology and the balance of power between religious groups dominate other considerations in matters of appointment to civic offices and the like. Personal initiative and personal liberty are limited in a closed system which exposes the individual to only one world view and one interpretation of religious life.

It seems clear that these consequences should be recognized and weighed in the forming of judgments when Americans are urged to approve policies favoring the growth of denominational schools at the expense of the continued support of the public schools. Whether these consequences follow from all varieties of material support for the efforts of denominational schools is also a matter needing fuller study. A large part of the problem in American policy concerns how these and other similar consequences can be avoided while improving the quality of denominational education.

Certain aspects of Dutch experience suggest that Americans might work at their problems by encouraging fruitful ways of framing these problems. In an area highly charged with convictions, commitments, and emotions the educational concern with the way in which people come at their problems is particularly central. An important part of the educator's responsibility concerns the building of a climate favorable to the informed and thoughtful discussion of public policy. Since in the Netherlands the discussion of policies about religion and schooling has been so central in national life, we may learn not merely what their policies are but what various aspects of their experience indicate about American approaches to policy problems.

It will be recalled that in the last part of the nineteenth century in the Netherlands efforts to support a unified system of public education directed by a policy of neutrality toward religious convictions brought forth a reaction in the form of a coalition between Protestants and Catholics. One of the elements of this coalition put the school question in the form of an antithesis, that is, as an ultimate and clear-cut choice for or against Christ. He who favored the private school supported Christianity; he who favored the public school was un-Christian. More recent movements in the Netherlands have sought to remove the school question from the denomination of the antithesis.

Arguments over religion and schooling in America frequently presuppose a premise similar to the antithesis. In many instances an antithesis between religion and public education is taken for granted. Charges that the public school is Godless, or that if it is not rooted in Christian doctrine it must be irreligious, or that its character is inherently hostile to spiritual and religious values express the logic of the antithesis. In this view no intermediate grounds are available between promoting doctrinal religious belief in the school and hostility to religion.

Perhaps certain people, including some teachers, seek to indoctrinate secularism as a doctrine in the public school, just as some may seek to implant uncritically any particular religious, nonreligious, or anti-religious views. Such instances of the uncritical planting of belief under the name of education are indefensible. However, the point being made here is that according to the premises of some religious interests, if the public school is not favorable to their doctrine, it is *ipso facto* hostile to them.

The logic of this view is that if you are not with us, you must be against us. An antithesis between religion and public education is presupposed. This unwarranted assumption denies all other alternatives concerning the school's role in contributing to understanding, tolerance, and respect for the varieties of religious experience. If we permit an inalienable opposition between the public school and religious belief to dominate our thinking, we might well recall the consequences of the antithesis in Dutch experience.

Another consideration comes from the fact that some in the Netherlands are saying that the difference between a public and a private school is so diminishing that it is no longer apparent in the work of the school. Aside from a difference in the planning procedure for secondary schools and in the religious aspects of the school, the nature and quality of the education given is, as they see it, less a function of the religious versus public school question and more a function of a complex of other factors.

Some think that "the school of the parent" has not produced, as its name might imply, a close relationship between the upbringing of the home and the spiritual outlook of the school. The Dutch complain about the lack of support in the home of the religious attitude of the church school. In this regard, the religious school has become more like the public school; in both institutions the engagement of the parent in the support of the work of the school and the promotion of its prosperity has in recent years been actively encouraged.

Further, the instructional program, largely under the influence of the examination system, is for the most part identical in public and in private schools. Parents of students in denominational schools are likely to complain that their children do not stand as good a chance in the examinations since they spend some time studying religion at the expense of other subjects. The difference between public and denominational schools is further obscured since, as we have noted, there is opportunity for doctrinal religious instruction in public schools as an optional subject.

Moreover, as we noted in our description of the legislative debate on the new secondary education bill, the private schools are treated in the same terms as the public schools in regard to their characteristics of good quality.

In short, the educational differences between the two types of schools, save for matters of ecclesiastical doctrine, are narrowing to the point where some thoughtful people begin to wonder whether the dual system is worth its cost. A number of Dutch educators have difficulty in seeing how their role as educators is different in public and in private schools. They find themselves inheriting a dysfunctional system of split schools.

All of this argues that a very high price may be paid for separate religious schools. Some believe that the disadvantages of the system as appraised by thoughtful religious people in the Netherlands may outweigh the gains. It is possible that much more conciliatory attitudes might develop in the United States if more attention were given to these assessments in the Netherlands rather than to one-sided claims that oversimplify the consequences of subsidies for private schools.

The power alliance based on the historic school struggle has, so to speak, fixed on the Netherlands a pattern of political and social life based on certain theological doctrines. It is not merely that religious differences are recognized and given a considerable measure of just treatment in educational policy. There is a difference between giving adequate attention to the problems of religious conviction in modern life and designing educational policy in conformity with the demands of theological positions. We have seen that some thoughtful Roman Catholics in the Netherlands are concerned with an increased lay control of schools and with less ecclesiastical domination. They see the encyclicals of the Catholic Church as historic documents conditioned by factors of time and place. Perhaps, they suggest, in an era of basic ecumenical thought, it is not ideal that every Catholic child should be in a Catholic school. This suggests that more discussion in America in the vein of critical reappraisal of commonly accepted doctrine might result in a much more sympathetic understanding of current educational problems.

We have also seen that the theological doctrines of sphere

sovereignty on the Neo-Calvinist side and subsidiarity on the Roman Catholic provided the rationale for an alliance of political power over a considerable period of recent Dutch history. It continues to give priority in educational planning to denominational secondary schools. We have noted that the legislature recently was called upon to decide whether the humanists could be considered religious equals with the main-line churches. This kind of mixture of religion and politics, acceptable though it may be to the Netherlands' form of democracy, is what Americans since the time of the founding fathers have tried to avoid.

Furthermore, conceptions of sphere sovereignty and of subsidiarity, which may have had a democratic orientation in the periods in which they were developed in European countries, are considerably less appropriate in the context of American life. The historic tradition of local control of public schools in America and the considerable success of organizations and movements seeking to bring parents and citizens into close touch with the schools undercut the relevance of these doctrines to American problems.

NOTES

1. See the chart and five pages in English by the Ministry of Education, Arts and Sciences, *From the Family by Way of Education Towards Society: Bill for Regulating Continued Education* (The Hague: Press and Publicity Department, 1960).
2. *Ibid.*, p. 2.
3. *Ibid.*, from the Constitution, Chap. 12, Article 208.
4. Ministry of Education, Arts and Sciences, *Dutch School System* (The Hague: Netherlands Government Information Service, 1960), p. 10.
5. *Ibid.*, p. 9.
6. Detailed in Maurice Couve De Murville, "Aspects of the Dutch System of Education," *Catholic Education: A Handbook* (Catholic Education Council for England and Wales, 1962–1963), pp. 32–40.
7. Ministry of Education, *Dutch School System*, p. 33.
8. Figures reported from *Digest of the Kingdom of the Netherlands; Education, Arts and Sciences* (The Hague: Netherlands Government Information Service, n. d.), p. 23.

9. *Ibid.*, p. 8.

10. Ministry of Education, *Dutch School System,* p. 8.

11. *Ibid.*, p. 22.

12. Philip J. Idenburg, *Schets van het Nederlandse Schoolwezen* (*Outline of Dutch Education*) (Groningen: J. B. Wolters, 1964) , p. 130.

13. A discussion of the legal regulations for secondary schools is given in D. N. van der Neut, *"De Wettelijke Mogelijkheden"* (*"The Legal Possibilities"*) , *Opdracht: Tijdschrift Voor Het Godsdienst Onderwijs* (*Magazine of Religious Education*) , 2 (December 1954) , pp. 69–75.

14. Idenburg, *Schets van het Nederlandse Schoolwezen,* p. 130.

15. B. van Gelder, *Spoor Zoeken In De Bonte Wereld Van Geloven En Denken* (Amsterdam: J. M. Meulenhoff, 1960) , 229 pages.

16. Ministry of Education, *Dutch School System,* p. 5.

17. David O. Moberg, "Religion and Society in the Netherlands and in America," *American Quarterly, 13* (Summer 1961) , p. 175.

18. van Gelder, *Spoor Zoeken,* p. 69.

19. I. Gadourek, *A Dutch Community: Social and Cultural Structure and Process in a Bulb-Growing Region in the Netherlands* (Leiden: H. E. Stenfert Kroese, 1956) , 555 pages.

20. *Ibid.*, p. 82.

21. *Ibid.*, p. 93.

22. *Ibid.*, p. 95.

23. *Ibid.*, p. 112.

24. *Ibid.*, p. 209.

25. *Ibid.*, p. 545. It should also be reported that, quite apart from Gadourek's study, an objective history jointly written by a Roman Catholic, a Protestant, and a Jew is widely used in Roman Catholic, Protestant, and neutral schools as well as in public schools.

26. See Gadourek, *A Dutch Community,* pp. 212–215.

27. J. A. A. van Doorn, "Verzuiling: een eigentijds systeem van sociale controle" ("Columns: A Present System of Social Control") , *Sociologische Gids, 3* (March–April 1956) , pp. 41–49.

28. D. I. Schöffer, "Verzuiling, een specifiek Nederlands probleem" ("Columns, a Specifically Dutch Problem") , *Sociologische Gids, 3* (July 1956) , pp. 121–127.

29. H. Verwey-Jonker, "De psychologie van de verzuiling" ("The Psychology of Columns") *Socialisme en Democratie* (*Socialism and Democracy*) (December 1957) , pp. 30–39.

30. J. P. Kruijt, "Sociologische beschouwingen over zuilen en verzuiling" ("Sociological Considerations about Columns and Formation of Columns"), *Socialisme en Democratie* (December 1957), pp. 11–29.

31. *Ibid.*, p. 15.

32. *Ibid.*, p. 21.

33. Sjoerd Groenman, "Calm Amidst the Raging Waves," *Delta, 2* (Winter 1959–60), p. 13.

34. J. P. Kruijt, "The Influence of Denominationalism on Social Life and Organizational Patterns," *Archives de Sociologie des Religions, 4* (July–December 1959), pp. 105–111.

35. Bisschoppelijk Mandement (Episcopal Mandate), *De Catholiek in het Openbare Leven van Deze Tijd* (*The Roman Catholic in the Social Life of These Times*), May 1, 1954, 47 pages.

36. Mandement, p. 43.

37. Kruijt, "The Influence of Denominationalism," p. 110.

38. *Ibid.*, p. 110.

39. J. P. Kruijt and Walter Goddijn, "Verzuiling en Ontzuiling als Sociologisch Proces" ("Pillarization and Depillarization as a Sociological Process") in *Drift en Koers* (*Drift and Course: A Half Century of Social Change in the Netherlands*), edited by A. N. J. den Hollander *et al.* (Assen: van Gorcum & Co., 1962), pp. 227–263.

40. *Ibid.*, p. 238–239.

41. *Ibid.*, p. 244–245.

42. *Ibid.*, p. 248.

43. See H. Daalder, "Parties and Politics in the Netherlands," *Political Studies, 3* (February 1955), pp. 1–16. Also Robert C. Bone, "The Dynamics of Dutch Politics," *The Journal of Politics, 24* (February 1962), pp. 23–49.

44. Frits Kool, "Communism in Holland: A Study in Futility," *Problems of Communism, 9*, (September–October 1960), pp. 17–24.

45. Idenburg, *Schets van het Nederlandse Schoolwezen*, p. 79.

46. *Ibid.*, pp. 123–124.

47. Richard L. Wing, *Recent Changes in Dutch Education* (unpublished doctoral dissertation, Harvard University, 1959), pp. 103–105.

48. The following paragraphs draw heavily upon A. C. de Ruiter, *Kaart van het Onderwijs in Nederland* (*Chart of Education in the Netherlands*) (Kampen: J. H. Kok, 1963), p. 46–54.

49. L. W. G. Scholten, *"Verwarring of Dictatuur"* ("Confusion or Dictatorship") *Christelijk Gymnasiaal en Middlebaar Onderwijs, 36* (April 11, 1959), pp. 509–518.

50. de Ruiter, *Kaart van het Onderwijs,* p. 57.

51. *Ibid.,* p. 65.

52. *Ibid.,* p. 69.

53. Philip J. Idenburg, "Financial Equalization in the Netherlands," *Yearbook of Education,* edited by Robert King Hall and J. A. Lauwerys (Yonkers: World Book Co., 1956), p. 418.

54. Philip J. Idenburg, "Democracy and Education in the Netherlands," *Delta, 3* (Spring 1960), pp. 16–17.

55. *Weekblad van de A.V.M.O. (Weekly Magazine of the Neutral Teachers Organization for Teachers of Preparatory Higher and Secondary Education),* 57 (February 7, 1964), pp. 513–515.

56. A. Hegs, "Discriminatie voor de openbare scholen — Wie bezet de Onderwijstroon?" ("Discrimination Against the Public School — Who Occupies the Throne of Education?") *Weekblad van de A.V.M.O.,* 57 (May 15, 1964), pp. 912–914.

57. J. A. Ponsionen, G. M. J. Veldkamp, and W. K. N. Schmelzer (eds.), *Welvaart, Welzijn en Geluk (Welfare, Well-being, and Happiness)* (Hilversum-Antwerpen: Paul Brand, 1963), Part IV, p. 295.

58. Geert Wielenga, "The Christian Schools of the Netherlands," *Yearbook of Education* (1958), p. 220.

59. André de Beurs, "La Situation Actuelle de l'Ecole Catholique en Europe Occidentale: Quelques réflexions sur les Raisons d'être de l'Ecole Catholique," *Sint-Bonaventura, 30* (December 13, 1963), p. 1167.

60. *Ibid.,* p. 1168.

61. *Ibid.,* p. 1169.

62. *Ibid.,* p. 1175.

63. *Ibid.,* p. 1177.

64. Moberg, "Religion and Society," p. 172.

65. Michael P. Fogarty, *Christian Democracy in Western Europe: 1820–1953* (Notre Dame, Indiana: University of Notre Dame Press, 1957), 461 pages.

66. Moberg, "Religion and Society," p. 178.

67. David O. Moberg, "Social Differentiation in the Netherlands," *Social Forces, 39* (May 1961), pp. 333–337.

68. In January 1964, a satirical television broadcast by the socialist network drew forth extensive and sometimes vituperative responses in letters to the newspapers. The broadcast, similar to one which had hardly stirred a ripple of excitement in England, satirized the worship of the television set as a new ecumenical religion. The language of the broadcast was frequently modeled on that of the Scrip-

tures. For example: "All come to the picture who are taxed and burdened and the picture will give you rest." Or, again, "Give us now our daily program. Be with us, O picture, for we do not know what we should do without you." (See J. van den Berg, Han Lammers, and Harry Mulisch [eds.], *Zo Is Het* [Amsterdam: de Bexige, 1964] p. 6. The Minister of Education, who in the Netherlands is responsible for the control of broadcasting, was criticized for not cutting the program off the air and was encouraged to take disciplinary action against the broadcasting company. A very popular television performer who had appeared in the program received such a reversal of popularity that she has apparently withdrawn from television altogether. The language of the letters to the papers was observed by some more thoughtful letter writers to reveal a mass of repressed feelings of hatred, the broadcast creating an occasion for expression of them.

CHAPTER 4

Religion and Public Schools in Sweden

Although arguments about learning from patterns of policy in Europe usually refer to those of the English and the Dutch, one might well also consider the policies of other democratic Christian countries. The picture obtained by studying England and the Netherlands would be balanced by looking into the situation in a Scandinavian country. In Sweden policies did not develop as a consequence of the kinds of pluralism found in England and the Netherlands. The nation as a whole seceded from the Roman Catholic Church in 1527 and embraced Lutheranism.

Furthermore, it seems desirable to look into policies of church and schooling in the context of the Scandinavian way of life, that is, in a democracy where the free enterprise system has been extensively modified by social reforms and where government enterprise, public ownership, and cooperative societies are, by American standards, much advanced. Not only does Sweden have a history of the growth of a democratic life in some aspects reaching back into the Middle Ages, but it also has developed unique ways of combining its democratic traditions and forms of social life with the more active role of the state in the public welfare. It should be interesting to see how a society characterized by the "middle way" [1] and the "politics of compromise" [2] takes care of the problems of religion and schooling. It has also been observed that until about 1900 the Scandinavians looked to America as an example of an ideal social republic — except for its treatment of the Negro — but that since 1900 the Scandinavian countries have been in many ways more of an example to Americans. [3]

A third reason for the study of Swedish policy relates to the large-scale and detailed reforms of the educational system in recent years. The length of compulsory schooling has been extended to nine years. A new type of institution, the comprehensive school, is to supersede completely the former elementary school by 1972–1973. When the Riksdag established the comprehensive school in 1962, it also provided for the "continuation school," offering general education with a practical emphasis. Later, a large committee was appointed to inquire into the future pattern of vocational training. A new organization of the gymnasium is being proposed. Higher education is being restudied and reorganized. Involved in all this is the study and report on the relationship of the Swedish church to the public school. In view of this effort to study and revise policy on a national scale, it is appropriate that Americans should try to understand various aspects of the teaching of religion in Swedish schools.

In the study of policies in Sweden, many conditions of social life and movements of thought, past and present, are involved. Some, such as an increasing tendency toward secularism in the latter half of the nineteenth century, but particularly after 1919, are directly related to current policy. Others, exemplified in the effort of the Nordic Association to correct mistakes and omissions in interpretations of Scandinavian history in textbooks, are more indirectly related to changes in policy about religion and the schools. Movements within the Church of Sweden toward more liberal policies, such as the ordination of women clergy, which raises problems about faithfulness to the Scriptures and to confessional doctrines, are related to policies about the place of religion in the schools. In 1958 a special parliamentary investigation was appointed to study the entire relation between church and state in Sweden. Various aspects of Swedish life and history bear with varying degrees of directness upon policy about the place of religion in the schools.

Although comprehensive school law was enacted in 1962, the full significance of its provisions about religion and schooling is not yet fully apparent since teaching materials reflecting recent developments in school policy have not yet appeared.

Furthermore, the bearing of Swedish experience upon American problems may be found not only in the content of their policies but also in the process whereby national policies are built. Present efforts to revise and unify the educational system exemplify the way social problems are studied and discussed by the Swedish people. Provisions for the wide participation of the Swedish people in the study and discussion of matters of public policy are a highly significant aspect of the settlement of policies in Sweden.

General Background Concerning State and Church in Sweden

A brief overview of the general character of Swedish national government may help us understand the nature of national educational policy and how it is developed.

Sweden is a parliamentary democracy with the King as the head of the state. The King-in-Council, that is, the King and the cabinet, is the chief executive authority, although, basically, decisions are made at preliminary meetings of the ministers. Legislative authority is shared between the cabinet and the Riksdag (legislature) with the latter in control of matters of public finance. The legislature is bicameral, the lower house having 232 members, elected directly; the upper chamber having 151 elected by county and city councils. The chambers have equal powers; they have an equal number of members on joint committees which play an extremely important role in the work of the legislature. The cabinet consists of fifteen members. The Prime Minister, appointed by the King, is usually the leader of the majority party. Five parties are represented in the Riksdag. Party distinctions tend to follow occupational differences rather than ethnic, religious, or regional cleavages.

In Sweden there is a separation between the function of legislative policy making and the administration and implementation of policy. The Swedish pattern of government differs from other Scandinavian forms in that there is:

> . . . sharp formal division between the policy-making executive departments of government and the entirely independent administrative boards and agencies. The latter, which are charged with the daily administration of existing laws and policies, are not obliged to seek the advice or opinion of any particular minister but are responsible directly to the government, which appoints a director general for each body.[4]

In education, legislative policies are managed by the Ministry of Ecclesiastical Affairs and Public Instruction; the National Board of Education is the independent, subserving administrative agency.

There are many avenues for interaction between the Ministry and the National Board of Education. One of them consists in the appointment of "royal commissions" which undertake thorough study of a matter, provide information for the guidance of the legislature, predict probable effects of legislative proposals, and obtain public reactions. Reports are widely distributed according to a "so-called 'publicity principle' whereby all state and municipal documents shall be accessible to whoever desires to see them — whether that person has anything to do with the matter or not — unless there is an explicit legal provision to the contrary."[5] Thus in the development of the comprehensive school and in policy related to religion in the school, the state issues publications in which policies are clarified and different views about them recorded. Extensive use of selections from these materials is made in the following pages.

The Church of Sweden "is fully a state church in the sense that it is the only one established by law, and the only one having the government as its highest organ of administration." [6] The Church performs a number of secular functions such as keeping the vital statistics and maintaining burial grounds for the entire population.

Unless his parents have formally renounced membership in the Church, one is a member by right of birth. The church tax is collected with the state taxes; those who withdraw from the Church pay only 60 percent of the church tax on the basis of its secular functions. Many members of the Free Churches as well as those of more secular persuasions retain nominal membership in the Church of Sweden.

The legislature decides many ecclesiastical matters. It enacts canon law with the consent of the General Synod. The government convenes the General Synod, pays its costs, and ratifies its decisions such as authorizing its ecclesiastical books — its translation of the Bible and its hymnal. [7] The clergy are paid by the state, various parish incomes augmented from central funds being used for this purpose.

In the last decade there has been much concern with the relationship between church and state. The problem debated within and without the Church concerns the degree and kind of separation which would give the Church more freedom from state interference — as exemplified in the government's support for the admission of women into the clergy — and yet provide sufficient financial support for the work of the Church. The Free Churches are particularly concerned since they do not have the privilege of support from taxes collected by the state and hold that a state church violates the principles of religious freedom. Heldtander, however, observes that "many free-church groups recently have accepted certain connections with the state in the form of church marriage privileges and state support for their educational programs." [8]

The Swedish Church is composed of thirteen dioceses. The cathedral chapter is the working unit of the diocese. The bishop is the chairman; lay representatives are included. The Bishop of Uppsala is archbishop, chairman of the church assembly, and spokesman for the Church in relation with the state and in ecumenical matters. The responses of various cathedral chapters to the government's educational proposals about religious teaching will be noted in later pages.

One of the conditions of policy about religion and the schools in Sweden, which is not immediately apparent to a visitor, concerns differences in religious faith and in the strength of religious feeling in different sections of the country. Other issues include the culture of the Lapps in the north, the presence of Free Churches and their societies, the differences between urban and rural settings, and the historic differences among the more metropolitan areas. There are distinctions between High Church and Low Church, Young Church and Old Church within the Church of Sweden, Old Church piety being strongest in west-coast Sweden.[9] These differences which have some bearing on policies in the public schools should alert us to the hazards of thinking of membership in the Church of Sweden as homogeneous.

Religious Education in the Comprehensive School

The nine-year compulsory basic or comprehensive school consists of three departments of three years each: lower, middle, and upper. The main features of the school are summarized by Jonas Orring, who was secretary-general of the commission responsible for the design of the new school.[10]

In the first eight grades the subject "Knowledge of Christianity" is taught twice a week. In the ninth grade, where some specialization begins, it is taught once a week for those preparing for the gymnasium or for further study in humanistic, technical, mercantile, or socioeconomic lines of study.[11] In general, the subject seems to be given less attention in the last year because of pressure from other specialized subjects related to the careers of the student. Some aspects of the study of religion in the higher grades are included in other subjects such as sociology.

The organization of the subjects in Swedish school law indicates the way in which religious instruction is related to other subjects in the curriculum. In the lower and middle departments of the basic school "Knowledge of Christianity" is listed as one of the orientation studies; in the first three grades, along with "regional study" (geography and folklore) ; in grades four, five, and six, along with six periods a week drawn from the fields of sociology, history, geography, and natural science. In the upper department it is listed as the only subject of general orientation, the other orientation subjects being divided into social and natural sciences. Thus, the way the curriculum is specified in school law indicates that the study of religion is a foundational subject matter serving to orient that student in the cultural life of his time.

The National Board of Education has indicated the aims of religious education. Its statement of orientation says:

> The teaching of religion aims at guiding the pupils in the essential content of the sacred Scriptures, in Christian faith and ethics, in the chief outlines of the history of Christianity, in the forms of congregations and in important non-Christian religions. It shall give knowledge too of the currents which have called into question the value of religious truths and give insight into fundamental ethical and religious questions and currents of ideas of the present day. Instruction shall be objective in the sense that it gives knowledge, founded on facts, of the meaning and substance of different outlooks on faith, without trying to influence the pupil authoritatively to embrace a certain way of thinking. It ought to be marked by broad-mindedness and tolerance. It ought to be given in such a way that the pupils comprehend the seriousness and significance of the questions at issue, and so that it promotes their individual progress and contributes toward creating understanding of the value of a personal conception of life as well as understanding of and respect for different views in questions of conceptions of life.
>
> The work in religion ought to be directed to giving the pupils such a skill that they will be able to acquire knowledge independently.[12]

After directing in these terms the general objectives of religious education, the school regulations continue by stating the major characteristic subject matters and patterns of teaching for the different levels of the comprehensive school. The effort is to give the schools some fairly clear direction as to what they should do in the particular area of instruction.

For the lower grades directions run to the effect that conversations should be undertaken on ethical and religious topics suitable for children. Simple narratives from the Bible, something about church festivals and modern Christian customs, some hymns and songs suitable for children should be given. Trips should be made for the purposes of study. A variety of study methods and work materials should be used.

For the middle grades selected materials from the Old and New Testaments and from the history of Christianity are indicated. Something about religious views, circumstances, manners and customs in non-Christian religions should be given. Discussions of moral and religious topics, suitable for the pupils, and initiated by other aspects of school work or from events and facts brought to the fore by pupils, should occur.

In the higher grades study of different Christian communions and important modern non-Christian religions should be undertaken. The Christian mission in the modern world should be emphasized. Deeper knowledge of the Bible and of Christian outlook on faith and life, with attention to cultural and social life and other outlooks on life, should be provided.

In short, directives are given for an increasingly broader and deeper understanding of Christian and other religions in the years of the comprehensive school.

The implementation of national policy about religion and schooling, as other subjects in the school, is directed by providing more detailed suggestions which teachers may use selectively in carrying on their work. At this level of advice, teachers are expected to be guided by suggested activities rather than to use the proposals for a desirable curriculum as a fixed course of study. Suitable activities for each grade are suggested. Suggestions are more extensive for the first seven grades than for the last two years of the basic school. We shall be more specific by sampling these proposals at various levels.

Suggestions for the content of religious education in the first grade of the comprehensive school indicate that talk about matters close to the child's experience, such as speaking the truth, being honest, considerate and grateful, being able to ask a person's forgiveness, refraining from gossip and the like may be encouraged at a positive and realistic level. They ought to terminate in a religious application, but only if they do so naturally. Relationship with other instruction should be sought. Stories of the birth of Jesus, materials showing the conditions of life in Palestine in the time of Jesus, narratives showing what kind of man Jesus was, should be used. Learning about Advent, Christmas, and Epiphany and hymns and songs appropriate to these church festivals should be included.

The proposals for study in the middle department of the basic school, suggest considerably more detailed study of the Old and New Testaments and the history of Christianity. Talks about moral and religious topics, characteristic of instruction in the first years of the lower division, seem to give way in the middle grades to more detailed and precise study of such topics as the parables, the Passion of Jesus, the Ascension, and Christian martyrdom. The study of Paul, the ancient church, Luther and the Reformation in Germany and Sweden are suggested for the fifth year. Attention to non-Christian religions is first mentioned for the sixth grade. It is clear that instruction in Christian knowledge is to be coordinated as far as possible with instruction in other subjects; history and geography specifically are mentioned.

In the seventh year's course the dissenting revival movement in Sweden, the origin of Free Churches, and different tendencies within the Church of Sweden are specified. The forms of religious life within leading modern Christian churches and in various countries are to be studied. The religion of primitive peoples, of Islam, Buddhism, Hinduism, and the religions of China and Japan are mentioned. Modern Jewish religion and the unique position of Judaism in relation to Christianity and the non-Christian religions are to be studied.

The eighth and ninth years' courses provide comprehensive treatments of the Bible, early Christianity, and the content of Christian faith and morals. Relations between religion and other aspects of cultural and social life are emphasized. More study of "other conceptions of life" is indicated. Religions of ancient peoples are also suggested.

The general proposals for the content of religious instruction in each of the years of the basic school are followed by a section giving instructions and comments about the management of the teaching.

Instruction ought to give *knowledge* of Christianity and to an extent of other religions. Christianity is a constituent part of the basic religious, moral, and social estimations, on which our culture, our society and our living together are being built, and knowledge of it is necessary to the understanding of Western cultural and social life in the past as well as in present times. The teaching of religion ought for that reason to be centrally teaching of Christianity, but knowledge of non-Christian religions is also part of the direction that the school should provide. This is particularly urgent at a time when the contacts between peoples and civilizations become more and more active and indispensable.

The teaching of divinity should have, as the teaching of any other subject, an *educating* effect on the pupil. The pupil's own attitudes toward life are at stake. The norms and ideals of life, which are important to the individual and to the search for truth and earnestness in life, are being molded. The teaching should relate the insights of modern religious and ethical study to the personal and social problems of real life. Pupils should know also about the currents of thought that have called into question religious truths of the past. Moral commandments ought to be so studied that they are not seen as arbitrary, but as the products of the human social condition. The pupil should be awakened to responsibility without fear or the paralysis of guilt. One-sided moralistic teaching should be avoided.

Religious education ought to be carried on so that it does *not infringe the individual's right of thinking and believing freely*. Therefore, it should be *objective* in the sense that it provides knowledge founded on fact about the content and significance of different ways of looking at life without trying authoritatively to influence the pupils to accept a certain way of thinking. The educational principle is that the pupil should be led through personal activity and independent thinking to search for his own conclusions. By presenting objectively and with tolerance knowledge of different beliefs, the pupil should be led to appreciation of and respect for people holding beliefs different from his own.

The teacher ought always to remember that the homes from which the pupils come represent different ways of looking at religious matters. He ought carefully to avoid everything which may seem a hurtful attack upon a personal way of thinking.

The *Bible* shall stand in the center of the teaching. It is vitally important that the pupils become well-versed in the Bible's religious and ethical message and get a good all-round Biblical education. Above all, the teaching ought to give them a complete picture of the personage of Jesus, his life and preaching. Also, the history of Christianity ought to be linked up with Biblical thoughts and texts so that it illustrates in a natural way the spirit of the Biblical texts. Students will thereby get a better understanding of and respect for people holding opinions different from theirs, and they may see that people who have tried to live after the message of Jesus have understood it in different ways. They will also get an idea of the influence the *Bible* has had through the ages.[13]

Following this further clarification of the general point of view to be taken in religious instruction, the recommendations deal in greater detail with the methods and resources for this instruction. Instruction should deal with what is central to the comprehension of the pupils. It should avoid a one-sided historical emphasis and seek to link up with the pupil's life. The teacher should plan what is a basic curriculum common to all pupils and what is to be undertaken above the basic standard. Relationships with other subjects are encouraged. The section ends with the suggestion that at the level of the ninth year, where divinity is not taught as a subject, questions concerning ethics and philosophy of life should be treated in other courses — courses in Swedish and other literature, sociology, and biology where problems of the individual's style of life will naturally arise in the nature of the subject.

It is clear from these sections of the report on the curriculum of the comprehensive school that Swedish policy combines a range of interests in such a way that the school is given considerable responsibility for the development of the student's knowledge of and life-attitude toward Christianity and religion in a more general sense. Swedish youth, through the work of the school, should know and understand the Christian character and background of their culture. They are to learn this critically and functionally as it relates to the personal and social problems of the day. It is repeatedly emphasized that the school's effort is to promote freedom of thought, tolerance and respect for the variety of Christian and non-Christian religions. The need to understand the religious basis of other cultures today is clearly recognized. The desirability of coordinating religious and ethical with humanistic and scientific knowledge is also clearly evidenced.

The teacher's freedom of teaching within the objectives of national policy is clearly stated in the description of the curriculum of the basic school. The teacher's freedom is coordinate with his duty to plan and carry on his teaching within the context of the long-range purpose of Swedish policy. The proposals for religious instruction provide a framework for the program of all nine of the school years so that there may be planning, continuity, and coordinated direction. Concurrently the freedom of the teacher within that framework is to be fully operative.

Before dealing in greater detail with the discussions leading to the settlement about the place and character of religious instruction in the comprehensive school, it seems desirable to consider the way in which problems about the religious character of morning assemblies in the school are handled. The character of religious instruction and the meaning of religious freedom are to a considerable extent revealed in the way in which policies concerning religious worship in school are interpreted.

Two statutes reveal the nature of Swedish policy in this matter. One of these states:

Before the first lesson of the day a time not to exceed ten minutes shall be spent for morning assembly; or if the meeting is common for several classes or for other special reasons it may be held for at most fifteen minutes.

The common morning meeting shall be conducted in the order the headmaster decides, by the teacher of religion, or by another teacher willing to do so or by another suitable person.[14]

The other statute states:

> The pupil in the comprehensive school may at the parent's request be exempted from taking part in the morning meeting if there is full reason for it.
>
> The pupil shall at the parent's request be exempted from taking part in instruction in knowledge of Christianity, if the pupil belongs to a religious community which has been authorized by the Crown to stand in the place of attending religious instruction in the school.[15]

Both of these statutory provisions are the result of much discussion concerning the new comprehensive school and also of discussion and enactments in the 1950's concerning the teaching of Christian knowledge, morning prayer in school, freedom of dissent, and religious freedom.

An article in the yearbook of the Society of Teachers of Divinity clarifies the way in which the right of exemption from divinity is interpreted. The articles points out that the Board of Education distinguishes between three groups of children: (1) those from "admitted" religious communities, (2) those from other religious communities, and (3) those without any confessional affiliation.

Concerning the first group, the statute just quoted provides that at the parent's request the child shall be exempted if the religious community has been authorized by the King to attend to religious instruction. Now, the article inquires:

> Which are the communities which have been authorized? In a royal letter of the 17th of April, 1953, the *Roman Catholic Church in Sweden* and the *Jewish Congregation* in Stockholm, Gothenburg and Malmö have the right to provide instruction in divinity instead of the school for pupils belonging to these respective religious communities.
>
> There are, however, certain conditions laid down. (a) The Board of Education and the proper county education authority shall have the right to get information about the instruction. (b) The instruction — save for the variance caused by differences in religious interpretations — shall correspond to the instruction in divinity at school. (c) The pupils shall be given a requisite certificate of the instruction they have received.

Since no other religious communities have applied for permission to give instruction in divinity instead of the school, it is in practice only Catholics and Jews who get this freedom.

The right to employ this provision has been delegated to the headmaster, so strictly speaking, the parents need only to apply to the office of the school and announce their desire.[16]

Concerning the children in the second group, those from other religious communities, they:

. . . may apply for this freedom . . . directly to the Government. The application is submitted to the Board of Education, which recommends according to the following assumptions: (a) That the conditions in the royal letter of April 17, 1953, ought to apply. (b) Further, the Board makes certain demands upon the religious community. It shall have stability in organization; it shall work with a certain intensity; it shall have "come of age." In return, the number of members is of less importance; as a lower limit one would expect twenty recorded members. If these conditions are fulfilled and if nothing else recommends against their freedom, the Board considers itself able to recommend the application, which as a rule will probably imply the sanction of the Government.[17]

Concerning children from the third group, those from confessionless families, the situation is different.

Even if parents pledge themselves to arrange instruction under the consideration of directions, which might be thought to be issued, the Board will not recommend such an application for freedom. Accordingly, it is less probable that the Government would sanction the application.[18]

Thus exemption from instruction in Christian knowledge is not uniformly given to any and all who seek it. Only those who belong to a substantial and enduring confessional group are likely to be exempted.

In regard to the morning assembly, the remarks of a member of the school drafting committee, Stellan Arvidsson, who is headmaster of an elementary teachers' normal school and a member of the Social Democratic Labor Party, give a clear indication of the considerations that entered the 1962 statutes. He reports:

The school drafting committee has not in its reports taken up the question of the character of the morning meetings. By doing so, the present condition of things is maintained. The school day is to be started with a morning meeting which may have different character, but there prayer, religious discourse and hymn-singing may exist. In most schools this is probably the content of the introduction to the day's work.

At the time of the report of the school drafting committee of 1946, six members of the committee supported the view that instruction in divinity ought to be objective, that common prayer ought not to exist in school, that the morning prayer ought to be replaced with other forms of meeting and that the regulation providing that the teacher of divinity must belong to the State Church or profess himself an adherent of the pure Evangelical faith ought to be rescinded. Since that time, the Riksdag has approved a new law of religious freedom in which the teacher's religious affiliation was pronounced to be properly the individual's private affair. By this was meant that instruction in divinity ought to be objective. Curriculums and instruction in this subject have hesitatively been changed in this direction. The school drafting committee has in its proposal distinctly supported objectivity and neutrality in instruction in religion. The earlier designation of the morning devotions has been changed to morning meeting, and the teacher has the liberty to shape this after his own opinion.

Under these circumstances, the right for the schools and teachers to arrange morning meeting with prayer and hymn-singing seems a contradiction.

Attendance at prayer and hymn-singing presupposes a fixed religious attitude. The constraint of attending morning prayer is a categorical interference in the freedom of faith. 'Just as you would not now-a-days force adult people to attend services, so you ought not to force young people, who are far more easily suggested and guided than older people, to attend devotional exercises,' said the six members of the 1946 committee.

When those from the church or religious community still claim the right for teachers to preach Christianity at school, this presupposes an antiquated conception of the Christian's sole right to the preaching of conceptions of life. Such claims are irreconcilable with democracy and freedom of religion. They are also irreconcilable with fundamental pedagogic principles: pupils ought as far as possible to be allowed to try by themselves to move forward and acquire conceptions founded on their own insights; they ought to be educated to independence of thought and to learning to take a critical stand on questions where different views abound and the influence of authority is felt. The school drafting committee has urged these points of view in regard to the subject, 'divinity,' itself. In my opinion they ought to have pronounced the same opinion in regard to the morning gathering.

As the drafting committee has not discussed this problem and accordingly not made any proposal in the matter, I propose: that the prescriptions about morning meeting will be shaped so that they eliminate all possibility of deviating from the principles of religious freedom.[19]

The point of view expressed in this passage indicates some fundamental problems that have been considered in the design of Swedish policy. Earlier school regulations had prescribed prayer and the singing of hymns for morning devotions in the school. In the 1950's the terms "morning prayer" and "morning devotions" were changed to "morning meeting" or "morning gathering" and it was ruled that the form of the meeting should be extended to provide for other kinds of content — music, literature, and talks without elements of religious worship.

At this point we should be reminded of the process by which policy is prepared for enactment in Sweden. In the development of policy the report of a committee for the drafting of legislation is published. It explains the grounds on which the committee bases its recommendations and includes minority or dissenting views such as that of Arvidsson. After this report and its associated "special remarks" are published and are widely discussed, a special committee of the legislature reviews the work of the drafting committee, solicits other comments from heads of departments, and recommends the legislation to be enacted. Thus the discussion of controversial aspects of policy occurs publicly, with maximum opportunity for all to engage in it, before the legislation is acted upon in the Riksdag. The time consumed in debate and passage of legislation in the Riksdag is very brief.

The report of the special committee indicates its weighing of various demands, among them some concerned with exemption from instruction in Christian knowledge and the morning assembly. The committee referred approvingly to the 1951 statute affirming the right of exemption for those whose faith was found by the government to diverge so much from what the schools were doing that children should be withdrawn. But for children of families without any confessional faith, the committee thought that they ought to know about the religious aspects of modern cultures and that objective instruction would not infringe their freedom. Furthermore, to divide children into "heathen" and "Christian" camps was seen as hardly compatible with the ideal of a common, unified, comprehensive school. The report suggests that the morning meetings ought to be characterized by the objectivity desirable in religious instruction so that all pupils could in good conscience attend.

Among the materials submitted to the special committee reviewing the proposed legislation about the comprehensive school, a statement by the president of the board of education indicated his approval of the principles and directions of the drafting committee's report. However, he wanted particularly to emphasize the principles at stake in instruction in "Knowledge of Christianity." He emphasized the need to understand the Christian character of Western culture, the varieties of its forms and the urgent need to know also non-Christian religions. Today contacts between peoples are more readily made, more lively, and more indispensable. He stressed the importance of personal development in religious and ethical matters. He wanted to emphasize more sharply than the drafting committee its pronouncement:

. . . instruction in divinity must be carried on so that it does not conflict with the demand of freedom of thought and faith. Therefore, it shall be objective in the sense that it gives knowledge founded on facts of the meaning and content of different confessions without trying authoritatively to influence the pupils to embrace a certain way of thinking.[20]

The content of the report of the special committee is of considerable interest for it reveals the nature of some of the demands made upon the committee and the way the committee responded to them. These demands concerned among other things: the changing of the name of the subject from "Christian knowledge" to "religion"; the dropping of the subject as a separate course and substituting the study of religion in other basic guidance or orientation subjects; the proclamation by the legislature of the importance of teaching Christianity and the interpretation of the need for "objectivity" in its instruction; the exemption from instruction in Christianity of children whose parents ask for it on the grounds of their atheistic beliefs; the proportionate number of school hours given to religion in the higher grades, particularly in view of the pupil's preparation for confirmation on the one hand and the pressure for preprofessional and practical subjects on the other. The committee responded to these suggestions, after expressing appreciation for the thoroughness and great sincerity of the drafting committee, in the following manner:

> . . . The aim of the school . . . must from time to time be revised; its tasks must continually be kept up-to-date. They thus cannot ever be finally stated. In older times the influence of the milieu of the home, the circle of comrades and of school upon the young could be built upon a firm system of norms accepted by all. The conception of life was uniform and the rules of action were to be interpreted only in one way. Education for life could and had to be given by impressing these rules and norms upon the young. Today within our people different opinions about conceptions of life are asserted, and old systems of norms, which many people still consider valid, should, as others see it, be replaced by new ones. The ideals of humanity and democracy are nowadays sometimes difficult to define but there are some undisputed estimations upon which the work of the school has to build. As a basis for its educational work, the school can no longer assume a view of the conception of life common to everybody; this has got to give way to a commonly acknowledged and accepted way of viewing society.[21]

This way of viewing social realities, which the drafting committee had worked thoroughly and attentively to present, is summed up in the demand for objective knowledge. Teaching in divinity should be done with the same aim as teaching any other subject. Policies about teaching divinity should be guided by "objectivity" and "matter-of-factness" which also characterizes the teaching of any other subject. This concern with objectivity, the special committee considered, reaches into the heart of the matter more fully and productively than other concerns which do not touch on the fundamental educational reason for the activity of the school in this matter.

The appeal to "objectivity" or "matter-of-factness" as a basic educational principle enabling a common policy about religious instruction and attendance at morning assemblies is a fundamental aspect of Swedish policy, and one not without its difficulties. The special committee seems to be saying that in order for the comprehensive school to live up to its function in the modern period, it should be guided by an educational principle, equally appropriate to the teaching of any subject matter, that it should be taught with a view to enlightening the pupil. Instruction in the knowledge of Christianity should in this respect have the same purpose as any other teaching.

It is interesting to note that the meaning of objectivity in the teaching of Christian knowledge is subject to much discussion and involves sharp differences of opinion. Among educators it is discussed reasonably but forcefully in an effort to develop operating policies that will guide the school as it seeks to come to grips with the conditions of modern life.

Some seek to have objectivity mean that the subject divinity is not to be given any privileged place in the curriculum. In this view Christian knowledge is not to be reinforced by acts of worship or by elements of evangelical, missionary, or redemptive purpose. It is to be taught factually, as a field of knowledge of Christian and other religions and is to stand on the same basis in the curriculum as any other subject. The teaching is to help the individual to think for himself, to develop his own interpretation of life.

On the other hand, some interpret objectivity and matter-of-factness within the context of the educational responsibility of the church. Faithfulness to the teaching mission of the church and to the living character of Christian commitment prevents the reduction of Christianity as a school subject to something less than personal involvement in a living faith. Objectivity means tolerance and respect for religious differences but not standing outside the religious experience and tradition within which lies one's redemption.

The discussion of policy between school people holding these views, which the writer heard through the generosity of these Swedish educators, was spirited, challenging, and responsible. Although all talk in Sweden about this matter may not be of this quality, one cannot help thinking that as dialogue of this order continues and is expanded and shared, a viable meaning of objectivity is being forged and demonstrated. As Swedish youth encounter the different values expressed by their teachers, they share the quest for objective religious education. Teaching at the higher levels of the school's classes presents opportunities for the objective discussion of such conflicting views. The greater difficulties in implementing objectivity in religious teaching are encountered in the lower grades.

The reports of the government's committees on religious education had not been able to take a clear-cut position on the act of worship in the lower grades of the comprehensive school. A committee composed of those with varying views is trying to develop examples and alternative ways to implement objectivity at the younger age levels. The committee seeks to help teachers to bring Swedish traditions and developing policies into relationship in the design of new practices rather than to leave teachers to their own devices in the matter. Educational leaders are much concerned with the work, and many agree with the chairman of the committee that what is done in this matter is a crucial test of the main direction of modern policy. It seems safe to say that the search for policy is moving in the direction of experiments with various kinds of morning meetings expressing the human aspects of religious faiths rather than their intellectually debatable aspects.

In Swedish policy, preparation for confirmation is separated from the teaching of Christian knowledge in school. In order to see how this works out in practice, a quotation from Sten Rodhe, a leader in the educational work of the Church of Sweden, is appropriate.

Of the newborn children in Sweden 85 percent are baptized into the established church — part of the remainder is baptized later into the established church or some free church. Practically every baptized child is later confirmed in the church. The usage of confirmation is as strong as is the usage of baptism, accepted by the great majority of the people, though only a small minority (about 3 percent) will regularly attend the Sunday services of the folk church. This means that the instruction given for confirmation reaches almost as many as the instruction given in the schools. School laws make no provision for confirmation as they do in Norway and Denmark, and with an expanding school system it is becoming increasingly difficult to find time for an effective confirmation teaching. The typical age of confirmation is 14, and though there is no strict rule, the confirmation is usually combined with the first Holy Communion. As a normal number of hours for preparation the bishops recommended 60 though the shortage of clergy means that often this amount of time is not reached. The usual way is to teach in the afternoons during a winter, from autumn to spring. But summer confirmation schools in diocesan homes, boy scout camps and the like are becoming more and more used and give evidently better results. In the last ten years committees appointed by the church have done much to help this teaching, which centers around the content of the catechism. Instructional courses for pastors are given; handbooks and teaching aids are published.

The free churches have "Bible schools" as an equivalent to the confirmation of the church. But it is not unusual that children from free church families are confirmed in the folk church.[22]

Thus the churches are able to reach a very large percentage of Swedish youth outside the school where the church may not engage in missionary activities.

An article by Gösta Lindeskog, director of the Institute for Religious Teaching at Uppsala, reveals the attitude of progressive religious teachers to the need for objectivity in religious teaching.[23] He points out that in the new regulations a direction which had been operative in large measure in teaching was legally confirmed. Since religion is an obligatory subject in an obligatory nine-year school and since the pupils in this basic school come from families of established church, Free Church, and professionless backgrounds, the situation calls for an objective religious lesson. Representatives of Christian interests, as well as secularists, have good reason to approve a policy of objectivity for this protects also their interest, particularly in the instance where a teacher of religion is an outspoken atheist.

Lindeskog points out that some see the religious lesson of the free confessional or denominational school as the final solution to the threat of secularism. He does not hold this view on the grounds that religious teaching would then disappear from the basic school and only a minority of pupils would receive a religious education. In addition, he believes that objective religious teaching is of great value to religious interests. In the hands of well-educated teachers, it not only teaches tolerance but also an objective or impartial basis for criticism of spurious religiousness. It promotes a fuller general awareness and understanding of genuine religious reality (*echte religiöse Wirklichkeit*).[24]

In discussing the meaning of objectivity Lindeskog contrasts it with the kind of religious teaching appropriate to a confessional religious lesson. He distinguishes between the content and the method of teaching. There is a difference, although not an absolute one, between a sermon and a lesson in religion. A sermon tries "to edify, to exhort, to awaken, to call for decisions, to warn, and to punish."[25] A lesson, aims to convey knowledge, to stimulate the intellect, to facilitate learning. While one cannot make a decisively final separation between a confessional and an objective lesson, the former is more typically limited to clarifying dogmas, to teaching a catechism, while objective teaching seeks the maximum of impartial justice to all views. Objective teaching seeks a general presentation of Christian belief and, at the higher school levels, of other religions and weltanschauungen. It has an historical orientation to the larger range of religious experience.

Since the subjective factor — that is, the personality of the teacher — is involved in both the confessional and the objective lesson, no absolute distinction can be made between them. The objective lesson can be a powerful experience in approaching the message of the Gospels. The confessional lesson may be turned into "an impersonal, dry, boring, caricature of the Christian message." [26] In the teacher's control of his values lies the difference. The objective lesson can let the *majestas materiae,* the sovereign majesty of the material, come to the fore. It can attend to the right of pupils of different backgrounds to form their own opinions of the profound questions of life. It can prepare pupils for what only they themselves can experience in the Gospels. The instructional function of the school can be combined with its function in upbringing. Only if objectivity stands for valueless neutrality, impersonality, ignorance of the character of the Gospels, does it become opposed to the more limited function of the teaching of a particular church.

Lindeskog's position goes a long way toward revealing the frontier of religious thought about educational policy in Sweden today. It carries forward positively the role of religious interests while attending centrally to the freedom of the enlightened mind to formulate its deepest convictions. It seeks to work out a meaning of objectivity which avoids on the one hand an overly narrow neutrality in matters of fundamental values and on the other hand the advancing of a predetermined religious faith that needs only to be perpetuated. The ingredients of his approach to problems of teaching religion in Sweden seem appropriate to problems in other countries, including our own.

A recent government publication [27] relates some of the representations made in response to the drafting committee's suggested regulations concerning the basic school. Criticisms centered in four concerns. A number of them represent the views of Cathedral Chapters of the Church of Sweden.

First, several statements supported the view that the school should have a clearly Christian character. In this view, it should be decided first of all that the Swedish school is a Christian school. "Education is an empty concept if it is not decided where it shall lead." Those holding this view think that the proposal of the committee contained a view of man which assumed that "man in his own nature is good and will develop good qualities to the extent that his milieu allows them to find expression." Such an anthropology, it was maintained, "is hardly realistic and is directly inappropriate as the aim of the school." This view is not satisfied by the explanation that these "smoothing-over and noncommittal" words had to be used because the culture is split by varied, well-established conceptions of life or the lack of them. "Swedish society is still at bottom so dominated by values derived from the Christian Gospels that it must be regarded as a principle task of the school to set forth in its activities the norms of a Christian way of life." [28]

The point of view of a Free Church committee is indicated by the following. When the drafting committee undertook as its purpose to provide a clear conception of the moral norms of a democratic society, they started as a matter of fact from fixed assessments and assumed that certain moral norms are necessary for that democracy to function. No more thorough analysis of the bases of democracy was made, and the norms were only suggested. What the drafting committee said about the Christian religion being a basis for our ethical and social values ought to have been allowed to define the aim of the school and especially of upbringing.

The second grouping of statements submitted as responses to the work of the drafting committee contained some penetrating questions concerning objectivity in instruction in divinity. Some observed that the drafting committee did not hesitate at all in stating that education for democratic citizenship should influence the pupil to take a certain point of view. It was then peculiar that the committee fenced instruction in Christianity with restrictions exceeding those needed for instruction founded on facts. Furthermore, the way the drafting committee justified the demand for objectivity in the teaching of Christianity could lead to consequences unfavorable to teaching Christianity.

Another response indicated that it was more correct to use the expression "correct instruction, founded on fact" than "objectivity." Still another response considered that the drafting committee was hardly successful in arguing for objectivity and in its proposals indicated a secularization of the subject. A further view expressed satisfaction with the proposals and stated among other things that the demand for objectivity was as much a protection against anti-Christian propaganda as against proselytizing for particular Christian opinions.

Responses to the report of the drafting committee also included one from the Swedish Social Democratic Students' Society. In their view, instruction in Christianity ought, because of the principles of religious freedom, to become religious knowledge both nominally and in reality, and this would mean that knowledge of Christianity would be removed as an independent subject in the curriculums and schedules of the schools.

A committee of Free Churchmen declared that they upheld the instruction in Christianity which had been in force for a number of years and disapproved of what had been stated about objectivity in the instruction of different age groups in the basic school.

A third matter that received criticism concerned the number of class hours allotted to knowledge of Christianity. Criticism was directed against the failure to include the subject in some of the technical curriculums of the ninth year. In a comparatively large number of comments it was held that the subject should be given in all ninth year patterns of study. A brochure to this effect carrying the signatures of about sixty thousand persons was delivered to the National Board of Education. However, the Swedish Social Democratic Youth's Society held that the subject ought not to exist in the ninth year's offerings. The Swedish Social Democratic Women's Society thought that the hours given to the teaching of religion in the middle department ought to be reduced.

The fourth focus of criticism concerned regulations about the right of exemption. Some thought the law ought to state that every pupil should get some kind of instruction in religion. Others thought that instruction should be so comprehensive and objective that all pupils were able to attend it.

As for the morning meeting, there was criticism of the view that pupils could be exempted from morning meetings which were conducted by a person who was a member of the pupil's own religious community. To distinguish between morning meetings with religious elements and those without was also considered to cause practical difficulties.[29]

The New Gymnasium

The committee concerned with drafting new curriculum regulations for the gymnasium also considered as part of its work the character and function of the study of religion. Its proposals were based on a considered analysis of and adjustment between the demands made upon the gymnasium by different groups of consumers, by society in general, and by individuals. The requirements about religion should be seen within this weighing of interests and also within the general aims and divisions of the curriculum.

Among these, it recommended that the gymnasium ought to go beyond the comprehensive school in developing the personality of pupils and especially their critical abilities. Pupils need good habits of planning and carrying on independent study. They need to be prepared for the realities of social life through study of sociology, technical and natural science, and cultural studies including literary, aesthetic, religious, philosophical and psychological matters, and through attending to international relations and historical developments.

The curriculum should gradually lead to self-dependent study and work on long-range scholarly activities. The hours spent in classes should therefore gradually be reduced in the three years. Thirty-four, thirty-two, and thirty hours a week were specified, and this meant an overall 10 percent reduction in class hours a week from the existing pattern.

Consequently, considerably less time should be given to the study of religion. Topics in church history should be transferred to courses in history. Religion should be largely devoted to the study of present conditions and the treatment of non-

Christian religions should above all be strengthened. This was why the committee suggested that the name of the subject should be changed to "religion." [30]

The altered nature of the subject which justified the recommended new designation is indicated in the following passage:

Religion as a self-dependent subject shall give knowledge of the function of religion in the life of the individual and of society in different cultural milieus. It should be characterized by a marked concern to provide guidance in the modern world and will concentrate on the description of the most important non-Christian religions as well as a treatment of the essential features of Christian faith and ethics in connection with Biblical texts and a discussion of actual problems and conceptions of life. Historical reviews will be given to the extent that they are necessary to elucidate important aspects of religious life within different churches and religions or to illustrate religious problems, which meet modern man within or outside our cultural milieu.[31]

The committee making proposals about the new gymnasium also suggested that the customary morning meeting should be abolished and replaced with a common meeting. At such a meeting, which might not occur daily, information about the school and plans for its work would be announced. Part of the meeting might consist of musical presentations, the showing of films, readings and short lectures. Primarily, the meeting should give a feeling of unity in the school. The proposal also suggested that attendance ought to be voluntary, and the report indicated that the Synod of 1963 approved of changes in this direction.

However, the committee drafting the plan for the new gymnasium also recognized that many people have a considerable interest in questions connected with religious and ethical questions. They recommended that:

The school ought to contribute in such a way that the pupils' interests in this regard will be satisfied. The committee therefore proposes that school halls be put at the disposal of pupils for meetings of this kind. These ought to be purely voluntary — attendance ought to depend upon every single pupil's initiative. The frequency of such meetings ought also to be the pupils' private affair.[32]

Further details about the considerations involved in the reduction of the number of hours in religious teaching are summarized in the fifth part of the report of the 1958 investigating committee dealing with the church and the state. In its second chapter the regulations pertaining to the gymnasium, as well as those about the comprehensive school and schools for teacher education, are summarized.

In the new gymnasium the former pattern of three main lines of study — general, commercial, and technical — are to be replaced by five — the humanistic, the social science, the natural science, the economic, and the technical lines. The new gymnasium is to be a three-year course except for the technical line which should be four.

In the older pattern "Knowledge of Christianity" was taught a total of five hours a week in the three-year course of the general gymnasium. The committee for the new gymnasium has suggested that a total of two and a half hours a week should be used for teaching Christianity in the humanistic and social science lines and one and a half in the natural science line. Thus a reduction of between three and a half and two and a half hours a week will be achieved.

The report also indicates that the committee conducted an investigation into the pupils' own interests in respect to the teaching of Christianity. The result showed a lack of interest.

Another investigation was made to find the opinions of citizens between the ages of fifteen and seventy-five about the extent of the teaching of Christianity. The results of the interviews showed that 2 percent favored no teaching of Christianity at all; 15 percent favored one hour a week in each class; 42 percent favored two hours a week in each class; 12 percent favored three hours a week; 6 percent, four hours a week; 3 percent, five hours a week; and 6 percent favored six hours a week. No opinion was expressed by 14 percent of those interviewed. The average came to 2.4 hours a week in each class. The answers from parents were distributed in the same way as those from citizens in general.[33]

The main considerations in the teaching of the subject in the gymnasium are said to be: to build upon the education that the comprehensive school began; to contribute to social maturity; to bring about a critical and inquiring attitude. The demand for objectivity is seen as a general rule in all gymnasium teaching.

The content and development of the teaching of religion as a subject should be judged in terms of the pupil's conduct of life and his valuations. The goals of the teaching are as follows: to give knowledge about the function of religion in the life of the individual and of the society; to give insight into the fundamental ideas of the various religions; to deal with the different forms of religious life within or without Christianity; to introduce the problems that exist within the present religious situation; and on the basis of the study of biblical texts to explain the characteristic content of the Christian belief and ethics and to relate this to other perspectives on life and to important problems in contemporary culture.

The effort to combine objectivity with the need for confrontation is clearly an important part of the considerations about teaching of religion in the gymnasium. The pupil is to become engaged in basic concerns about a philosophy of life without being led to accept a predetermined view. The teaching is to help the student to think and to take a position independently and to develop his own interpretation of life.

Objectivity is seen as consistent with the teacher's expression of his own opinion. The teacher is not directed to communicate only the dry facts about different perspectives. He is to engage the students in the problems of belief but also to protect their freedom of belief and thought. It is pointed out that this problem is encountered in the teaching of other subjects, especially those dealing with teaching about society. It is better that teachers should work at the matter rather than having the young people get their knowledge without control on the part of the society. If it were done by some means other than by the teachers there is little chance that the various religious perspectives would be made believable. The young would be more likely to be provided with a certain outlook. The school's neutrality can be achieved if it bases its education on values that do not have their source in any special religion or perspective.

In connection with the recent developments concerning religion and the schools in Sweden, one observes that considerable attention has been given by Swedish leaders to what is called the "co-Christian name-gathering" of 1963. This refers to a petition against reducing the number of hours devoted to teaching Christianity in the gymnasium. The petition was circulated by some 10,000 of those sympathetic to maintaining the traditional number of hours, five hours a week, for teaching divinity. The petition was signed by some 2,100,000 Swedish people. The total population of Sweden numbers about 7,500,000. The petition was transmitted to the president of the board of education by its primary sponsors, the Joint Christian School Committee. The petition represented, as the president of the board of education said, a very great expression of opinion, one that could not be overlooked in the final settlement of the matter.

An article by the editor of *Church and School*,[34] the journal of the Church Teachers' Society and the Future Teachers' Christian Union, is interesting because it interprets the response of the press to this petition. The author reports some 5,000 news items and articles have dealt with the matter in the Swedish press. In his opinion, as a result of this considerable attention in the papers, the petition was the product of an informed public opinion. People did not sign without knowing what the matter was about. He found the disinclination to take it seriously in the more culturally radical press a "morally dubious form of political pressure." The local papers first recognized the seriousness and considerable extent of public opinion. The author finds that the attention given to the matter in the Stockholm papers, particularly those associated with social-democratic political views, and in the state's television broadcasts was too little and too late. The article expresses some surprise on its side at the large number of signatures. Perhaps the reluctance in Stockholm to take the petition seriously was the difficulty involved in "fitting it into the usual conception of the state of opinion in the country." It concludes that the real political effect remains to be seen; that the struggle is not ended.

Also of interest is the opinion, particularly on the part of those supporting the government's position, that the pressure exerted by the petition was unnecessary. In the legislative processes the recognition of the importance of Christianity as the religious basis of the culture would have been taken care of without this additional pressure upon parliamentary processes in Sweden. In this view, the parties are so divided, with the Social Democrats holding a bare majority, that there is no hard and fast grip upon a movement toward secularism in the Swedish parliament. On religious questions certain members of the dominant party cross over to the opposition. Parliamentary leaders are careful to keep away from situations where Christian members of the Social Democratic Party would vote in opposition to the party's general position. In a sense, then, the will of the people in regard to the teaching of Christianity is expressed somewhat apart from political party affiliation. However, those more actively concerned with upholding the place of the Church of Sweden in national life see the extent of the petition as evidence strongly supporting their position.

The Role of Voluntary Organizations

We have already noted several aspects of Swedish political life making for the kind of compromise or "middle way" in matters of public policy. The commissions of inquiry engage in thorough study, using the products of research and holding hearings to elicit a wide range of expressions of views and proposals in forming their recommendations. The separation of administrative boards from the policy deliberations of the Ministry provides for the consideration of policy in the light of the practical experience of administrative agencies. The principle of publicity means that extensive public documents are accessible to the press, to interested groups, and to any individual who wants to be concerned with the forming of policy.

One of the outstanding characteristics of Swedish society contributing substantially to the development of policy consists in the number and variety of voluntary associations. Dankwart Rustow says that the Swedes have "a universal inclination to form societies in the pursuit of impersonal objectives." Swedish society is:

> . . . saturated with voluntary associations. Almost the entire working population is organized according to its function in the productive process — the wage earners in trade unions, white collar workers in associations of salaried employees, farmers in agricultural marketing societies, and industrialists in employers' associations. One million four hundred thousand voters are card-holding members of the several political parties and their affiliates, 1,000,000 consumers belong to the cooperative movement, 800,000 sports fans to the National Alliance of Sports Federations, more than a quarter million Protestant dissenters to the various low-church sects, and 300,000 teetotallers to the many temperance societies — not to mention academic, philanthropic, philatelic, convivial and innumerable more casual societies.[35]

The representatives of voluntary organizations serve on various committees and administrative boards and are elected to the legislature, and the views of the organizations are recorded in the official publications of the government. Thus the interests, which in America take the form of pressure groups, are in Sweden built into the process of public debate and have a responsible part to play in the structure of democratic policy making.

In addition to voluntary associations relating to the occupational and economic groupings of Swedish life — labor-management groupings, the cooperative movement, the agrarian associations — there are the so-called idealistic associations.[36] Among these are the Free Church societies, the members of which typically retain their membership in the established church. Originating in the late eighteenth century, the Free Church movement became more powerful at about the turn of the twentieth century and had a considerable impact upon loosening the hold of the established church upon religious teaching in the schools. The Free Church movement had the effect of emphasizing personal decision and individual obligation in religious life — in this sense it supported the pietistic movements within the established church. The Free Church movement also sought the independence of religious life from the state. In more recent years the Free Church societies have cooperated with the Church of Sweden in opposing the secularizing tendencies of modern life.

The Roman Catholic Church and its societies, although showing the greatest increase of any group in recent years, "finds itself still on the fringe of Swedish society." [37] Although it numbers today about 28,000 members, compared with 5,000 in 1940, and, according to Gustafsson, has made a definite impression on Swedish spiritual life, it has not yet gathered the strength to enable its political influence to be felt.

The voluntary organizations, both those representing occupational-economic interests and those of a more "idealistic" order, have played an important part in Swedish life. Although membership is voluntary, strong social pressures upon the individual encourage him to identify with societies whose efforts benefit the members of the group. An identity and solidarity in common effort is experienced. Heckscher observes that there is no important interest which is not expressed in an association and that it is a common experience to hold office at some time in one or more of the subdivisions of those societies.[38]

Furthermore, membership provides experience in the resolution of conflicts between organized interests. Thus a basis is laid for working out conflicts through consideration of contending views and a process of give and take leading to common policy. "Informal yet intensive training in the arts of orderly debate and group decision provides a solid foundation for Swedish democracy." [39]

Moreover, it is significant that much of the process of weighing and judging issues in policy is achieved below the level of governmental regulation. As voluntary associations extend their efforts in this adjudication of interests, they are able to take over some of the functions which in other societies are managed by governmental agencies and institutions. Thus the process of developing public policies is widely shared and the risks of having policies determined by governmental bureaucracies in the absence of public concern and debate are minimized.

Political Parties

The political parties in Sweden have also played an important part in the development of policy concerning religion and the schools. There are five political parties presently represented in the Riksdag, although in the period of unrest at the time of World War I several farmers' and liberal parties were represented. Rustow provides a general picture of the character of the current parties.

All of the five present-day Swedish parties have a relatively stable and well-defined social base. The Conservatives are a party of the upper and upper-middle classes, appeal strongly to the higher age and income groups, and have their main strongholds in the south of the country and in the large cities; however, they receive some support from the poorest workers. The Liberal party, although built around a strong middle-class core, is the only major party to receive substantial support from all three social classes. It appeals to both urban agnostics and rural conformists, and to farmers as well as to small merchants; its strongholds are in the North and in the cities. The Agrarian (Center) Party is almost exclusively a countryside party of small farmers; it is strongest in the southern rather than northern agricultural districts. The Social Democrats are predominately a working class party with support from both industrial and agricultural workers. they appeal more successfully to young people than to old, and to married couples (especially to the wives) than to single persons. The Communists derive their main support from workers of all income groups; they are strongest in the extreme North and in the two largest cities (Stockholm and Göteborg).[40]

The Social Democratic Labor Party has been the dominant party since the early 1930's. In several periods it was in coalition with others, chiefly the Center (formerly the Farmers') Party, but since 1957 it has been in office alone. The percentage of the electoral vote and the percentage of members of the Second Chamber in 1960 showed the following distribution: Conservatives, 16.5 percent; Liberals, 17.5 percent; Center Party, 13.6 percent; Social Democrats, 47.8 percent; Communists, 4.5 percent. In the First Chamber in 1962 there were 23 Conservatives, 29

Liberals, 19 Centers, 77 Social Democrats, and 3 Communists.[41]
Most voting follows party lines. Of 383 seats in both houses, Social Democrats carry 191 votes against 184 for the combined other
democratic parties (excluding the Communists). The Communists usually abstain in order to avoid forcing out a socialist
government.

The chief pressure in the party system for lessening the
church's control and influence in education has come from the
Social Democrats. In the party's description of its ideological
development we read:

> . . . lively discussions have taken place on the Party's attitude to re-
> ligion. In the early years of the Party, anti-religious views were fairly
> strongly expressed. The Party has, however, never given any official
> directive on religion but always urged freedom of thought in this
> respect. In the earliest statements on this question, religion was sim-
> ply stated to be a private matter for the individual. In 1905, a de-
> mand was added for the abolition of the State Church. This demand
> still appears in the programme while the Party's standpoint is defined
> otherwise as "religious freedom." Opinions undoubtedly differ in the
> Party, not over the principle of religious freedom but where the
> State Church is concerned. On the initiative of the Social Democratic
> Government new legislation was introduced in 1952 stating that
> everybody has the right to cancel his membership of the State Church
> and to be relieved of taxation paid to the Church.[42]

As Tore Heldtander expresses this position, "It cannot be said
that the Swedish labor movement has been directly hostile to the
church . . . but the labor movement has taken a quite indifferent position towards the works and services of the church." [43]
Others refer to the labor party's leadership in supporting secularism in the schools and to attacks from "rising secular atheism"
appearing in one of the leading newspapers, *Dagens Nyheter*. It
was also the present government which appointed a committee in
1958 to look into the problems of church and state and to appraise the consequences of changes from present patterns.

The major opposition to the Social Democratic Labor Party
comes from the Conservative Party. The preface to the program
of the Conservative Party states:

The Swedish Conservative Party asserts that the people of Sweden are of old a *Christian* people and that the Christian faith is an indispensable, sustaining and purifying power in society.[44]

Items 14 and 16 in the party's program further affirm its position on religion and schooling.

14. The school's task is to provide a full education and, together with the home, to arouse and strengthen the sense of personal responsibility and the consciousness of ethical values. Within the framework of the school sound religious instruction is to be given, whilst observing the principles of religious freedom as regards respect for those who hold different opinions. . . .[45]

16. Religious freedom is to be maintained and all denominations are to have the right to work in their own way. The Church of Sweden, as a free national church collaborating with the Swedish State, will work for the Christian education of the people of Sweden. The agencies of the Church of Sweden are to have the full right of decision in the internal life of the Church and a decisive joint influence over the form of connection between State and Church. The self-government of the parishes will be preserved.[46]

It is clear that the Conservative Party places "the principles of religious freedom" within the context of the school's responsibility to offer "sound religious instruction" and that the established church is to have "decisive joint influence" over the relations of church and state.

The Liberal Party also calls itself the People's Party. It is founded upon the principles of freedom of the individual and the right for justice for all. It bases its position upon Luther's insistence upon the individual's direct responsibility to a higher power and upon the long traditions of liberalism in English and German thought as well as upon Swedish traditions. It expresses its support of the major popular movements, the right-to-vote reforms of the last part of the nineteenth century, the "evangelistic movement and its fight for existence against the striving of the state church to get monopoly on exercise of religion," its association with the temperance movements, the Free Churches, and the older labor movements.[47]

Liberalism's demand for freedom for all puts it in opposition to general collectivistic or socialistic conceptions, although where the individual's freedom is not in jeopardy, it supports certain movements toward centralization. The railway, postal, and telegraph systems are cited as examples. However, it opposes a "far-reaching centralization of the administration." It opposes the setting of interests in opposition and favors a cooperative, peaceful, and juridical coexistence among peoples, both nationally and internationally.

Its emphasis on character building and individual development in education is supported by a general respect for individually interpreted spiritual and religious values.

> . . . The respect for spiritual, religious and ethical values must be kept up, preserving and widening the serious outlook on life which belongs to the most valuable inheritance of our people, having its strongest foundation in the Christian culture.[48]

It is clear that its efforts for "liberty, justice, and humanity" have been closely associated with the efforts of the Free Churches to obtain religious freedom and with the "dissenter legislation" in the 1950's. In addition to the right to leave the state church, this legislation included the right to civil funeral, the dissenting ministers' right to solemnize marriages, the right to teach religion in the schools although one is not a member of the established church.

The positions represented by the three political parties which we have mentioned are sufficient to indicate the range of party positions on questions of religion and the schools. The parties of the left are more likely to contain members who, somewhat apart from the platforms of the parties, push more militantly for a treatment of religious instruction which will bring it on a par with other courses of instruction in the school. The parties of the center and of the right are more concerned with affording religious teaching a more centrally Christian interpretation and character. Most of the discussion comes to a focus in the interpretation of "objectivity" and in the question about the amount of time given to the study of Christianity in relation to other subjects. In addition, discussion concerns the study of world religions and philosophies appropriate to the moral and spiritual decisions of young people growing up under the conditions of modern life. Although Sweden does not have confessional parties, it manages to discuss in serious political terms some of the basic problems of policy about religion and the schools which are common to us all.

If our interpretation of what some leaders in Sweden were saying is at all correct, it might be put in this way: As questions about religion are dealt with in legislative measures, the members of the political parties are not likely to be subject to party discipline. They are less guided by party positions than by their sense of the enduring spiritual character of Swedish life. They are likely to reaffirm the importance of a traditional Swedish religious unity. In a sense, they do not want to depart too far from the faith of their fathers.

Although they may favor the study of world religions appropriate to Sweden's place in world affairs today, although they may want matters of doctrinal conviction to be engaged in the church's instruction for confirmation rather than in instruction in the public school, although they may appreciate a principle of objectivity in religious instruction, yet when it comes to school policy and regulations, they are not disposed toward a radical break with their Christian past. The "middle way" is being worked out. Although some new emphases and directions may be encouraged in religious teaching, in the basic school it will still be called "Christian knowledge," and it will still have a special position in setting the tone of the school.

Selected Aspects of Historical Background of Swedish Policy

The teaching of religion in the folk school, enacted in the Primary School Act of 1842, consisted of the teaching of the catechism and the morality approved by the Church of Sweden. Even before this time there were trends that moved away from the use of the school as a means for promoting the faith of the

Church. Pietism emphasized the importance of the ability of the people to read the Bible for themselves. Various reform movements appeared under the liberalizing cultural movements associated with the term "enlightenment." These urged the religious upbringing of children so that they could use rational argument rather than a mechanical acceptance of belief. Children should be led to think independently, to find genuine reasons to be convinced as a result of their own religious search.[49] But the majority view looked to the Lutheran catechism and the historic evangelical interpretation of the Bible as the direction of the religious responsibility of the school.

In the second half of the nineteenth century the influence of dissenting congregations, at first the Baptists, but later the Pentecostalists and the Swedish Mission Covenant, became much stronger than the numbers of their memberships suggest. These groups strongly opposed the way Christianity was being taught in the schools. In addition, in the early part of the twentieth century various leaders of the "Young Church Movement" developed a more ecumenical outlook in the Church and looked to newer interpretations of biblical Christianity rather than the fundamentalism of Lutheran orthodoxy, which still dominated the teaching of Christianity in the schools. The very important work of the Sigtuna Foundation, establishing contacts between the Church and the new groups in society, including the workers movement, dates from this period (1917). It contains today a flourishing folk high school and serves as a retreat and a center for study and for discussion between various groups in Swedish cultural life. Although under church auspices, it has complete freedom from church authorities and exemplifies the contribution of the Church to the national life on a voluntary basis.

The year 1919 marks a turning point in the development of the teaching of Christianity in Swedish schools. The period of close relation between church and school was ended.

It was now decided that the catechism should no longer be taught; the Bible should be taught as a historical book; the instruction should be objective, which means being bound to no denomination although an Evangelical Christianity was presupposed as a common basis. Time given to religious instruction in school was reduced.[50]

Thus after 1919 the sense of "objectivity" in the teaching of religion became, as it continues to be, controversial. At first it presupposed a common Christianity about which the Church of Sweden and the free Churches could agree. More and more it became interpreted as a kind of neutrality, which to some meant indifference to conviction but to others meant an uncoerced search for enlightened conviction. Increasingly it meant teaching about Christian and non-Christian religions. However, the widened range of the content of religious education has not even today settled the question of the character of its impact upon the lives of students particularly at younger levels.

In 1919, however, the tendency of future concerns was indicated.

If instruction is objective and is sustained by the spirit of tolerance, there is yet in Christianity so very much in common for different religious thinking that such planned instruction ought, without losing anything in earnestness and firmness or in properly instructive import, to be able to satisfy the great majority of our people, at the same time that it ought to enable our children to find a deeper and truer conception of religious and ethical problems.[51]

Although in the years between 1919 and the 1940's there were occasional efforts to return to the more dogmatic lines of earlier years, the overall tendency was to loosen the hold of orthodox belief and to bring the teaching of religion more relevantly in touch with the newer movements and demands of modern Swedish life.

As one reads the record of proposals, discussions, and enactments, after 1919, one sees recurrent concern with questions about the number of hours a week to be allocated to teaching Christianity, the use of Luther's catechism as a text, whether knowledge of Christianity and the morning devotions should be compulsory, whether and in what sense instruction should be nonconfessional, and how responses to these matters are to be related to the cultivation of respect, tolerance, and the freedom of thought.

One school commission followed another in considering these matters, some being appointed before the earlier one had finished its work.

The 1946 School Commission, of which Tage Elander was initially the presiding officer, proposed the combining of the *folkskola* and the *realskola* into a single united school having a nine-year compulsory course, a proposal which has now resulted in the comprehensive school. The policies proposed in 1946 regarding religious education were largely those which became the general policy in the 1960's. The 1946 report observed that religious education given under other auspices than the public school could not guarantee to be as broad-minded or pedagogically sound as that which could and should be given in the school.[52] The problem of morning devotions inherited from 1919 was recognized, and rules were formed which retained its character as worship, yet tried to make it more acceptable to all parents. A minority reservation was recorded by six delegates who thought group prayer should not be held in school and that obligatory participation in morning devotion constituted a categorical interference in liberty of thought.

The freedom-of-religion law of 1951 is an important milestone in the development of modern Swedish policy. Since its passage cabinet ministers, with the exception of the minister in charge of church affairs, no longer have to be members of the Church of Sweden. Although since 1860 it was permissible to withdraw from the Church of Sweden and either join another approved Christian denomination or found another congregation after obtaining the sanction of the government, it was not permissible until 1951 to leave the Church without joining another religious community.[53] Prior to 1951 teachers of religion had to belong to a Protestant faith. A heated debate resulted in the decision that there should be no rules whatever on the faith of teachers of Christian knowledge. Rodhe states that there are now teachers who are Roman Catholics, Jews, atheists, and agnostics although most belong to the established church, and further, that there is no way to determine how many teachers represent any group.[54]

It is interesting to observe that it was about a hundred years earlier, 1858 in fact, when the Conventicle Edict of 1726 was rescinded. This edict, directed against the pietists who established "conventicles," or worship in private groups, had prohibited such private worship at the peril of fines, imprisonment, or exile.[55] Only family devotions in a strict sense were permitted. Thus, in a period of 100 years Sweden had moved from patterns of severe repression of dissent to patterns supporting a considerable measure of religious freedom.

The committee proposing the law about religious freedom also stated that it had worked against the disintegration in the teaching of religion, which would have come about if Christianity, traditionally taught in the schools, suddenly would have been taught by the different communions. It would have meant giving up the basic principle of a unified school. The Free Churches had attacked the teaching of Christianity partly because of its strongly confessional character under the influence of the established church. Since the teaching was changed so that it was acceptable to most Christian communions, it could remain as an obligatory subject without violating the principles of religious freedom and freedom of conscience of the various Free Churches.

It was, as the committee on religious freedom saw it, a matter of how the teaching was done, its content and the spirit of the teaching. It should be done so that constraint of conscience was excluded. This could be done to the satisfaction of the Protestant groups, but it might be different for Jew, Roman Catholics, and those who belonged to no communion. There might be a reduction of the freedom of religion for these groups. The committee noted a tension between society's responsibility to educate in a common united school program and the freedom of religion of even small groups who should also be protected against constraint of conscience and oppression of opinion.

To reach an adjustment the committee thought it best that under certain circumstances release from participation in the teaching of Christianity might be given as long as the exceptions formed only a small number of all the students. In this way it would not constitute a breaking up of the united school, which had been accepted as a principle by the Riksdag.

The period of the 1950's was marked by experimental development of comprehensive schools. Jonas Orring, who has occupied several key positions in the growth of the comprehensive school movement, reports that the number of school districts having experimental comprehensive schools grew from 14 in 1949–1950 to 30 in 1952–1953, to 59 in 1955–1956, to 142 in 1958–1959, and to 295 in 1960–1961. There are slightly more than 1,000 school districts in Sweden.[56] He indicates that the change to the comprehensive school was planned to continue from 1962 to 1968 with 1972–1973 as the year in which all school districts will have established the full nine grades. The development of policy in its operating context in the life of the schools has thus been promoted by planning directed by the National Board of Education. The experience gained in the process has been accumulated and published and thus made available to school commissions and various committees that continue to study and refine policies and to make the results of their work available to the schools.

A wide and accumulating experience in the careful balancing of interests has played an important part in the Swedish settlement of the religious question so that major advances in the extension of educational opportunity could occur. Experts have been drawn upon to develop basic curriculum recommendations and these have been widely distributed and extensively commented upon by many kinds of voluntary groups in the country.

. . . Study associations and adult education organizations have, for many years, spread information about and understanding for the fundamental ideas of the reform; commercial and industrial enterprises and labour market agencies of different kinds have actively participated by organizing courses and distributing information among their employees and members in order to bring about direct co-operation with the school. The public debate in the daily press and other publications during all these years has not only reflected the general interest in problems of education, but has also contributed to greater understanding for and interest in practical problems and principles that are an integral part of the reform.[57]

Thus the problems in teaching religion, such as the questions about objectivity and how it is related to the expression of faith in acts of worship, have been widely discussed and the people have participated in the operating settlement of them.

Significance of Swedish Policy for Americans

It is clear that new dimensions of experience concerning religion and schooling are introduced as one moves from the policies of England and the Netherlands to those of Sweden. In Sweden policies regarding the teaching of religion in the unified comprehensive school are of maximum concern.

In contrast with English policy, Swedish policy seeks to teach a common undenominational but generally Christian religion which shall, however, be taught objectively. Rather than having boys and girls emerge as convinced Christians, as English policy proposes, the function of religious education in Swedish public schools is to enable them to think for themselves about questions of faith. The schools are to enlighten, to encourage the forming of convictions, but more and more they are not to predispose belief by fostering the acceptance of doctrine, such as that involved in a generous interpretation of the Apostles' Creed. However, the consequences of Swedish policy, when measured in terms of church attendance, do not seem much different from those in England. Although 99 percent of the Swedish people belong to the church and more than four-fifths of all parents have their children baptized and later confirmed in the Church of Sweden, only one of every five Swedes worships at least once a month in church.[58] In terms of the criterion of attendance at church, the policy involved in the agreed syllabus approach does not seem to produce any greater results than the objective neutrality of Swedish policy.

Teaching religion objectively has been extensively studied and experienced in Sweden. What Americans mean by "teaching about religion" and how this is to be planned and controlled under public school auspices might be promoted through consideration of Swedish experience. For the sake of brevity combined with comprehensiveness let us assert without elaboration some main considerations.

A common and united school program in which all persuasions participate with the least possible sorting out on religious as well as social class and income differentials is seen to be of central importance in extending Swedish patterns of democratic life.

The Swedish example has shown that it is not impossible for a people to work together and achieve in large measure an operating policy of teaching objectively about religion.

The Swedes have shown that the kind of neutrality toward religious faiths and creeds involved in objective teaching is neither hostile nor indifferent to religion.

A distinction between religious teaching in the public school and religious teaching by the church as preparation for confirmation may be desirably maintained so that the former supports the latter.

The educational value of an informed uncoerced search for independent judgment does not necessarily indicate either a cold presentation of facts without exercise of critical judgment or a lack of involvement in questions involving convictions.

Swedish policy has been gradually and experimentally developed with a wide participation on the part of varied interests and groups which have studied and contributed to the direction of national policy. A similar tolerant, experimental, participant process might well be stimulated and extended in the United States.

Swedish experience in teaching religion objectively also helps to bring out some of the problems encountered in "teaching about religion." For example, Swedish leaders are concerned with whether religion is a subject of equal standing with other academic subjects or whether it has a privileged position. Some see it as a subject with a unique position in the curriculum on the grounds that its nature demands its pervading everything else in the life and curriculum of the school. Others think that this extension of its range as a subject matter is a claim in excess of objectivity. The scientific attitude toward openness of inquiry should also be pervasive as should the aesthetic quality of experience involved most clearly in art, literature, and music. In this view, when one is considering the qualities that pervade the school's efforts and program, the attention to perspectives on life should be seen as a philosophical rather than a religious dimension of the school's work.

Although we have underscored the wide participation of voluntary groups in the discussion of Swedish policy, it should also be noted that considerations about religion in the schools also become involved in political affairs in such a way that interests are not ready to join in a common and shared effort. Not all expressions of religious views are as open and friendly as those conducted by teachers. Some take the form of polemics and might quite readily be found in this form in the journals and papers. There is an important segment of Swedish opinion holding that educators should lead in the reasoned discussion of questions of religion in the schools. This of course requires that teachers should be educated and experienced in a respectful weighing of the conditions and values involved in those questions.

Finally, Americans might profit from the Swedish concern with other countries and with foreign relations that promote peace and understanding between peoples. The Swedish people, particularly educators, sense that one cannot deal effectively with other countries unless he understands their cultures, including their religions and the problems conditioned by those religions. Swedish policy in extending the basis of religious literacy is particularly attentive to its international and sociocultural relationships with many other peoples.

NOTES

1. Marquis W. Childs, *Sweden, the Middle Way* (New York: Pelican Books, 1948), 198 pages.
2. Dankwart A. Rustow, *The Politics of Compromise: A Study of Parties and Cabinet Government in Sweden* (Princeton, New Jersey: Princeton University Press, 1955), 257 pages.

3. Bryn Hovde, "We Americans and Scandinavia," *Scandinavia Between East and West,* edited by Hennring Friis (Ithaca, New York: Cornell University Press, 1950), pp. 336–341.

4. Joseph A. Lauwerys, "Lands and Peoples," *Scandinavian Democracy,* edited by J. A. Lauwerys (Copenhagen: The Danish Institute, et al., 1958), p. 44.

5. *Ibid.,* p. 45.

6. Berndt Gustafsson, *The Christian Faith in Sweden* (Stockholm: The Swedish Institute, 1963), p. 9.

7. Robert Murray, *A Brief History of the Church of Sweden,* translated by Nils G. Sahlin (Stockholm: Diakonistyrelsens Bokforlag, 1961), pp. 79–80.

8. Tore Heldtander, "Church and State in Sweden," *The American-Scandinavian Review, 50* (March 1962), p. 20.

9. See Gustafsson, *Christian Faith in Sweden,* pp. 14–16.

10. Jonas Orring, *Comprehensive School and Continuation Schools in Sweden,* translated by Albert Read (Stockholm: Ministry of Ecclesiastical Affairs and Public Instruction, 1962), 154 pages.

11. Specified in *Curriculum for the Comprehensive School,* "Svensk Författningssamling" (Swedish Statute Book; hereafter SF) (1962, No. 480), pp. 1316–1321.

12. National Board of Education, *The Curriculum of the Common School* (Stockholm: The National Board of Education, 1962), p. 217.

13. *Ibid.,* pp. 221–222.

14. *Regulation for the School* (SF 1962, No. 439, paragraph 35), p. 1095.

15. *School Law* (SF 1962, No. 319, paragraph 27), p. 721.

16. Sven Alsparr, "Rätten Till Frikallelse Från Kristendomsundervisningen" ("The Right of Exemption from Divinity"), *Yearbook of the Society of Teachers of Divinity,* Stockholm, 1963), pp. 53–54.

17. *Ibid.,* p. 54.

18. *Ibid.,* p. 54.

19. *Special Remarks,* "The Morning Meeting in School" by Stellan Arvidsson (SOU [i.e., Official Publications], 1961:30), Stockholm, p. 832.

20. *Supplement to the Official Records of the Riksdag,* 1962, 12th Collection, Statement No. 1, 1962, pp. 37–39.

21. *Formal Report of the Special Committee of the Riksdag,* No. 1. 1962, pp. 155–156.

22. Sten Rodhe, *The Scandinavian Churches: Church and Education* (unpublished manuscript, n. d.), p. 16.

23. G. Lindeskog, "Religionsunterricht in einer säkularisierten Welt," ("Teaching Religion in a Secular World") *Opdracht, 9* (No. 5), pp. 154–159.

24. *Ibid.,* p. 156.

25. *Ibid.,* p. 157.

26. *Ibid.,* p. 158.

27. *Teaching Christianity* (SOU, 1964:30), 182 pages.

28. *Ibid.,* p. 62.

29. *Ibid.,* p. 63.

30. U. Dahllöf and L. Sandgren, *Gymnasiereformen* (The Reorganization of the Gymnasium) (Stockholm: Bonniers, 1963), pp. 50–51.

31. *The New Gymnasium* (SOU, 1963:42), p. 361.

32. *Ibid.,* p. 405.

33. *Teaching Christianity,* pp. 77–79.

34. Carl Gustaf Boethius, "The Co-Christian Name Gathering and the Press," *Kyrka och Skola, 24* (No. 3–4, 1964), pp. 7–9.

35. Rustow, *Politics of Compromise,* p. 7.

36. Gunnar Heckscher, "The Role of Voluntary Organizations in Swedish Democracy," in *Scandinavian Democracy,* edited by Lauwerys, p. 131.

37. Gustafsson, *Christian Faith in Sweden,* p. 19.

38. Heckscher, "Voluntary Organizations," p. 133.

39. Rustow, *Politics of Compromise,* p. 7.

40. *Ibid.,* p. 143.

41. Ernest Michanek, *Swedish Government in Action* (Stockholm: The Swedish Institute, 1962), pp. 15–16.

42. Frans Severin, *The Ideological Development of Swedish Social Democracy* (Stockholm: The Swedish Social Democratic Labour Party, 1956), pp. 54–55.

43. Tore Heldtander, "Church and State in Sweden," *The American-Scandinavian Review, 50* (March 1962), p. 16.

44. Conservative Party Information Service, *The Conservative Party in Sweden* (Stockholm: Högerpantiets Informationstjänst, 1963), p. 14.

45. *Ibid.,* p. 20.

46. *Ibid.,* p. 21.

47. The Swedish Institute, *The Swedish Liberal Party* (Stockholm: The Swedish Institute, mimeographed, n. d.), p. 2.

48. *Ibid.,* p. 6.
49. *Teaching Christianity,* p. 14.
50. Rodhe, *Scandinavian Churches,* p. 13.
51. *Teaching Christianity,* p. 30.
52. *Ibid.,* p. 40.
53. Murray, *Brief History,* p. 68.
54. Rodhe, *Scandinavian Churches,* p. 15.
55. Murray, *Brief History,* p. 52–53.
56. Orring, *Comprehensive School,* p. 146.
57. *Ibid.,* p. 149.
58. Gustafsson, *Christian Faith in Sweden,* p. 16.

CHAPTER 5

Some Problems of Policy in the United States

What we have seen of the social and historical determinants of policy concerning religion and schooling in selected European countries suggests a variety of concerns with the character of policy in the United States. Rather than attempting to set up a balance sheet summing up the benefits and liabilities of European patterns of policy which we have noted in preceding chapters, we shall attempt to look again at the current situation in America. Perhaps a perspective refreshened through the investigation of policies abroad may help to sort out some of the ingredients of our problems and some of the opportunities before us today. The study of European policies may have helped to alert us to what we ought to avoid and what we might be able to achieve in the United States.

We have seen that present policies in the countries we have studied have grown out of the relatively unique historical conditions of the particular nation's culture. The United States has escaped, for the most part, the long and bitter struggle which is the background of policy in England and the Netherlands. The history of religious pluralism in this country is in sharp contrast with the relative homogeneity of church membership in Sweden. If the historical background of American experience is adequately appreciated, it points to conditions which are significantly different from those in other countries. These conditions include a number of valuations contributing to flourishing church life and freedom of belief and thought in this country.

Although a thoroughly grounded expression of our unique conditions and valuations would call for much more than we can do here, we may be briefly reminded of four main interrelated premises supporting American policy.

1. The American people have rejected policies entangling religion and politics in an effort to avoid allowing religious differences to become the source of civil strife and discord. To achieve this end policies in the United States have adhered to the view that religion and government can best advance their purposes when each is free in its sphere from the control and support of the other.

2. The people of the United States have built a system of common public schools open to those of any race, creed, or social class, comprising in this sense a single comprehensive system under public control, financed by tax funds, and devoted to the enlightenment of all so that they can think for themselves.

3. Our conception of a free and open society includes the protection of religious freedom, the right for each to believe and practice his faith including his dissent from any or from all faiths, as he sees it.

4. We have achieved a life of law under due processes, including judicial review, whereby, as conditions change, conflicting interests may be adjudicated.

Despite some differences in the interpretations of the meanings of these generalizations and some qualifications concerning the relations between them, they offer a basic framework of American policy that has carried us forward in the past and continues to be treasured by the vast majority of our people.

Each statement individually and the meaning of all of them collectively merits considerable refinement. What we have referred to as the rejection of entanglements between religion and politics, for instance, does not deny that the churches have an important and legitimate role in the criticism of public policy. Nor are religion and government so distinct in their spheres of operation that there are no grounds for maintaining such traditional practices as chaplains in the armed services, prayers at presidential inaugurations, and certain common civic services for church schools, although these may be questioned by some. Our purpose is not to set forth a self-regulating set of principles but to call attention to interrelated conditions of American policy which are sometimes overlooked in the heated exchange of views between opposed interests. We should keep centrally in mind what is uniquely valuable in American experience, for it provides a context for moving ahead responsibly with the refinement of policies appropriate to new conditions.

In short, the people of the United States face the situation of extending educational opportunity appropriate to a flourishing society while doing so within the context of their historic patterns of public policy and the continuing welfare of institutions essential to them.

Viewing our problems in this light provides several further appraisals of our present situation. One of these points to what has been called the American experiment in designing a free and open society. This means that our traditions in large part point to a willingness to break with European views of the relations between church and school and to adopt a responsible experimental attitude toward devising new approaches to problems that have plagued European democracies. Historically, among these new approaches are our traditions of religious freedom, the separation of church and state, and the development of a public school responsive to the needs of a growing pluralistic society. Today we should be guided in our responsiveness to changing conditions by a primary care for the policies and institutions that have contributed so fundamentally to our present ability to expand and extend the benefits of our way of life.

None of this means that public school policy should be merely maintained without change resulting from responsible criticism and efforts to expand its benefits. Nevertheless the public school has contributed a measure of unity in a context of diverse peoples and creeds without which we would be a very different people. Hence, we should appraise carefully the probable consequences for its continued welfare as we make new efforts to provide a fuller extension of educational opportunity to more and more of our people. We have noted European efforts to achieve comprehensive schools with the unifying social consequences that mark our system of public schools. We have noted the conditions contributing to the decline of the public schools in the Netherlands. These experiences indicate the desirability of preserving and enhancing rather than depreciating and limiting the role of the public school in the development and maintenance of the free and open society as we know it.

As we work in this country toward some fuller refinement of our policy, we need to be concerned with how we can extend opportunities to the greatest range of our people while avoiding threats to the integrity of a wide variety of religious believers and dissenters as well as the fracturing of our society into separate ways of life each seeking to maintain itself against the extension of advantages to the others. How can we, through the judicious modification of policy within the framework of our values and the institutions supporting them, move ahead without infringing upon the freedom of groups and individuals, freedoms we presently enjoy in large measure and seek to extend and strengthen? How can we extend educational opportunity without incurring the consequences of various forms of political preference for religious faiths found in European countries?

We have seen that not only do our European ancestors have a long history of bitter discord and persecution over religious differences, but that conflict frequently has centered about policies concerning religion and schooling. Many evidences point to continuing struggle underlying current compromises.

In England, persistent and diligent efforts by Roman Catholics to raise the level of public support for their schools have raised the question with Anglicans and Free Church men as to whether they should not reverse the tendency to turn their schools over to public authorities. Many question whether the compromise of 1944 could be achieved today. In the Netherlands, policies favoring the establishment and maintenance of the religious school have elicited organized reactions from the friends of public schools and from liberal movements within Roman Catholic and Calvinist circles. In Sweden the Cathedral Chapters of the Church of Sweden have predicted continuous struggle over policies favoring diminished time for study of divinity in the gymnasium. Thus controversy continues and settlements are uneasy. This suggests that Americans might become more critical of the notion that in European countries a pattern of settlement of the problems of religion and schooling has been found.

However, the presence or absence of conflict over policies about religion and schooling is not the key concern here. Democratic societies, although they may not always thrive on controversy, have due processes for hearing the clash of interests and achieving some kind of settlement by peaceful means. Presumably in a free society settlements of social problems are compromises in which some demands by some interests are unfulfilled. The more important concern is whether in the course of public deliberation the full consequences of alternative lines of policy are made fully clear. We would do well to encourage the full, responsible discussion of problems of policy about religion and schooling rather than asserting our intransigencies or failing to come to grips with the deep social, political, and educational issues.

As provisions in American policy move toward increased indirect support for private religious schooling, as is the case in recent federal enactments, experiences in other countries indicate that pressures will continually be exerted in the direction of more complete support for parochial schools. English experience suggests that as Roman Catholic pressure increases, Protestant and Jewish sectors of the population will not sit idly by without seeking their measure of public support for their schools.

It is therefore not simply a matter of the reduction of conflict over policies about religion and schooling, but a question as to the consequences for both democratic government and the quality of education of movements in this country to extend the use of public money for denominational schooling.

Since federal legislation provides a more extended use of public money for indirect benefits to parochial schools, there is a question as to whether we are not in essence enacting a partnership leading to a much expanded parochial school system. The enlargement of indirect benefits, exemplified in provisions for textbooks and instructional materials and for special services to religious schools, will permit the expansion of the parochial school system as well as an upgrading of its quality. More widespread programs of dual enrollment will provide a saving of parochial school funds through use of public school facilities for the most expensive parts of education. Despite recommended guidelines, we do not know whether parochial school students will, because of problems of scheduling, be receiving instruction in secular subjects in classes composed of parochial school students, or whether they will be integrated as individuals into the normal classes of the public school. If the former, programs of dual enrollment, involving the use of public funds, will be further expanding the range of religious segregation.

These considerations, among others, suggest that in extending public funds to private schools we may through legislation be encouraging forces making for religious columnization of American society. As increased aid from public funds enables denominational schools to expand, fewer children will grow up within a common, unsegregated school in which they rub elbows with children of different faiths and learn to respect those from religious backgrounds different from their own.

This probable expansion of schooling under the control of religious interests may remind us of some of the consequences of increased governmental support of church schools in England. There, not only are Protestant groups reassessing the release of their schools to public controls, but an interdenomination Protestant counteraction to Catholic pressure appears to be growing.

We are reminded that a Roman Catholic leader has reported that during the 1960's Catholic students will account for 63 percent of the total increase in the school population and by 1974 for one sixth of all school-age children. He predicts that the government should spend the bulk of its educational funds providing more schools for Catholics. Perhaps an affluent America can afford the costs of increased indirect aid to private schools. However, when we think of a parochial school system enrolling a school population roughly proportional to the membership of its churches, the adroitness in the use of power manifested by the Catholic Church in England, and the spreading effect of this use of power in the reactions of other religious groups, a concern for the welfare of the public school might well be alerted.

Recent legislation in this country may well encourage the social consequences that we have observed in the Netherlands. There, as we have seen, social life is splintered into religiously columnized sectors. The institutions and organizations of social life are marked off so that people of the same religious group interact with each other rather than with members of other religious faiths. We recall that in the Netherlands it is of extreme importance as to which religious orientation is represented in the person of the Minister of Education. One can advance through elementary and secondary levels of Dutch education without coming in contact with a student or teacher of another faith. Only 28 percent of primary school children are in public schools. Coalitions of confessional political parties characterize political life.

Surely, policies involved in federal legislation in the United States need to be looked at very carefully if we are to avoid encouraging consequences of this order.

In the effort to extend the range of indirect support of church schools we should be alert to the character of organized political efforts by religious interests. We have noted that the drive for increased subsidies for church-controlled schools in England has resulted in considerable pressure being put on members of Parliament and public officials. Organizations have been formed whose primary function is to provide propaganda for full support of

Catholic schools and to bring pressure upon local educational authorities. Pilot studies were made to appraise the effective strength of opposing religious groups.

In the Netherlands we have noted the efforts of confessional parties to have their religious doctrines given a preferred place in national educational enactments. The legislature was called upon to decide whether the Humanist League had the same standing as that of a church. An ecclesiastical letter brought pressure upon voters to conform to the political efforts of a confessional party. To be reminded of these findings of our inquiry in European countries is to be forewarned of consequences in the United States that may follow from some organized political efforts by religious groups.

In view of the tradition in the United States of local control in education, when decisions about forms of indirect support of religious schools are made at the local level — in regard to bus transportation, provision of textbooks and teaching materials from public funds, and other indirect benefits — the door is open more widely to pressures on public officials, to religious bloc voting, to considerations about the religious affiliation rather than the full qualifications of the public official or candidate for office. Since religious groups are not evenly distributed in this country, and since the character of their political activity varies with circumstances of time and place, problems are likely to be more intense in some places and times than others. In short, as indirect support increases and is managed at the state and municipal level, there is more need for clearly defined nationwide policy if undesirable consequences are to be avoided.

Yet, as Edgar Fuller, executive secretary of the Council of Chief State School Officers, has pointed out, federal enactments concerning higher education in 1963, economic opportunity in 1964, and especially elementary and secondary education in 1965 raise questions of fundamental policy about government financing of public and private education.

It is not unusual for federal officials to present strained and legally elusive interpretations of federal requirements that clearly favor private schools. To qualify for federal funds, more than one state attorney general has thus been led to do likewise in interpreting his own state constitution.[1]

There are a number of practices involving the blending of public and sectarian private education which have not been tested by the courts. Especially in regard to provisions in the Elementary and Secondary Education Act are policies concerning the co-operation of public and private sectarian school authorities unclear.

As Fuller points out, in the absence of statutory provisions for more direct judicial review an imbalance between the three major divisions of government is created in favor of the legislative and executive branches. Furthermore, "The strategy of those who favor increased federal tax support of private and sectarian educational institutions without judicial review under the First Amendment has been to prevent such cases from getting into court." [2] In the absence of judicial review, recent federal legislation passes on to the vagaries of state and local authorities what has not been clarified at the level of nationwide policy.

What we have seen of the experience of European countries indicates that they have accepted detailed control by the national government of policies regulating religion and schooling. The English have extensive and carefully formulated governmental provisions for making the local educational authorities the arm of the Department of Education. Debate over the Mammoth Law in the Netherlands shows much concern with whether sufficient room remains to distinguish the confessional from the public school. In the United States a curious situation may be building up in which those most concerned with the maintenance and expansion of the private sector of schooling adopt strategies that have as their consequences increased public control over sectarian schools.

Furthermore, if efforts to promote the quality of education provided by religious schools are to be advanced through indirect aids and justified in part on the grounds of the public service rendered by these schools, presumably the people should know how these aids promote the educational aspects of the work of these schools. One of the difficulties appears to be that it is unclear whether this aid on the basis of the fulfillment of the civic functions performed by these schools contributes to these civil betterments or to the church as an ecclesiastical institution.

However, if it is possible to distinguish the more secular subjects from those in which sacral concerns are more central and if the religious school fulfills the obligation of a public school and in addition suffuses its work with a religious quality, then the public which supplies funds on the basis of the parochial school's civil responsibilities should be able to be satisfied that its funds fulfill the public as distinct from the churchly interest. The government does not supply funds for vocational education, for instance, without being entitled to be satisfied that its support is used for this purpose. In this sense a measure of public control is involved.

This is a matter of concrete specific means. Experiences in other countries indicate that the means for assuring the fulfillment of the civic responsibilities of religious schools are not without consequences. The experiences of the Dutch with "requirements of good quality" suggest that as one becomes more specific about the characteristics of good quality, the difference between public and private schools becomes less perceptible. The liberty to do as one's doctrines indicate in one's own circle is brought more and more under common, public control. The religious society finds that its conception of freedom is limited by the assurances the state requires in return for its subsidy.

In short, there is a difference between public funds used to subsidize education under ecclesiastical controls and the use of public funds to support that aspect of privately controlled education which fulfills public requirements and is subject to public controls. If policy moves in the direction of the former, it would constitute a major departure from the main direction of interpretations of our constitution. If it moves in the direction of the latter, problems about public control of aspects of parochial schooling arise. At this time in our national experience the problems following from this dilemma need to be given careful consideration.

Another related matter deserves mention. The extension of

educational opportunity may be sought by providing indirect support such as educational materials for religious school pupils from public funds under the "benefit to the child" justification. Some indirect support, such as police protection, protection against fire, and provisions for school lunches presumably do not involve major dimensions of doctrinal religious interpretations. Other varieties of indirect support — the provision of textbooks and other educational materials — may involve the introduction of doctrinal views. The use of particular forms of religious symbols in visual, auditory, and written materials is introduced. Presumably textbooks involve interpretations and explanations as well as purely factual or neutral presentations. We have some evidences through George R. La Noue's investigations [3] that existing materials in parochial school textbooks express religious doctrines in a rather complete range of subjects. The use of public funds to provide textbooks expressing a particular religious view and seeking explicitly or implicitly to secure adherents to that variety of religious belief constitutes a support of religion as distinct from a benefit to the child.

Again, this is a matter of specific means to put into effect criteria expressing a clear educational policy. In Sweden, for instance, a textbook commission supervises the books written for school use and judges whether the directives of the legislature are carried out. We are reminded that the Nordic countries have been cooperating for several decades in producing history textbooks that adhere to objectivity, faithfulness to fact, and the promotion of peace and understanding between their nations. This suggests the desirability of a sustained and coordinated effort in this country to articulate criteria of objectivity in educational materials and to define their use in ways which support our values as a free people.

There is another matter observed in the dialogues carried on in Europe that bears upon the development of educational policies in this country. We recall that there is some expression, particularly on the part of Catholic laymen in the Netherlands, of a view concerning the nature and function of Catholic education in a period of reconsideration of the Church's responsibilities in the modern world. In regard to education this view has been concerned with policies of the Roman Catholic Church which separate its educational work from the efforts of all people to build a more humane society. It sees the Church's role in education in terms of conditions of time and place. It suggests that the encyclicals expressing the educational policies of the Church are historical documents responsive to conditions of a period. These conditions may change. This view is not directed toward eliminating church schools but is concerned with whether the conditions of modern life indicate something other than a single uncompromising effort to have every Catholic child in a Catholic school.

It appears that this view may be related to efforts to extend educational opportunity in this country. Programs of shared time under certain conditions might provide an appropriate means to extend educational opportunity without endangering the public school or providing preferential treatment of religion, and they might counteract tendencies toward columnization in American life. The American people might be able to find a way to extend their traditional unique experiment in a free society under the terms of the First Amendment. However, these programs involve many unknowns which might become of considerable importance if shared time were to typify our policy.

One issue concerns the stance taken by American Catholics toward the traditional educational policies of the Church. If the position expressed by the Church were interpreted by American Catholics in terms of the conditions of American life today, it might recognize more than a single, monolithic Catholic school system as an appropriate means for the fulfillment of the Church's educational mission. Some Dutch Catholics have pointed out, as have some in this country,[4] that the school is not the church. There may be more than one means to fulfill the Catholic educational function. The kind of pluralism of means may be exemplified in America by a shared time approach, not as a temporary expediency on a route to the fuller support of church-controlled schools but as a policy of taking pluralism of means seriously.

These considerations suggest that before we are too far committed in this country to what may be profound changes in national policy, we need to study together in greater detail and under clearly designed patterns of inquiry problems associated with programs of dual enrollment. We need to know what educational conditions or controls are related to the development of informed minds, to learning respect for other people's beliefs, and to learning the right to share without duress in public affairs. Carefully designed and controlled efforts to test the consequences of specific aspects of policy should be created. Until we are guided by studies of the ingredients and variables in the newer patterns of cooperation. educational policy development will remain a matter of crude trial and error.

Policies concerning the teaching of religion in public schools are related to those about the support of religious schools. In both matters public funds are expended. The teaching of religion also involves questions about the control of that teaching and about the meaning of religious freedom. If the problems of policy involved in these matters were clarified and appropriate responses to them developed, the schools would be able to undertake a more active role in promoting religious literacy. This in turn might well advance the discussion and understanding of policy about religion and public education to new levels.

In questions about the teaching of religion in public schools, as in questions about the support of church schools from public funds, the conditions and values of the American context are of central importance. Some aspects of policy within this context have been clarified and for our purposes can be briefly asserted. The Supreme Court has determined that official acts of worship or such aspects of them as Bible reading and the recitation of prayers are violations of our constitutional provisions. The Court has further tried to make it clear that this judgment does not mean the establishment of secularism as a religion. The policy of neutrality toward all religions does not mean hostility to them. Nor does it mean the exclusion of the study of comparative religion, of the history of religion, or of the bearing of religion on various conditions and problems in our own and other cultures. It does not exclude the study of the Bible for its literary and historical qualities. Presumably, religion, as any other subject, may be studied objectively. The schools, as is commonly said, may teach about religion.

What we have seen of the teaching of religion abroad suggests that we need to be further concerned with policies of teaching about religion. We can take it for granted that teaching about religion means that the advocacy of particular forms of religious creed, belief, or doctrine is to be avoided. An objective effort should be made to inform the student of the religious ingredients of his and other cultures. Yet questions remain concerning the interpretations and explanations involved in providing information. To say that the school's function in teaching about religion is to be nonpreferential in regard to religious faiths may give some direction as to what the schools should avoid. It does not, however, give sufficient direction for the positive role of objective teaching about religion.

We might be clearer about two related aspects of the matter. One relates to the nature of the authority involved in such teaching. Instruction in this as in any other subject matter is authorized by some claim to knowledge of a specialized kind and to some view of how the field is brought into relationship with those who do not possess that knowledge. Presumably the teacher of mathematics or of history or of any other subject not only knows his field but knows it in terms of bringing it to bear upon the student's need for that knowledge and the society's concern that that knowledge be conveyed in ways appropriate to the values of that society. In teaching about religion we should try to be clear as to the authority for that teaching.

We cannot here develop a full analysis of the relations between the various dimensions of the nature and sources of the teacher's authority for instruction about religion. Presumably this matter merits further inquiry if we are to ground teaching about religion in a sound theory about its policies. However, we can point to a difference between the kind of authorization claimed by the church or the parent as a member of the church and that of the public school.

In general, ecclesiastically based claims to authority in matters of religion stem from particular historic creeds and doctrines, ultimately theologies, expressed by an organized group of believers who seek to maintain and extend that belief and the organized forms of its expression. The teaching mission of the church is to be distinguished from the educational function of the public school. The latter is authorized to bring an area of knowledge and concern before the student in such a way that he can think for himself as an informed and critically responsible person.

While the authority of the church may not be opposed to that of the school, the two patterns of authorized control over the lives of others may be said to intersect or perhaps converge at particular points rather than be congruent or coincident throughout. The function of the public school under its patterns of authority may support and extend the interests of the church. The ability to think and choose for one's self need not be inversely related to the church's pastoral, liturgical, and teaching functions. The function of the church in securing belief and, as the English say, membership in a worshipping community, may under some conditions, promote the work and welfare of the public school. However, the educational function of the public school differs from the teaching function of the church, and American policies concerning teaching about religion should reflect the differences.

This distinction between the character of the control of religious education under ecclesiastical and under educational patterns of authority may not need to be further refined in order to relate it to different dimensions of the meaning of religious freedom.

What we have observed in European countries suggests two meanings or frames of reference in regard to religious freedom. It may refer to the freedom of the church from interference by the state in the control of its teaching mission; or it may refer to the freedom of the individual to think for himself in religion as in other matters. Policies about state-supported teaching of religion may express the freedom of the church to engage in and direct the teaching of religion under ecclesiastical authorities.

This is the dominant pattern of policy in the Netherlands. Policies may instead express the freedom of the individual to develop his understanding of religion under the control of religiously impartial educational authorities. This characterizes modern Swedish policy. Policies may express some mixture of the two as they do in England. Presumably, American policy has sought a balance between the two without confusing one with the other or limiting one meaning of freedom by allowing it to be dominated by the other.

In this regard the development of policy in Sweden is most relevant to the American policy of teaching about religion. There, educational considerations, including the freedom of the individual to think for himself, are central in public school policy, and the churches are free to engage in confessional religious teaching. The meaning of objectivity and related concepts is much discussed, and policy has favored the nonpreferential teaching about religion and life perspectives under the control of educators rather than the church. An active concern for the development of materials and forms of expression within the framework of this policy is clearly evident.

Teachers of religion in Sweden point out that objectivity in teaching not only promotes religious freedom in the sense of individual informed choice, but also promotes desirable consequences for the interests of the church. Objectivity in teaching religion not only serves to prevent proselytizing for particular religious views but is also a protection against efforts to implant anti-religious doctrines. It teaches understanding of religion and respect and tolerance for various religions and provides for the exploration of questions that challenge religious beliefs and doctrines. It counteracts superficiality and hypocrisy in religious belief. Impartial investigation of man's search for a faith to live by promotes the individual's ability to understand his own life situation. The teaching of the church has something to build on.

Some are willing to grant that teaching about religion may bring understanding of religious questions under educational control. They agree that the religious freedom of the individual is centrally served, and through it, the freedom of organized religions. They see that the individual's concern with religious questions is another matter than the church's interest in maintaining its life and functions. As they see it, however, questions remain as to whether religion is a subject comparable to others and whether it ought to be treated educationally as a subject of equal standing with others. Because it deals with convictions and commitment and with matters of ultimate concern expressed by institutional forms and creeds, religion is seen by some as different from other subjects. One has to grow up within it and experience it in upbringing in order to know and understand it. Objectivity in how it ought to be taught should be of another order from that pertaining to other subjects.

Others argue that although teachers may be required to extend critically their conceptions and practices of objective teaching, the educational problem is not different in kind from that in other areas. The teacher should deal objectively with expressions of conviction and the values of life wherever they arise, and he should when appropriate state his own views without inculcating them as preferred commitments. Such impartiality does not mean indifference to religious values but a loyalty in this area as in others to the uncoerced search for truth. Problems of instruction here are not different from those in other subjects where questions concerning orientation to life and choices concerning values arise. To attempt to extend the teaching of history, sociology, and literature in the understanding of the value problems of life is not to displace the aspects of upbringing for which the home and church are responsible, but to undergird them with the knowledge that one needs to think for himself.

The discussion of these considerations in committees at national and local levels and the wide participation of the Swedish people in the development of policy about the teaching of religion suggest the need to extend the study and discussion of similar problems in this country.

Although there have been some efforts in teacher education to extend the teacher's understanding of religion and what is involved in teaching about it, educators could profit from considering what European countries have done, particularly in producing materials for use in the schools and for the guidance of the teacher. This means that teachers need not only the kinds of knowledge and understanding contributed by ecclesiastical interests but also insight into the many aspects of educational policies appropriate to teaching about religion. The production of materials for use in the school, apart from thoroughly penetrating study of the problems of policy, is hazardous. If the American people are to participate in the understanding and development of policies appropriate to their context, the teacher must be prepared to make very clear the considerations that guide the school in its efforts. We need to clarify how the educational interest under the guidance of educational values is to work out in practice and in judgments of practice.

This calls for an educational effort in research, discussion, and experimental practice, an effort grounded not only in knowledge of the content and forms of expression of religious belief. It demands a considerable grasp of the anthropological, linguistic, and philosophic resources, among others, that may be drawn upon today. A continuing effort by some institute, corresponding to those in England and Sweden, might supply the leadership needed today. If it could bring together the contributions of the various disciplines, it could, among other things, help educators see what moves they could make in experimental practice and what requires further theoretical analysis in the development of American educational policy. This in itself would be a significant contribution.

NOTES

1. Edgar Fuller, "Government Financing of Public and Private Education," *Phi Delta Kappan, 47* (March 1966), p. 366.
2. *Ibid.,* p. 370.
3. George R. La Noue, "Religious Schools and Secular Subjects," *Harvard Educational Review, 32* (Summer 1962), pp. 255–291.
4. Mary Perkins Ryan, *Are Parochial Schools the Answer?* (New York: Holt, Rinehart and Winston, 1964), 176 pages.

Index

A B C D E F G H I J   5 4 3 2 1 7 0 6 9 8